ROSSLYN

ROSSLYN

ANDREW SINCLAIR

Birlinn

This edition first published in 2005 by
Birlinn Limited
West Newington House
10 Newington Road
Edinburgh EH9 1QS
www.birlinn.co.uk

ISBN10: 1 84158 417 7
ISBN13: 978 1 84158 417 1

British Library Cataloguing-in-Publication Data

A catalogue record for this book is available from the British Library

Typeset by Hewer Text, Edinburgh
Printed and bound by Creative Print and Design, Ebbw Vale, Wales

To the Sinclairs, whoever,
and wherever they were and will be

The Thistle shall rear her rough front to the sky,
And the Rose and its wearers at Roslin shall die

JAMES HOGG

Contents

Prologue

This is the history of the flowering and the falling of a place and a name. These are Rosslyn church and castle south of Edinburgh, along with Sanctus Clarus or St Clair or Sinclair. The period covers two and a half thousand years of battles and weapons, from the Trojan War to King Arthur's Camlann and the Crusades on to Bannockburn and Culloden and Yorktown. The clashes of faiths begin with the pagan Apollo and Mithras, then on to the Christian combat between Rome and the Greek Byzantium and Islam. Moreover, the great rebel heresy is examined, the belief in the direct approach to God without state or church, which led to the Cathars and the trials of the Knights Templars and the Protestant Reformation.

The frontiers are a factor, the Borders between England and Scotland, also the North Sea. All these strands are tied together in the building of the mysterious and flamboyant Gothic church at Rosslyn, where the Templars merged into the medieval crafts and guilds, including the gypsies, to create a third Temple of Solomon, under the patronage of the St Clair lairds. Loyal to the Stewarts and the Catholic creed and the Jacobites, they took in their falling the militant Scots Lodges to America and France, where these groups became major leaders in both revolutions against the tyranny of kings and religion. With their wealth and records destroyed, the Sinclairs of Rosslyn saw their church and castle lapse into ruin, leaving behind many false interpretations of what they had believed and done.

I

The Labyrinth and the Bull

We do not choose our names. We are given them after our birth. We cannot select the genes which make us what we are. These are our inheritance. We grow within a tradition and sometimes an old place. After much research and writing a couple of books on Rosslyn and the St Clairs, I found that the more I knew, the less I knew. Our name did not date from the Viking invasion of France in the 10th century, but from Homeric times. There lay the beginning of an entry into a maze of queries.

I had the luck and the grace of a classical education. So I returned to old myths and a map of ancient Greek cities in Asia Minor, where Troy had been attacked in the *Iliad* in that primal conflict of the West against the East. I discovered that there was a shrine to Apollo at Claros to the north of the Athenian colonies of Colophon and Ephesos on the mainland off the islands of Samos and Chios. According to the historian Pausanius, the Clarians claimed to be descended from the Cretans, where Minoan culture stretched back to the 4th millennium BC with its labyrinth and its bull worship. Certainly, when I reached the stubs of the fallen columns of the ruined temple of Apollo in its swampy ground, four rows of a hundred sacrificial stone blocks still held iron rings to tether their victims. Overlooking these remains, the vast and headless statues of Apollo and his sister Artemis and his goddess mother Leto still reigned in disdain.

In their ceremonies in ancient Crete, young men had leapt over the horns of huge bulls, while the mythical founder of Athens, the hero Theseus, redeemed the sacrificial victims of his city by killing the

Minotaur, the shag-headed and hoofed and tailed monster at the heart
of a maze. That great beast was the offspring of Queen Pasiphae, who
had lusted after Poseidon's Bull of the Ocean, meant for sacrifice and
not for her bed. Her husband King Midas was the son of Zeus, who
had changed himself into a white holy bull to ravish Europa and give a
name to a continent.

The Minoans from Crete were the trading partners of the Egyptians. And at Saqqara, near the Nile and the ancient capital of the
Pharaohs at Memphis, the persistent bull cult of the Eastern Mediterranean can be viewed in one desert place. Near the original step-
pyramid designed by the high priest Imhotep in the 27th century BC,
there is the Serapeum, the catacomb of the bulls sacred to the divine
Apis, a creative force through which life reached this world. He would
later be called by the Greeks Serapis, in a combination with the god of
dying and rebirth, Osiris. Off dark vaults, side chambers hold twenty-
five huge granite sarcophagi weighing seventy tons apiece. Buried
within the tombs for 1,400 years were the mummified corpses of the
sacred cattle kept by the priesthood; one pickled beast remains in the
Agricultural Museum in modern Cairo. And outside in the desert, a
circle of Greek philosophers, now headless, can still be seen, as if in
silent approval.

The worship of the bull dated back to the Babylonians and the
Assyrians and the earth-mother Cybele, whose lover Attis was
castrated. Her cult had preceded that of Apollo in her cave at
Claros. The vengeful Bull of Heaven, sent by another primal earth
goddess Ishtar, had been killed by Gilgamesh, who had spurned her
divinity and lust. The genitals of the beast were eaten by many
worshippers, while a bath in its blood would become a pagan
precursor and response to the Christian communion of the Blood of
the Saviour. One ancient text stated, 'Reborn into eternity through
bull sacrifice'.

In the original Temple of Solomon, twelve bronze bulls would
support a huge basin, full of the waters of life, while live bulls were
also sacrificed as burnt offerings to Jehovah. That seminal belief
would persist into the visions of the Apocalypse in the Christian
Bible, with a bull-headed angel and demon in the *Book of Revelation*,
an Apis after the Cross. To this day, Jewish and Muslim people

purify their meat by slitting the throats of animals and draining the blood.

In Homer, the cult of Apollo, whose anger devastated the Greek camp outside Troy at the start of the *Iliad*, was associated with Κλάρος, a method of prophecy which used marked twigs taken from a bowl to show the divine will. Moreover, this was a way of dividing the spoils among the warlords by seeing who drew the long end, and not the short. At Delphi and Claros (probably the origin of its name), such a means of divination was common. It passed on to western Europe, for the Roman historian Tacitus noted that the Celtic and Germanic peoples divined the future by casting marked twigs. Also at Claros stood a blue-marble navel stone, the ᾿ομφαλος, the origin of this earth.

The temple there was so famous as an oracle that the Latin poet Ovid, in exile by the Black Sea, wrote of Clarian Apollo. The inquirers went underground to a sacred spring, where a male priest drank from the holy water and answered the question he was posed in a gnomic way. His trance may have been aided by the opium poppy or hemp or methane gas from the neighbouring marshes. Alexander the Great consulted the oracle before founding Pagos or Smyrna, whose inhabitants had this answer from the priest:

> You shall live three and four times happy
> At Pagos, across the sacred Meles.

And so they did for millennia, although Alexander died young, before he could see his new city grow, while his cavalry tactics would inform the Mediterranean world for many generations.★

As a matter of fact, when Alexander died in Babylon, his embalmed body was placed in a temple on wheels to be dragged back to Greece. His divine remains were diverted to Alexandria, where a mausoleum was built to house them. He had expressed the wish to be buried at the Oracle of Siwa, where another meteorite was the stone of prophecy. This one was beset with local emeralds, the precious stones of Hermes, the messenger of the Gods.

When the Alexandria mausoleum was burned, the holy corpse was said to have been spirited away to Siwa, where the oracle had

★ *See Illustrations.*

prophesied that the Greek general would become a god. In one Islamic miniature, Alexander was depicted as worshipping at a third meteorite, the black stone in the Ka'aba at Mecca. He fascinated the Islamic world and was identified with the Two-horned One in the Koran, who was 'given power on earth, and made his way to the furthest west and furthest east'.

The Mesopotamian, Egyptian and Hellenic mystery religions would become the forerunners of Christianity in some of their beliefs and ceremonies. During the dramas and celebrations over nine days at Eleusis, sacred vessels were produced. Clement of Alexandria and Plato both mentioned a ritual speech of the worshippers: 'I fasted, I drank the potion. I took it from the chest. Having tasted it, I put it away in the basket and from the basket into the chest.'

These sacraments were followed on the fourth day of the festival by a procession with a basket containing pomegranates and poppy seeds, cakes and salt and a live serpent. On the last day, two jars were filled with water and wine, and these were placed to the east and to the west. These were overturned to the words *ue kue*, 'rain' and 'conceive'.

These fertility rites were matched in the contemporary Orphic mysteries of Dionysus, the overlord of wine and the spirit. He was a similar god to the Egyptian Osiris and Attis and the Phoenician Adonis. They all died and were born again to become divinities of life and death, giving human beings an assurance of their own immortality. In Greek legend, the body of the child Dionysus was eaten by the Titans, who boiled and spitted and roasted his flesh. This was a communal and cannibal feast. The Titans were then destroyed by a thunderbolt from heaven, and humanity was born from the ashes. An element of this ancient blood sacrifice would reach the Christian religion.

The celebrants of Dionysus also ate the raw flesh of animals, as he was said to have done: the savage hunter as well as the maker of wine. When his follower Orpheus, with his lyre, was torn apart by the frenzied Bacchantes, his sacrifice was a prelude to eating the divine flesh and drinking the blood in an orgiastic mystery, at which some healing cures of the disturbed and the sick were reported by Plato. The singing head of Orpheus was said to have been washed up at

Lesbos, an event celebrated by Milton in his *Lycidas* – another version of the speaking heads of the Celtic gods and Christian martyrs.

The worshippers at the Orphic ceremonies affirmed the split between the corrupt body and the eternal soul, which descended into Hades and was sent back to this world in an endless recurrence until the spirit might be liberated to join the gods. An Orphic gravestone in southern Italy asserted: 'I am a child of earth and the starry heaven, but my descent is from heaven. This you know yourselves.' Clement of Alexandria again recognised this view of the flesh as the prison of the spirit, when he wrote that ancient theologians witnessed 'that for a punishment the soul is yoked with the body and buried in it.'

The way to heaven was through an ecstatic vision of God. An ascetic life of penance culminated in a religious celebration, in which wine and narcotics were used to induce the vision of the divine. The early ceremonies of the Orphic cult may have included Minoan and Anatolian sacrifices, where the blood of sheep and goats was poured from a jug into a cauldron in the ground. Later Orphics in Roman times were attracted by the Christian communion, when wine was translated into holy blood as a means of absolution, of freeing the spirit from the flesh.

Although the Romans defeated the Greeks, they surrendered their education to their slaves. 'When in Rome,' the saying went, 'do as the Greeks do.' Zeus became Jupiter and was called the Stone. The strongest oath was *Per Jovem Lapidem*, 'By Jupiter and the Stone'. Both Poseidon and Neptune were worshipped as a square stone, while Hermes and Mercury were represented by a plain standing-stone or a head placed on a square column.

The first oriental divinity accepted in Rome was consulted by the senate in 205 BC and thought to have won the Second Punic War against Carthage. The Sibylline oracle had declared that Hannibal would be forced out of Italy, if the Mother of the Gods, the Greek Rhea, could be sent from Phrygia to Rome. One more black meteoric stone representing the female principle of creation was delivered by King Attalos of Pergamon and installed in Rhea's temple on the Palatine.

Another important oriental cult figure for the Romans was the sun god Mithras. His worship derived from India and the Persian Maz-daists, who saw the world as a battleground between the forces of light and good and the powers of darkness and evil. Mithras was identified with the sun, the bringer of light to humanity, the mediator in the cosmic struggle. The Greeks called him *Helios* and the Latins, *Sol Invictus*, 'The Invincible Sun'.

The widespread Mithraic chapels of the Roman Empire were often built underground or in caves with the signs of the zodiac, set on mosaic floors. Part of the service was a communion with a consecrated cup and a loaf, symbols of the holy supper which Mithras had taken with the sun after his time on earth. The Christians claimed that the followers of Mithras had stolen their Eucharist, although the reverse might have been true. The pagans also believed in the survival of the divine essence in humanity, and in rewards and punishments in an afterlife. Mithras would descend on the warring world like Christ at the Last Judgement. Then he would awaken the dead, separate the virtuous from the sinners and rule over a heaven on earth.

We discovered an unknown Mithras temple in a cave beneath the ruins of a house in Jayce after the war in Bosnia. In the carving, the god can be seen at the ritual sacrifice of a bull with a sun disc behind his loose tunic. A dog swallows the blood of the beast as a symbol of the immortality of the soul. The reptile of resurrection, because it sloughs its skin from a renewed body, the Serpent of Wisdom is shown, turning about the sword-arm of this divine killer.★

Mithras wears a Dacian conical helmet with earpieces. This con-firms the passage of the light cavalry, who had once fought Alexander the Great, from the steppes through the Balkans as far as Hadrian's Wall in Roman Britain. Indeed, about AD 175, over five thousand Sarmatian horsemen reached that frontier, converted to animal god worship.★ Four Mithras altars and two legionary standards bearing the heads of bulls are still preserved in the museum at Maryport in Cumbria. Rudyard Kipling himself wrote a hymn to the beliefs of the 30th Legion, quartered about AD 350 on the Wall.

★ See Illustrations.

Mithras, the God of the Sunset, low on the Western main –
Thou descending immortal, immortal to rise again!
Now when the watch is ended, now when the wine is drawn,
Mithras, also a soldier, keep us pure till the dawn!

Mithras, God of the Midnight, here where the great bull dies,
Look on thy children in darkness. Oh take our sacrifice!
Many roads thou hast fashioned – all of them lead to the Light:
Mithras, also a soldier, teach us to die aright!

In pagan and Celtic Britain, two major cults were those of the severed head and the horned god. Along with the serpent and the stag, the bull and the ram were the divine symbols. Bulls' heads were also linked with hawks or eagles. The greatest of the supernatural bulls, the Donn of Cuálnge in Ulster, had fifty youths playing on its back or leaping over it as in ancient Crete. An effort to rustle the mighty beast resulted in an Irish civil war.

Iron was the most precious metal of its age, for it made the weapons by which one tribe destroyed another. Once tempered, the metal was fiercer and harder than the bronze weapons of Homer's heroes. In early Irish history, the Firbolg, who first invaded that island, were miners, who used bronze and iron in their weapons. Pushed out by other invaders from northern Europe, the Tuatha de Damaans, they passed over as Scotti to Dalriada or Argyll and the Borders. There they encountered the Picts, who claimed descent from the Scythians and the Thracians. These cavalry tribes had already been strung along Hadrian's Wall by the Romans, and there they joined units of the Tungri and the Batavians. As the historian Tacitus noted, they were so expert in swimming with weapons and horses that they could cross the Rhine, let alone the Humber or the Tweed. 'There is no strength in the Roman armies, but it is of foreign strangers.'

The Greek Herodotus noted of the Scythians that they were tattooed or painted with woad as were the original Picts, who met the Roman legions. They also cast slender javelins as well as swinging broadswords and heavy rounded spears, the forerunners of the fearsome bills of Border war. They became worshippers of the eastern sun-god Mithras. His weapons in the Zend Avesta were the gold club, the bow and quiver and arrows, and the axe, which slew the sacrificial bull that Zoroaster had called the principle of life in man. In northern Britain, the dog below the Mithraic altar also represented Cu'chulain, the great Irish hero; it was the hound of heaven, and the guide of souls across the divide between earth and sky.

The legendary god and king Lug, who had brought with him the Daghda Cauldron of Wisdom and the sacred spear and sword, defeated the Firbolg with his warriors, on St John's Day or Mid-summer. Their sea-deity was the Mithraic Ogmios of the sunlike face, who was said to have invented writing in the Ogham script. In Greek, 'ογμος meant a furrow, a straight series of things planted or the line of the reapers. And in both Greek and Latin letters, our only records of early Celtic history lie. Lug was also connected through the Latin *lux* with the cult of divine light.

In his account of Agricola on his British campaign, Tacitus alluded to battlefield tactics on the Borders. He claimed that three Batavian and two Tungrian cohorts dismounted and fought the enemy with their round shields, 'for the enormous native swords, blunt at the point, are unfit for close grappling and engaging in a confined space.' The bosses of the iron shields mangled the bare faces of the foe, who broke and ran. In the poem of *Beowulf*, a shield was known as a *hilde-bord*, round and small with hollow metal bosses, tapering to a point or knob, while in Gaelic, a *bord* also signified a shield.

With their iron weapons, the Picts and the Scots were prone to fighting and raiding sheep and cattle. The northern tribes justified their forays by continuing to worship the bull as a god, as can be seen on the seven carved stones retrieved from the ancient fort at Burghead in Morayshire.* When the Mithras cult arrived with the legions at Hadrian's Wall, where a whole temple to the Sungod is still preserved, they found previous worshippers of divine beasts, ready to oppose them.

Even at the time of the Crucifixion, the old animal sacred killings persisted in the Jewish faith. On Yom Kippur, the Day of Atonement, the High Priest entered the Holy of Holies in Herod's vast Temple, which enclosed the smaller one of Zerubbabel on Temple Mount in

* See Illustrations.

Jerusalem. He sacrificed a bull in the ancient ritual way as an offering to cleanse the sins of Israel. Then he uttered the Tetragrammaton, the hidden four letters of the name of God, and the people prostrated themselves. Afterwards, two goats were chosen for a holy role. One 'scapegoat' was loosed into the desert to die, while the other was slaughtered to purge the errors of the nation.

In *The Acts of the Apostles*, we read of St Paul proceeding on his mission to the Gentiles as far as Ephesos, south of the ancient temple at Claros. He was on his way to his martyrdom under Nero in Rome. There he condemned the worship of the Greek gods, particularly Diana of the Ephesians. But he converted the Greek-Jewish Timothy, who became the first bishop of Ephesos, and 'a certain Jew named Apollos, born at Alexandria, an eloquent man, and mighty in the scriptures'. This was a pagan, not a Christian name, and implied the translation of a man from the Apollonian Temple at Claros, who was well versed in Greek Gnosis. Ephesos and Alexandria would become the sources of spreading Gnostic doctrines through their chief preachers, Valentinus and St Thomas, as far as western Europe and India.

From his prison in Rome, St Paul wrote back to the Ephesians through his disciple, the Roman Tychichus, in Latin — St Paul also spoke Greek and Aramaic, the ancient language used in the recent film, *The Passion of the Christ*. We have the first mention of the Latin word *clarus*, which differed from its Greek meaning of 'prophecy'. It meant 'clarity' or 'light'. As St Paul wrote in almost a Gnostic way, 'for ye were sometimes darkness, but now are ye light of the Lord: walk as children of light.'

Such a message would be music to the souls of Apollos and Timothy in Ephesos, for the new bishop there received two more epistles, exhorting him to see the messenger to heaven as Christ, 'who hath abolished death, and hath brought life and immortality to light through the gospel.' These three messages from St Paul were written about AD 50 and predated the Gospels.

Until the Emperors Constantine and Justinian imposed a Canon of what should be in the Bible and what not, there was a struggle for centuries over the many texts of the time and their meanings. There was even a revival of paganism under Julian the Apostate, when the Temple of Apollo at Claros was deluged with bull's gore in old ceremonies, only to be cast down afterwards by Byzantine decree. The followers of Mithras were wiped out in their own blood.

In Rome, the Gnostic Valentinus from Alexandria nearly became the Pope of the Christian Church, but was beaten by Pius the First, otherwise we would not worship as we do now. Not until the end of the 2nd century AD was the first sustained attack on the Gnostics written by St Irenaeus, the Bishop of Lyon. He showed how much the doctrine of the Holy Light, the immediate way from the self to the divine, had spread to the South of France.★

In early Christian times, the passing of the communion chalice and the drinking of the Blood of Christ were uncommon, for this practice derived from the ancient mystery religions and the Jewish faith. By the 13th century, Rome would deny the giving of communion to lay people. The Body and Blood of Christ, the host and the chalice, would be reserved for the priest.

The carved head of a horned bull-god or Ba'al outside the 15th-century St Clair chapel at Rosslyn, wrongly ascribed to the Muslim devil Baphomet, would demonstrate the persistence of the Mithras cult along the Scottish Borders. From the time of Hadrian's Wall for fifteen hundred years, the cult of the bull has lingered in cattle-owning societies. As in the Roman Empire, the gladiators, called matadors, still fight the mighty beasts in Spain and Provence. The Ba'al at Rosslyn pointed back to millennia of heresy and probably indicated a labyrinth within the chapel, where the Minotaur was replaced by Lucifer and slain in the Mass of the Armed Man.

★ See Illustrations: Map.

2

Sanctus Clarus

A certain sense of the ancient infuses the past, and both affect the present. If we drive through the Langue d'Oc high into the Pyrenees, the mountains inform us of attempts to dwell there from cave people to pagans to Romans and the coming of Christians. Against these peaks and gorges, any human effort seems stillborn. Yet I did discover how my namesake Sanctus Clarus was held to have preached and died there. When the legend is written and carved in stone, at least it survives for the living. And when places are given their titles, they hallow a long tradition. As the Latin epigram stated: *In Nomen Numen*. In the Name, the Divine Will.

At the end of the 6th century, St Gregory of Tours wrote the first account of the historical St Clair. In the earlier *Gnostic Gospels*, the Blessed Joseph of Arimathea and Mary Magdalene were held to have brought the faith and the Grail to eastern Aquitaine, landing at Marseilles. According to Gregory, two other saints from Ephesos, Martin and Clarus, went with St Paul to Rome and were later dispatched to western Aquitaine at the time of the Gnostic doctrine reaching Gaul. Clarus may well represent the 'Apollos' of *The Acts of the Apostles* by the simple change of a pagan to a Christian name at his baptism by St Paul. Both names signified the search for the light of wisdom.

A later manuscript of the 11th century from the Benedictine monastery of Saint Sever on the Cap de Gascogne in the Landes stated that Sanctus Clarus came from Greece, where his family had been converted by St Paul. The disciple went to Palestine to convert the Jews, but he was expelled, and so he proceeded to Rome. There the Pope Anacletus consecrated him as a Bishop and sent him to convert western Aquitaine with six other priests, who would become martyrs.

The site of their harbour on their mission was meant to be the island of Cete near Narbonne in the Langue d'Oc. This hill, covered with a pine forest near a plateau of white stones, was a landmark for sailors, who called it Mons Setius, although now it bears the name of Mont Saint Clair. Once topped by a Roman fortress and the home of the 7th Legion, after the 12th century the crest supported the oratory chapel of Sanctus Clar or Cler. A hermit, Hilarion, would live there on alms given by the faithful, who bathed their sore eyes in the holy cistern as a cure. The blessed saint was meant to heal the blind by a miracle.

A wild herb of St Clar did grow on the sides of the hill at Cete. The extraordinary abbess St Hildegarde of Bingen recorded St Clar's wort as a remedy for weeping and red eyes. On his Saint's Day of 12 July at Gondrin in the Gers, pilgrims still wash their eyes with water from the holy well in the village. Sanctus Clar was also the protector of crops. Wearing a scarf covered with black crosses and carrying a pallium on his shoulder, his statue can be seen, chasing the clouds from the harvest, at the church of St Privat de Salces in the Lodève. There he was held to be a weather forecaster, with the worshippers chanting on the date of his festival:

> If the sun shines on Saint *Clar's* Day,
> For forty more, it will stay that way.

Traditionally, Sanctus Clarus and his six disciples, Justin and Girons and Sever and Polycarp and Jean and Babyle, proceeded along the Roman road to Albi, where he became the apostolic First Bishop. His relics and those of his companions are still carried in processions on his blessed day in the diocese of Auch, at Agde and Périgueux, at Tulle and Sorlat, at Rodez and Lectoure, where all seven apostles were murdered for their faith. On the wall of the church of Sainte Eulalie in Bordeaux, an inscription reads: *Charlemagne founded this chapel and placed behind the altar the blessed bodies of the fortunate seven who had received the crown of martyrdom.*

In the fortified cathedral of Albi, which rears as a brick battleship above the city, and beside the largest mural of Heaven and Hell in all of France, one of thirty chapels off the soaring nave is still dedicated to Sanctus Clarus, and there his relics lie, although some of his bones are still at Bordeaux and Lectoure. In the commune of Quins near Averyon a woodland chapel of the 11th century, dedicated to St Clair de Verdun, has been restored in his honour, while the Abbot of Rodez testified to the cult being observed in nine surrounding villages. En route to his ending, the apostle of Aquitaine named two towns of the Langue d'Oc, Saint Clar de Rivière in the Haut Garonne and Saint Clar in the Gers.

At Lectoure, where his sarcophagus is preserved, St Clar and his six companions met their fate, while trying to convert the nine pagan tribes of the region. He refused to make a sacrifice in the Temple of Diana. Instead, he fell on his knees in prayer, and the statue of the goddess crashed down in pieces. Accused of sacrilege, he was stripped, dragged behind a horse through thorn bushes and whipped and put in prison. Then he and the other six priests were beheaded, as St John the Baptist had been.

When I saw my namesake's stone coffin at Lectoure, I could hardly believe my eyes. It was covered with many of the symbols of the Gnostics and the Masons. There was Jesus holding the Grail plate at the Last Supper. There were Adam and Eve in Eden with the Serpent of Wisdom, or the Sophia. There was Solomon or David with two lions between the twin pillars, Joachin and Boaz, of the first Temple. And outside tradition, when the orthodox faith was still being decided in Aquitaine, research in Albi told me that a historical St Martin had founded an abbey at Marmoutiers in the 4th century, while a Gallo-Roman aristocrat with the name of Sanctus Clarus had set up a nearby priory. Both were accused of being Gnostics and of preaching the heresy of the direct approach to God by the individual self without the need of the Church of Rome. They would become the heralds of the Cathars and the Albigensians with their doctrines of the Perfect Ones and the Elect.

During the spread of early Christianity, there was a multitude of interpretations of what the Gospels meant. Many of the Gnostic texts were excluded from the final Bible. One of them, *The Epistle to*

Rheginos, began by stating that there were some who wanted to learn much, but they were occupied with questions, which had no answers. They had not stood within the Word or Logos of Truth. They sought their own solution, which could only come through Jesus Christ, who had denied death, although that was the law of humankind.

'Those who are living shall die. How do they live in an illusion? The rich have become poor and the kings have been overthrown, everything has to change. The cosmos is an illusion.' All was a process, the transformation of things into newness, which would create a heaven from a corrupt society.

The authors of the Gnostic texts chose insight rather than the sermons of early Christian bishops as the way to interpret the Gospels and reach revelation. On this count, they were denounced in the late 2nd century by St Irenaeus for 'inventing something new every day'. His chief target was Justin Martyr, who had been a Stoic and a Platonist before becoming a Christian philosopher. Justin praised the heresies of Simon Magus, the magician and enemy of St Paul, while Christ was treated as the Logos or Word, who mediated between the sinful earth and the light of paradise.

These inspirations were called Gnosis, which now came to mean a personal vision, a direct and individual perception of truth. The first appearance of Jesus to Mary Magdalene in the garden after His Crucifixion was interpreted in her apocryphal Gospel as no actual event or even a spiritual flash; she saw Him in her mind. This vision she reported to His disciples. They could now see the risen Christ as she had; any believer could see Him. Of course, the direct approach to Christian revelation put in doubt all religious authority. Why listen to a bishop if an inner voice told you what Christ wanted you to do?

In St Mark's Gospel, it was stated that Jesus had given the disciples the secret of the kingdom of God, while He spoke to the rest of the world in parables. While Saints Peter and Paul professed to pass on these secrets to the Churches later established in Rome and Byzantium, the Gnostic Gospels claimed that the living Jesus could at any time reveal His hidden mysteries to a woman, who was not even a disciple. He could appear to a Mary Magdalene, who represented the ancient female principle of generation, and the Sophia, the goddess of

Wisdom. He would show Himself to the person, who was fit to see and hear the divine message.

For the Gnostics, there were two distinct worlds, split by a war zone and a veil between heaven and earth. On the shining and dividing screen were the pictures of things, created by the Logos or Word and interpreted by Christ. Flaming walls separated wisdom from matter with angels as messengers across the horizon between sky and sea and land. The problem of evil allowed by a just God was solved, for life below was already hell.

While the Christians were still secret sects persecuted by the Roman Empire, such heresies could flourish among a larger heresy. Yet after Constantine established Christianity as the official faith, these subversive cults, which declared that authority was evil, had to be extirpated. Yet the Byzantine Emperor would call his new basilica Sancta Sophia, not after any saint, but the wise goddess.

The more extreme of the sects were persecuted – the Orphites, who worshipped the wise Serpent; the Adamites, who held their ceremonies in the nude; and the Cainites, who cast aside all civil authority to venerate Cain carrying out the divine will by killing his brother Abel, as well as Judas, who was forced to denounce Jesus. As St Irenaeus wrote of the teaching of the Gnostic 'Gospel of Judas', 'He alone was acquainted with the truth as no others were, and so accomplished the mystery of betrayal. By him all things, both earthly and heavenly, were thrown into dissolution.'

For the philosophers of the Kabbalah, the Shekinah was the Sophia, the principle of the Divine Mother united with God, and eternal, and indivisible. As St Irenaeus also wrote of the Gnostics, they said that the Sophia spoke of Jesus descending from 'the incorruptible light of heaven'. The Sophia was also the serpent in the Garden of Eden, which brought wisdom with the apple to Eve and Adam, and led to their expulsion from paradise to a Satanic earth.

The cult of Sanctus Clarus spread to the north-west of France. Such doctrines of the personal revelation of a secret knowledge and of a continuing revolution were to be the motive forces of heresy within Christianity for two thousand years. Every state and each Church had to reject the rebellion of the cults. Once the Bible was defined within the limits of the Old and the New Testaments, allowing only the messianic and apocalyptical *Book of Revelation* inside its covers, all deviations from that holy norm might be pursued with fire and sword. The deviants would be terrified into dissolution. Fear will drive men to any extreme, as George Bernard Shaw noted – as faith will, too.

The cult of Sanctus Clarus or the 'Holy Light' did reach Albi, which would become the centre of the Cathars and the Elect and the papal crusade against that revolt. And curiously enough, another legend was born in Provence, because of the emigration of members of the House of Levi there with the collapse of the Roman Empire. The Elect of Israel were the Bnei-Zadok Levites, also called 'the Sons of Light'. They were responsible for guarding the Ark of the Covenant with the Holy of Holies, the Shekinah. Their arrival would raise many myths about the blood-line of Jesus and the Ark reaching the west of Europe.

By the 3rd century, a St Clair became the first bishop of Nantes. Very little is known about him historically. According to Breton legend, about the year AD 280, the Pope had him sent to Amorica, entrusting him with a relic: the nail used to pierce the right hand of Saint Peter at the time of his crucifixion.

Legends concerning another saint preceded this founder of the diocese. In Brittany, it was said that in the year AD 69 another Sanctus Clarus was consecrated bishop by St Linus, St Peter's successor as the head of the church, and that apostle died thirty years later. This oral and traditional way of having Sanctus Clarus alive in the 1st century has allowed a fabulous hagiography, in which he is placed in a relation with a disciple of Joseph of Arimathea called Drennalus, who went to Great Britain at this time. No wonder that the first of the romances about King Arthur and the Grail were chanted by Breton minstrels.

This other Sanctus Clarus of legend was reputed to have died at Réquiny, in the district of Vannes, on October 10th of the year, which became his Feast Day in Brittany. The church of that parish still preserves a trepanned skull attributed to him, as well as a cenotaph, which is consecrated in his name. The latter bears the following inscription: *Saint Clair, buried here October 10th, 868.* For the corpse of the blessed bishop was transported from Nantes to Angers at the time of the Norman invasions. Until the French Revolution, it was protected in a silver reliquary in the Benedictine Church of St Aubin. In the 17th century, however, his skull was venerated in the Cathedral of Nantes. The historian La Borderie saw in these two skulls 'an unimpeachable proof of the duality of two personages'.

This other St Clair was also invoked for the recovery of eyesight and for weather favourable for good harvests. Until 1890 at Réquiny, people immersed the skull of the saint in a basin, and those suffering from eye inflammation or from blindness used this hallowed water for bathing their eyes. This custom has disappeared in our day. A Latin hymn from 1400 is chanted to implore the grace of the saint to bring back sight, or insight:

> We praise by pious hymns
> Saint Clair who gives light to blindness.

Certainly, the cult of the Holy Light spread from Aquitaine in place-names up to Lyon and the north-west of France. This progress was paralleled by the advance of the vision of the Grail through 150 shrines to Mary Magdalene all the way to Glastonbury through Fécamp across the Channel. There were five Norman towns called St Clair before the Viking invasions. In 911, Rolf the Ganger and his longship crews from Norway and the Orcadian Isles, including the Møre family, defeated the French King Charles the Simple. The Møres took the name of the town of St Clair, which was on the Epte river, where a peace treaty was signed, ceding the occupied territories to the raiders.

When I visited the town park, I found a statue of a St Clair, holding his severed head in the palms of his hands. Said to be a hermit from Kent, he was meant to have suffered the fate of St John the Baptist, after refusing the advances of the local Salome. The myth from over the Channel was clearly false. He represented the original Sanctus Clarus, beheaded in the Pyrenees. That was proved by a well near his original cell there; its waters were again used to cure eye diseases. Healing wells were always associated with the title of St Clair; there would be one dedicated to St Catherine near Rosslyn. There the Viking border barons, who had become Normans and taken on a new name, would build a castle in Scotland and a mystic chapel of the Grail.

3

King Arthur and the Grail

Charging against the invading English in the south, King Arthur won the great battle of Mount Badon. The later of his twelve battles were fought in the Cheviot hills north of Hadrian's Wall. In the *Annales Cambriae*, he is claimed to have brought Christianity to the north about 573 at the battle of Arthuret, later the site of a Templar commandery. The brief ancient chronicler of that fabled cavalry commander, the Welsh monk Nennius, made Arthur unite the Clyde kingdom of Dyfnwal in the early 6th century with the command of Camelot over the West Country and Wales, where he was known as Emrys and given a Celtic ancestry. His defeat came at Camlann, 'in which Arthur and Medraut [Mordred] perished. And there was a plague in Britain and Ireland'.

His tactics were commemorated in the Welsh poem, 'The Elegy for Geraint', a prince of Dumnonia or Devon.

> In Llongborth, I saw the clash of swords,
> Men in terror, bloody heads . . .
>
> In Llongborth, I saw spurs
> And men who did not flinch from spears . . .
>
> In Llongborth, I saw Arthur's
> Heroes who cut with steel . . .
>
> Under the thigh of Geraint swift chargers,
> Long their legs, wheat their fodder,
> Red, swooping like milk-white eagles . . .

Most probably, King Arthur had succeeded a Romano-British leader, Ambrosius Aurelianus. As the contemporary Celtic monk Gildas wrote of him, he was brave on foot, but braver still on horseback. Unlike the medieval legends of armoured knights in various colours with lances, these horsemen adopted the tactics and the light weapons which the Sarmatians had already used in the north – the thick leather jacket with a mail breastplate and a helmet, the javelin and the short sword, the curved bow and the small shield. They were highly mobile and raided the ranks of the Saxon invaders, equipped with broadswords and long spears. This was no joust of chivalry, but a charge against massed infantry. No heavy armour has been excavated from many early battle sites, which yield swords and spears and little else.

Historically, the Papacy often considered Britain as the home of heresy. The great offence to the Bishop of Rome was the idea of a direct approach to God without the intercession of the Church. In the early 5th century, two Celtic monks, Pelagius and Coelestius, were banished from the Holy City for preaching that through their deeds, human beings could perfect themselves. There was no original sin, as St Augustine was arguing. Therefore a priest, who might absolve sins, was unnecessary. The believer could reach heaven by his acts alone on a sinful earth.

'Everything good, and everything evil,' Pelagius wrote, 'for which we are either praised or blamed, is not born with us, but done by us.' This doctrine was condemned by the Council of Ephesos and was to breed the first crusade of Europeans against Europeans, when the Cathars would be destroyed by Simon de Montfort and the Inquisitors. Pelagius was also the forerunner of Calvin, who would split the Christian world with the doctrines of the Puritan and Protestant faiths.

The Celtic heresy of Pelagius denied the authority of Rome. There had already been British revolts against the Caesars led by the cavalry of Maximus and Constantinus, whose conquests in Gaul foretold the legend of King Arthur's victories on the Continent. In 429, Germanus, later called Saint Germain in his bishopric at Auxerre, was sent on the first of two visits to Wales to suppress the Pelagian heresy, which was backed by the paramount ruler Vortigern. Faced with an incursion by the Irish and the Pictish Scots, Germanus used his military

knowledge to destroy the invaders near Mold in Flint by a charge of
warriors shouting 'Alleluia!' After this victory, Germanus was called
Harmon in Wales. He set a precedent for later claims that King Arthur
won a battle bearing the image of Jesus Christ or the Virgin Mary on
his shield.

Yet Germanus failed to root out Vortigern's resistance to the rule of
Rome. The Welsh king invited the raiding Saxons to act as his
defenders against the Irish, who had already established a beachhead in
Wales, and against the Picts in the north. He ceded land and tribute to
the Saxons, who were later followed from the Continent by other
tribes of Angles and Jutes. The new settlers turned on the natives and
destroyed the late Roman urban civilisation of the south-east of
England. Gildas also wrote in *The Loss and Conquest of Britain* of
'the general destruction of everything good and the general growth of
everything evil throughout the land'.

The twelve battles, in which Arthur was the victor, can only be
surmised as being somewhere on the mainland of Britain. They have
variously been sited in Lincolnshire, Northumberland, Cheshire,
Strathclyde, Somerset, Wiltshire, Berkshire and East Anglia. Certainly,
a defence against the Anglo-Saxon incursion would have involved
fighting on a shifting frontier drawn from Devon along the Welsh
borders to the Firth of Forth, while the Irish pushing into Pembroke
and Argyll implied separate battles on the western shores. These were
cavalry actions against foot-soldiers, for Arthur probably took over the
tactics of Ambrosius. And he was successful, for in the late 6th century
Gododdin, Arthur was said to be supreme at slaughter and glutting
black ravens.

Keeping a force of hundreds of knights in the field involved
sophisticated planning and a wandering court. Recent excavations
at Cadbury Castle and other Iron Age hill forts have shown that Celtic
warlords returned to these ancient strongholds behind their ditches
and earth walls, adding stone and wooden ramparts along with gate
towers and halls. Fodder for the horses was easily found on the hill
slopes, although not for long. Surprise attack was unlikely over open
ground.

The feudal system was not yet in place, as in the later Grail
romances. So the court could not be supported by the local country

people for more than a month. King Arthur and his fighters had to ride from place to place to maintain themselves. Even in the late Middle Ages, the royal court was a moveable feast. In Arthur's day, Camelot was on the hoof all over Britain. That palace of later dreams went to where the next campaign was.

The probable sites of Arthur's travelling Camelot were these: the Roman city of Colchester, or Camelodunum, where he would have fought the Saxons in East Anglia; Cadbury Castle, where he might resist any advance into the West Country, with Tintagel as a last bastion; Carleon-on-Usk, where he would have struck against the Irish colony in South Wales; Dinas Bran, near Llangollen, which was called after the Celtic god of the speaking head and was given the name of the Grail Castle Corbenic in medieval times; Carlisle, where he would have contained the Danish invaders; and Arthur's Seat in Edinburgh, where he would have opposed the Picts from the north, and from the west the Irish, then called the Scotti. The necessity of feeding the cavalry would have kept Arthur in the saddle, as it did the original Celts of the Russian steppes, who had fought another legendary hero, Alexander the Great.

Tactics insist on movement. That was why the ancient chronicles and Grail romances altered places and names so frequently. And as these sagas and accounts were usually sung or spoken by many voices before they were set down in writing, the variations in spelling and in translation eddied as banners in the wind. What is certain is that the truth of Arthur was taken up by the Celtic bards to create the legend of a conquering hero, who would reflect his fame on to his people.

Already by the 7th century, four British royal families had given a son the name of Arthur. He became the Matter of Britain, as opposed to the Matter of France, which glorified Charlemagne, the supreme Emperor. And there was also the Matter of the classical age of Homer and Virgil, the heroes of Troy and Rome, and of Alexander the Great. These bardic tales would provide the synthesis of the European romances of the Middle Ages, where the Eastern traditions met the British, French and German to create the stories of the personal search for the divine.

The Celtic religious renaissance of the 6th and 7th centuries was based on the Atlantic sea routes, and was set against the authority of

Mediterranean Rome. The word was spread by holy pilgrims and hermits, the apostles of the later Grail romances. They spoke in resistance to the Nordic, Germanic and later Arabic assaults on the Celtic folk. They demanded a political hero, who would defend his people and their independent faith from their enemies. They chose Arthur, the *dux bellorum* and Christian leader, in this sustained period of Celtic resistance to Nordic penetration, which would become the stuff of legend.

King Arthur was a war hero among the native peoples of Cornwall, Wales, Ireland and southern Scotland. A different Byzantine rite had passed from the Mediterranean along the old tin-trade routes to these Celtic civilisations. From that Greek learning, the Irish monasteries were becoming the leading lights of what were later miscalled the Dark Ages. They were sending missionaries, pilgrim saints and hermits after the example of the desert Christian Fathers to Wales, the Isle of Man and Scotland. There in the time of King Arthur were concentrated the early Christian gravestones inscribed in the Ogham script, that writing in stone of grooves and notches, which may have derived from the Druids.

St Petroc carried the faith to the west of England and Brittany where Celtic refugees had already fled from the Anglo-Saxons; many churches were named after him. St Samson also sailed to Cornwall and Brittany with his Irish chariot: his voyage was commemorated on a stained-glass window in the Cathedral of Dol. Other pilgrim saints reached Galicia in Spain and even Iceland, while St Aidan founded an abbey at Old Melrose with monks from Iona, and St Cuthbert studied there before evangelising the Scottish Borders.

The roles of the Irish Saints Columba and Columbanus as bearers of the Greek and Gnostic doctrines of the divine light is a matter of history. In his early account, Adamman, the Abbot of Iona, who died in 704, declared that St Brendan saw 'a most brilliant pillar wreathed with fiery flares' preceding his fellow saint. A side-chapel was filled with light by Columba, and nobody could look on him any more than the midday sun. As the saint told another novice, 'Take care of one thing, my child, that you do not attempt to spy out and pry too closely into the nature of that heavenly light which was not granted thee.' And another peeper through the keyhole of the saint's cell was told that if prayers had not been said for him, he would have fallen dead before the door, or had his blinded eyes torn from their sockets. With Columba's death, the whole vault of heaven was illuminated, while an immense pillar of fire rose to the stars at midnight, so that the earth was as bright as under the summer sun at noon.

Such a confusion of the missionary Irish Columba with the sun-god Mithras heralded his coming to his famous monastery in Iona. There, the saint was also meant to have blessed a knife for the slaughter of bulls, although he hoped that it would not injure man or beast. Equally in the 6th century, from St Andrews to the Orcadian Isles, an anchorite and monastic movement of Irish monks, the Célidé or Culdees, established early Christian and eastern Greek practices in the first Scottish church, independent of Rome, before the Reformation. Their Greek names as priests, *papas*, are still commemorated on Papa Stour in Shetland and Papa Westray in Orkney.

These early differences were backed by later letters to the Pope, written by the Celtic St Columbanus, who took his mission from Ireland through Burgundy to Bobbio in Italy. He told Gregory the Great and Boniface the Fourth that they had limited authority, which did not extend to the Celtic Christian ways of worship. In his most famous letter, Columbanus disagreed on the dates of Easter. He was grieved at the ill repute of the contemporary chair of St Peter in Rome. 'It may be that in this affair, a living dog is better than a dead lion. For a living saint may correct the errors that have not been corrected by another greater one.' He also protested that the Celts were the recipients of pure and early Christianity. 'For all we Irish living at the uttermost ends of the earth are the disciples of St Peter and St Paul and of all the disciples who wrote the sacred canon under the inspiration of the Holy Spirit: receiving nothing outside the evangelical and apostolical doctrine.'

Pope Gregory the Great had sent a second St Augustine to Canterbury, and the Saxons would become the spearheads of the Italian version of Christianity in Britain. According to the Venerable Bede, the Pope thought that the nearby Angles should also join the angels in heaven. Certainly the Anglo-Saxons would confirm the supremacy of the Roman rite in England by the middle of the 7th century, at the Synod of Whitby. Yet in Scotland, Mass was still being spoken in Gaelic, the language used in the 11th-century illuminated *Book of Deer*, created in a monastery dedicated to St Columba and his preaching.

The fundamental Scottish heresy of salvation through good works would be the inspiration of the Knights on the quest for the Grail. By his virtue, each member of the Round Table might reach the light of God and the Holy Spirit without the need of a priest to absolve his sins. These wandering mailed horsemen were advised on their way to the Grail Castle by holy men, modelled on the travelling Celtic preachers who were spreading their independent faith over the northern Atlantic seaboard. The legends of Arthur and the Grail were to enshrine the resistance of many peoples to the authority of the Holy See.

Evidence of the Roman Church's growing suspicion of the legend of Arthur was apparent in later Welsh tales about him, in which he was presented as a trickster and a thief. And in various 'Lives of the Saints' he was shown to be evil. Before the writing of Geoffrey of Monmouth's favourable *History of the Kings of Britain*, Arthur was described in *The Life of Cadog* as full of lust and perversity, while *The Life of Padarn* turned him into a mean and despotic ruler. The Papacy continued to view Arthur as a rebel against its claims to supremacy.

The few who could read in the age of Arthur and in the centuries to follow were priests, and the language was Latin. Most people were illiterate. They heard what they thought, and they thought that was what they knew. Homer, and the bards who succeeded him at the courts of the later warlords of Europe, sang of the exploits of heroes. They also spelt out the genealogies of their patrons, connecting these families to the superhumans of past legend.

A strange legitimacy was conferred by Homer in the *Iliad* on the later dynasties of the Greek cities, connecting them to the gods as well as the myths. Virgil in his *Aeneid* performed the same sleight of birth for the Roman emperors. These revered epics persuaded the Greeks and the Romans that their rulers were blessed and came from divine ancestry. Such was the task of Geoffrey of Monmouth, when he wrote in 1135 the sourcebook of King Arthur and the Matter of Britain. He was providing proof that the Norman conquest had inherited the myths of blood and soil of the defeated North Sea islanders. The

Normans were the true heirs of the Celts. Both peoples had resisted the Germanic tribes and the power of Rome.

In diplomacy, a country usually allies itself with the enemy of its own immediate enemy. With *The History of the Kings of Britain*, the Welsh or Breton Geoffrey of Monmouth could build up the legend of Arthur to illustrate the fact that the Celts and the Normans had defeated the Anglo-Saxon incursion into England. He went much further and left out much more. The Normans were actually Vikings, who had invaded France and taken over Normandy and Brittany in the 10th century. Before that, they had destroyed and colonised Orkney, the Shetlands, northern Scotland, the Western Isles and parts of Ireland, as well as pillaging the monasteries and cities of much of northern Britain.

The victory of William the Conqueror in England was only the prelude to the spread of Norman rule to the south-west of France, Sicily and southern Italy, where they became the adversaries of Islam, then spreading its faith across Africa and the Mediterranean to the north of Spain. This clash between Christians and Muslims led to the crusades. Jerusalem had already fallen to Frankish kings, when Geoffrey of Monmouth concocted a European empire for King Arthur as large as the true one of Charlemagne.

From the syntheses of the epics to date, Geoffrey created the propaganda for the Norman Empire. By his invention, the mythological Brutus of Troy colonised Britain and released it from a race of giants led by Gogmagog. Telling many more tall stories, two of which Shakespeare used in *King Lear* and *Cymbeline*, Geoffrey took his fabulous tale on to Arthur. Inspired by the magician Merlin, who was confused with Ambrosius Aurelianus, this legendary emperor spread his dominion to Norway, where the Vikings had originated, and on to the Rhine in a mastery of France.

There, the British King defeated Flollo, the then Roman tribune of Gaul, in a brilliant joust. Arthur felled his enemy from his horse and was laid low himself. Covered with blood from a head wound, the British King struck the Roman with his sword Caliburn, or Excalibur, and so sent him to the ground and his soul to the winds. Normandy was given to his cupbearer Sir Belvedere, and Anjou to his seneschal Sir Kay. Thus the Normans were confirmed as the heirs of the Celts

and the Vikings, and as the opponents of Rome, which was only saved
from Arthur's advance by his death at Camlann and burial on the Isle
of Avalon.

Geoffrey of Monmouth insisted that the deeds of Arthur lay in the
memories and traditions of many people, as surely as if they had been
written down. He claimed to have read them in an ancient book given
to him by Walter, the Archdeacon of Oxford. Most of the troubadours and chroniclers of the Grail romances would claim ancient
sources for their endeavours. William of Malmesbury, who had
created his own *Deeds of the Kings of England* ten years before
Geoffrey's *History*, declared that his rival invented everything about
Arthur and his successors 'from an excessive love of lying, or for the
sake of pleasing the Britons'. But William also asserted that King
Arthur should be commemorated in true histories and not only in
Breton tables, because of his long resistance and restoration of Celtic
morale.

In later colonial empires, trade would follow the flag. But in the
12th century, song followed the sword. In the French and British
fiefdoms of the Normans, Welsh and Breton bards and troubadours
were predominant. They were like Widsith in the early English poem
of the Far Traveller, who claimed to have sung all over Europe and the
Near East. He glorified his peers:

> Thus wandering, the minstrels travel as chance will have it through the
> lands of many different peoples. Always they are bound to come across,
> in the north or the south, some person who is touched by their song
> and is generous with his gifts, who will increase his reputation in front
> of his henchmen showing his nobility of spirit before worldly things
> pass away, the light and the life. He who works for his own good name
> will be rewarded on earth by a strong and steady fame.

After the Dark Ages, Celtic minstrels were moving through the
Atlantic areas, spreading the legends of Arthur and his companions.
Transcendent among them at the court of Poitou was the Welshman
Bleheris. He was the 'fabulous translator' of Arthurian legend into
Norman French, and he was commemorated by two rivals as someone
who knew the history of all the counts and all the kings of Britain, and
'all the stories of the Grail'.

The term troubadour derived from the Provençal word *trobar*, to compose, to seek and to find. In that sense, the lays of the minstrels were quests for the Grail put to words and music. Certainly, their art was influenced by oriental singers from Spain as much as by Celtic bards or classical legends. Arabesques, with their tantalising sadness, became part of their musical technique, and the pilgrims and knights setting out to Palestine repeated the refrains. The wandering minstrels were the entertainers and reporters of their age, which rarely distinguished between fancy and fact.

The pilgrim Celtic saints had converted the Atlantic seaboard to the Greek rite. Now the Welsh and Breton troubadours spread the news of King Arthur, his exploits and his empire, from the ocean through the Continent by word of mouth. A French text, derived from Geoffrey of Monmouth's *History*, which was written in Latin, was set down by Wace of Jersey in the Channel Islands. He dedicated his creative translation of the Matter of Britain, *Roman de Brut*, to Eleanor of Aquitaine, the wife of King Henry II of England and Normandy. With her possessions, the king could claim an Anglo-French empire almost the size of that of the legendary Arthur. Wace added to the story the legend of the Round Table, which he had heard from other Celtic sources, and he ended his account with the hope of the undying King Arthur, ready to be resurrected when his people might need him.

These two seminal texts were copied out hundreds of times in the next centuries before the coming of printing. But in this illiterate era, it was the wandering minstrels who spread the word of Arthur, using Geoffrey of Monmouth and Wace as cue sheets. Since Homer, flattering bards had been the chief entertainers of the courts and the counts. From Poitou and Aquitaine, the fame of Arthur reached Italy, probably with the Breton contingent assembling at Bari for the First Crusade.

The early 12th-century arch over the north door of Modena Cathedral portrays Arthur of Britain, called Artus, and his knights, as they rode to deliver the Queen of Camelot from the Dolorous Tower. In 1165, a mosaic was laid in the cathedral of Otranto near Bari, showing Arturus Rex carrying a sceptre and riding a goat. This mocking description of the Celtic hero as a kind of devil on a playful pavement satirised the suspicion of the Roman Catholic Church in regard to British and Norman resistance. At the end of the century, Gervase of Tilbury visited the Norman court in Sicily and reported that King Arthur had been sighted living in the fiery crater of Mount Etna. Again, the Normans of the time were struggling with the Papacy for control of southern Italy, and the myth of Arthur's return suited their aggressive diplomacy.

Chrétien de Troyes created the story of the Grail in his *Perceval*, putting it together from many ancient and contemporary tales, as well as from his own imagination. His was a synthesis of genius, making molten many myths to forge for the chivalry of his time a justification for the search for glory and for God. He was fortunate in his birth and career. He was probably born about 1135 at Troyes in Champagne in France. The city was a crossroads of Eastern beliefs, which were returning with the crusaders to jostle with the Christian faith; also a frontier where the Matter of Britain and Arthur met the Matter of France and Charlemagne.

His early patron was the cultivated Marie, Countess of Champagne, the daughter of the French King Louis VII and Eleanor of Aquitaine, who later married King Henry II of England. Countess Marie and her mother were said to have presided at a Court of Love, which insisted – as did King Arthur's Round Table – on a knightly code of chaste behaviour to women.

Marie made Champagne the vineyard of the culture of courtesy and chivalry, but when her husband, Count Henry, went away to the Holy Land and died a week after his return to Troyes, she left public life, refusing to marry the new patron of her poet Chrétien. This was the widowed Philip of Alsace, Count of Flanders and a temporary Regent of France. He died of the plague on the Third Crusade without recapturing Jerusalem, now lost to the Muslim armies of Saladin. In one sense, the invention of the quest for the Grail would symbolise other crusades to regain the Holy City in Palestine.

Chrétien dedicated his last unfinished romance, *Perceval* or *The Story of the Grail*, to this Count of Flanders, whose father, Thierry of Alsace, had even brought back the Holy Blood of Christ – the sacred relic was his reward from the King of Jerusalem for valour shown on the

Second Crusade and on three other expeditions against the forces of Islam. In a great procession in 1150, he had donated the precious fluid to the city of Bruges.

The chapel built to house the relic still exists; round dark brick arches lead to a shadowy altar, over which a golden pelican now settles. The bird was a symbol of the Redeemer, as it was meant to feed its young with its own blood, as shown on the mosaic in Charlemagne's chapel at Aachen; it also represented a distilling vessel for the process of alchemy. Two black Grail tombstones on the floor, however, are badly worn from innumerable feet, but they recall the containers which once held Christ's Blood.

Influenced by the mass faith in the Holy Blood and the fierce stance against heresy taken by Philip of Flanders, Chrétien de Troyes turned the Celtic Grail myths of pagan cauldrons into Christian symbols. In fact, he claimed that he had merely put into verse a lost book loaned to him by his patron:

> He tried and tried time after time
> The best tale ever told to rhyme.
> The royal courts recount the tale:
> It is the story of the Grail.

Count Philip had fallen out with the King of France before going to the Holy Land. Chrétien also presented Perceval as a rebel against authority. A simple Welsh youth with a lethal proficiency with javelins, he badgered passing knights to find out what they did, and then deserted his mother to make his way to the court of Arthur. There he discovered that a Red Knight had insulted the King and had stolen a gold cup. He pursued the knight and killed him with a javelin through his eye, taking his armour and his horse. He also had the gold cup returned to Arthur. Untaught, Perceval went on his way towards the Grail Castle.

This ingenious opening prophesied the mysteries of the mission. Perceval was then too simple to see the quest for the Holy Grail as more than a fight to recover a stolen precious object. And so he was unaware when he met the crippled King of the Grail Castle fishing in a boat nearby. Directed to that place, Perceval found himself in the finest fortress this side of Beirut in the Near East. There he was given a sword of Arabian, Grecian and Venetian work. The following procession of the Grail was also associated with the East and the crusaders, such as Philip, Count of Flanders, for it was led by a squire carrying a white lance with a tip that bled drops of crimson blood.

The discovery of the Holy Lance below the cathedral of Antioch had saved the First Crusade from disaster. This relic was held to be the iron point which the blind Centurion Longinus had put into the side of Christ, only to have his sight restored by the Saviour's blood and water, running down into his eyes. That sacred flow was also said to have been collected by Joseph of Arimathea in the cup used at the Last Supper, a vessel which was to become the chief symbol of the Grail.

This blessed vision of Perceval was nearer to paganism than to the doctrine of the Roman Catholic Church. Although the bleeding lance was associated with the death of Christ, it also had a parallel in the magic Spear of Destiny of Welsh and Irish literature. This belonged to the god Lug, and was both lethal and life-giving. It could kill as well as make the desert green. It could destroy all the royal enemies, but also a whole kingdom. Its prick could ravage as well as regenerate. The harm of its point could only be blunted in a cauldron or bowl of boiling blood and water: the male principle creating birth from the female. Otherwise, its wounds might lay waste to the land of the Fisher King, who was incurably maimed by its thrust between his thighs.

Chrétien de Troyes went further by combining the Celtic and Nordic cauldron and horn of plenty with the communion chalice. He was not, however, the first to use the word 'Grail'. Meaning a 'dish', *graal* had occurred previously in a romance about Alexander the Great, and earlier as *gradalis*, or a bowl to serve delicacies. In *Perceval*, the vessel appeared to have a lid, which was removed before it served its inexhaustible food for the needs of all present. Platter or closed bowl, it was a giver of plenty, as was the Welsh *dysgl*, one of the legendary Thirteen Treasures of Great Britain. Yet it also contained the host or Body of Christ, the sole food of the Fisher King. And it was carried by a young woman.

This was anathema to the Church of Rome. The communion cup

could only be borne by a male priest. The Elevation of the Host to the congregation remained a sacred mystery, which would not be unveiled. Yet to Chrétien, all those in search of perfection might see the Grail themselves. He was associating the giving by Christ of His Body and Blood with pagan goddesses of fertility, the chalice representing the womb. He was also alluding to the Gnostic heresies from the Near East that were spreading across Flanders, Brittany, Champagne, Provence and Italy. These spoke of a Sophia who embodied divine wisdom. The Grail in her hands was the Word and the Light of God, which blazed like the sun on the darkness of this earth, where Satan was fighting for mastery of the flesh.

For the Gnostics, the most significant of biblical texts came from St John the Evangelist: *God is Light, and in Him is no darkness at all.* Their preachers saw themselves as John the Baptist in the Gospel of St John: *He was not that Light, but was sent to bear witness of that Light. That was the true Light, which lighteth every man that cometh into the world.* That was the Light that shone from Chrétien's Grail, carried in the female hands of wisdom and rebirth. The Gospel also contained the stories of Nicodemus and Joseph of Arimathea, so significant in the medieval romances about King Arthur and his Knights.

The Host within the Grail seen by Perceval was not the communion wafer of Catholic absolution, but rather the blessed bread distributed among all believers at the feasts of the early Christian communities, and later the Cathar heretics. It did not so much represent the Body of Christ as the miracle of the loaves and the fishes, where Jesus fed the multitude: the fish was a Greek sign of Christianity, while the Fisher King symbolised the search for salvation within his Castle. In *Perceval*, the maiden carrying the covered bowl of the Grail was followed by another young woman with a silver platter. They were serving sacred food to the Knights of the Grail, but it was not the Eucharist. And Perceval saw no priest, altar or cross inside the castle walls.

Although Chrétien de Troyes was a French-speaking cleric and poet, his influence came from Britain, Rome, Byzantium and the Jerusalem of the crusades. He might have visited the first two places; he knew of the history and creeds of all four. In the sacred objects of the Grail procession, he combined the Celtic and the Nordic with the

Christian, the Kabbalah and Islam. The bleeding white lance derived from the castle of the god Lug, as well as the hand of St Longinus, who let out the blood of Christ with it. The golden Grail set with gems was a Celtic cornucopia and a Christian chalice. The silver platter represented a cauldron of plenty and the dish, on which was once set both the head of John the Baptist and the sacrificial lamb of the Last Supper. The Grail held many sources and had many shapes.

Chrétien's last romance contributed to the spiritual awakening of Western Christendom at the time. There were discoveries or rediscoveries in science, mathematics and philosophy; the founding of convents, monasteries and Military Orders; the flowering of chivalry and courtly love; the making of the Gothic cathedrals; and the arrival of the crusades in Jerusalem, there to build a holy and heavenly city on earth. The quest of the crusaders fed on the quest for the Grail. Both were martial pilgrimages in search of the place of the Holy Spirit, also of peace and plenty on earth before a vision of heaven.

When King Richard the Lionheart came within sight of Jerusalem, he hid his eyes under his shield and turned his crusading army away, as Lancelot did before the Grail. He did not feel fit to achieve his desire. For only a knight without sin could reach the Grail, which ministered to the needs of its guardians in a castle on the Mount of Salvation. The way to the Grail was by trial and test. A knight had to survive sitting at a Last Supper in the empty Judas seat, the Siege Perilous. If he was a sinner, he was swallowed up. If he was stainless, he might search for the divine Light − in fact as well as in fiction.

Gillermus or William St Clair, the son of the original Lord of Rosslyn, went on the First Crusade. Many of the Møre line would join the Vikings from Orkney on other expeditions towards Jerusalem. They were inspired by the rise of the great neighbouring Cistercian abbeys of Newbattle and Melrose in Lothian, also by the Scottish headquarters of the Knights Templars at Balantrodoch or Temple, only six miles to the east of Rosslyn.

The family would become the stuff of other romances and legends. A truth of its past, however, occurred to me, when I stumbled over the first of fifty Templar gravestones, which I was to discover in

Scotland or the Borders. They mostly bore the signs of the broad-sword with the Rosy Cross and the Grail. Those original markings on a tomb lay in three broken pieces in a dark corner of Rosslyn chapel. Now restored, it is in pride of place.

4

The Knights of Black and White

The small carved Grail stone of WILLHM DE SINNCLER bore a battle sword with a Lombard hilt. From the steps of the Temple of Solomon, a long stem ran up to a chalice, enclosing the flowering octagon of the Rosy Cross.★ This was the memorial of a Templar knight, usually buried in this fashion. In Sir William's case, he had died twenty-one years after the Military Order had been condemned. He had been killed on a crusade in Spain, while trying to carry the heart of Bruce for burial in Jerusalem. His skull and bones had been returned by the Moors for interment at Rosslyn.

The crusaders and the Knights Templars were not the first westerners in the conquest of Jerusalem. The Vikings had formed the elite corps of the Byzantine Emperors for centuries. The Varangian Guard of these northern raiders and traders had sailed down the Vistula and Volga rivers through Poland and Russia and across the Black Sea. They were as significant as the Praetorian Guard had been in ancient Rome. They defended and made and broke these new Greek Caesars of the Balkans and the Near East. The most renowned of them was the royal Haraldr Sigurðarson, the later King Hardrada III of Norway, who was defeated at Stamford Bridge by another English King, Harold, in a clash before the Battle of Hastings, when armoured Norman knights and archers – nine of them St Clairs – would destroy the shields and broadswords of the thanes.

As many Norse war leaders, Haraldr entered Byzantium with a poem:

★ See Illustrations.

> The cool wind drove swiftly
> The black prow of the ship
> The iron-clad vessels
> Held up their masts in splendour
> The great king saw the metal roofs
> Of the city gleaming ahead . . .

With his men, Haraldr was taken into the service of the Emperor Michael IV to command the Varangian Guard. He was sent to Palestine, and he helped to take back Jerusalem into the Christian faith. Before the Knights Templars, his saga stated that he 'made an offering at the grave of Our Lord, and to the Holy Cross, and to other holy relics in Jerusalem, of so much money in gold and jewels that it is hard to compute the amount; he also put the entire way to Jerusalem at peace, slaying robbers and other evil folk.' Actually, the Emperor had made a truce with the Caliph of Egypt in 1036 to allow the rebuilding of the Church of the Holy Sepulchre by Byzantine masons. The Varangians were sent there to protect pilgrims, as the Templars would at a later date.

Haraldr's major campaigns were against fellow Vikings, the Normans who had conquered Sicily and Southern Italy. On one campaign, he wrote back to his queen:

> The ship was filled with blood
> By the cape where blood blew;
> The ships ran to the shore,
> The Lord fought nobly . . .
> The bodies of the dead let the blood
> Pour onto the planks of the keel.

Haraldr was later imprisoned for the theft of imperial funds. In his gaol, he was meant to have killed a lion and a Great Worm or dragon, as Theseus had killed the Minotaur. Released in a *coup d'état*, Haraldr slaughtered his enemies and blinded the pretender. In two Viking craft, he escaped to assume the throne of Norway by sliding over the iron chains across the Bosphorus. The Varangian Guard was later filled with Vikings, fleeing after the victory of the English King Harold, and with English warriors, also escaping the wrath of the Normans after King Harold's death at Hastings.

These two battles were to change the balance of warfare. From the time of King Arthur until the interminable Viking raids of the succeeding hundreds of years, the light horsemen and the spearmen and the archers had usually been defeated by the strength and weapons of the Nordic invaders, who were armed with broadswords and battle-axes, shields and spears and knives. They wore conical and ridged helmets over leather jerkins, sometimes reinforced with mail. Their armourers had to import superior blades from the Franks, who had better smelting techniques. Their rapid-fire small bows shot, as the Eddas stated, swarms of arrows, whining as angry bees. Such archery had been learned when the mounted cavalry of the Steppes had loosed hailstorms of shafts at the Viking ships pushing down the Russian rivers towards Byzantium.

Reaching Stamford Bridge near York in 1066 after a series of forced marches, King Harold faced King Hardrada, who had drawn up his men in a Norse phalanx or shieldburg. English cavalry attacks did not break the metal ring, but the flight of many arrows did. Provoked, the huge Hardrada led an attack on the English spearmen and almost hacked his way through the lines before being killed by a shaft through the throat – an uncanny prophecy of King Harold's own tactics and death against the Normans. And so Hardrada achieved what his mounted rival had promised: 'seven feet of English ground, or as much more, as he may be taller than other men'.

With more forced marches, King Harold returned to the southern coast to confront at Hastings another sea assault from William, Duke of Normandy. Now he adopted Viking tactics. Between two tracts of sea marshes, he blocked the Norman advance on London with a wall of the long yellow and red shields of his house carls, wearing helmets and hauberks, and armed with battle-axes and maces. Behind them were thousands of levies, carrying bills and scythes and clubs. There were few bowmen or horsemen.

William led off with an attack by his archers, but the shield wall held firm. A second assault by his men-at-arms with their spears was repulsed by thrown axes and javelins and stones. This was followed by repeated cavalry charges with lances, but these also failed. For the great battle-axes of the thanes could cut off a leg or a head of an armoured knight at a stroke, as can be seen on the Bayeux Tapestry, woven and thick with lopped limbs.

Either by a stratagem or the need to regroup, the Norman horsemen withdrew. The shield wall broke ranks in a charge after the defeated foe. But when the pursuers were killed, more Norman charges uphill were unsuccessful, except on a wavering left flank. Turning to meet this weakness, King Harold was killed in a cloud of arrows, fired high over the shield wall, or in a last stand around his raised ensign, The Fighting Man. The following massacre of his forces in retreat showed the superiority of heavy cavalry in most of the pursuits of the Middle Ages.

William, Duke of Normandy, thus became King of England. With his professional mailed knights and a system of fortifications and the feudal system, he would establish a successful European strategy for warfare and government, which would endure until the coming of cannon and gunpowder. The broadsword and the axe and the foot soldier would have few victories against the armed man on his charger, backed by spearmen and the terrible archers of the longbow, which could pierce chain mail a hundred yards away, without mercy or redress.

So the Vikings and the English and the Normans fought and fled and died. The St Clairs were of Viking descent from the Møre family and Norse warlords called Rögnvald, often mentioned in the Icelandic sagas. The most significant of these was the *Orkneyinga*, which dealt with a crusader who also became a saint. Earl Rögnvald Kali of Møre in Norway and Orkney began to build St Magnus Cathedral at Kirkwall in the 12th century. A poet as well as a warrior, he joined in the Viking surge to the Mediterranean, taking fifteen warships to Narbonne in south-west Provence on the way to the Holy Land. Here he met the heiress Ermingerd. As the saga related:

> The Earl was sitting feasting one day when the Queen came into the hall escorted by a group of ladies and carrying a serving-bowl of gold. She was in her finest clothes, with her hair falling loose as is customary with virgins and a golden tiara upon her forehead. She served the Earl, while her companions began to entertain them with music. The Earl

took her hand along with the bowl, and sat her on his knee, and for the
rest of the day they had a great deal to say to one another. Then the Earl
made a verse:

> I'll swear, clever sweetheart,
> you're a slender delight
> to grasp and to cuddle,
> my golden-locked girl.
> ravenous the hawk, crimson –
> clawed, flesh-crammed –
> but now, heavily hangs
> the silken hair.

Refusing the chance to marry Ermingerd, but promising to return to
Narbonne after the voyage to Jerusalem, Earl Rögnvald sailed away.
He had renewed the contact of the Far North with the St Clair cult
and the Cathar faith, before it was declared a heresy. As he wrote
again:

> In the Earl's ear the words
> of Ermingerd will echo,
> enjoining us to journey
> by water to Jordan.

After swimming across the sacred river and visiting the Byzantine
Church of the Holy Sepulchre and the Templar stronghold by
the Dome of the Rock in Jerusalem, the Viking warfleet sailed on
to Constantinople. There, Earl Rögnvald was pressed by the
Emperor to join with his men the Varangian imperial guard,
but he would not be another Haraldr Hardrada. He left six ships
and a thousand crewmen to the Emperor, and with one craft, he
set off for Rome. There he bought horses and rode back from
this other holy city on the pilgrim route all the way to Denmark.
He passed through Le-Puy-en-Velay, where the octagonal St
Clair Chapel was modelled on the Church of the Holy Sepulchre
and Charlemagne's Chapel at Aachen.* When he returned to
Orkney, he would see again the round churches at Orphir and

* See Illustrations.

Egilsay, built by St Magnus on Byzantine models before his betrayal and murder.

In 1158, Earl Rögnvald Kali's turn to die came about in Calder Dale in Caithness, where the outlaw Thorbjorn Clerk and his men killed him with a sword stroke on the chin and a spear thrust to the body. His reign of twenty-two years as Earl of Orkney had been distinguished by protecting his own state against the Kings of Scotland and Norway as well as many a pretender, including the Bishop of Orkney. His corpse was carried back for burial in St Magnus Cathedral, where the saga stated:

> Earl Rögnvald rested until God made manifest the worthiness of the earl with a number of wondrous miracles, whereupon, with the Pope's permission, Bishop Bjarni had his holy relics translated. On the boulder, where Earl Rögnvald's blood had poured when he was killed, we can still see it, as lovely as if it had been newly spilt.
>
> Earl Rögnvald was deeply mourned, for he had been much loved in the isles and in many other places, too. He had been a good friend to a great many people, lavish with money, moderate, loyal to his friends, a many-sided man and a fine poet.

He was to be an inspiration to two later Earls of Orkney, Henry St Clair, who would also be known as 'the Holy', and William St Clair, the builder of the Grail chapel at Rosslyn.

After the Varangian Guard had policed the pilgrim route to Jerusalem, the Byzantine Emperor had cleverly bribed the First Crusade to fight his battles against the Muslims in the Holy Land. Another guardian force was needed there, and that was to be the Knights Templars. The Military Order was created by St Bernard in the 12th century. The son of a nobleman from Burgundy, he built with his brothers and friends a monastery at Citeaux and an abbey at Clairvaux, which would become the spiritual beacons of the Europe of the crusades. The genius of Bernard was to put together the Church with chivalry. To defend his Cistercian Order of white monks, he had sanctified the Order of the Knights of the Temple of Solomon, with their black-and-white banner, *Beauséant*, of light and dark.

The Cistercian monks and the Knights Templars were always to be linked by place and sympathy, but not by history. For when the Templars would be proscribed as heretics and lose their thousands of commanderies, the white monks would keep their distance and their monasteries, including Melrose and Newbattle near to Rosslyn. St Bernard himself was always a disciple of Rome. He could not foresee the consequences of his diplomacy with the Vatican, when he secured papal blessing for the armoured guardians of pilgrims visiting the holy places in Jerusalem, where the Templars had their base.

In 1146, St Bernard preached the Second Crusade to King Louis of France and many nobles at Vézelay. His fervency and tongue of quicksilver, praising the remission of grievous crimes for all who took up the cross, provoked a gale of acceptance. His hearers cried out for the favours of Christ. Before too long, all the prepared red strips of cloth were finished. Saint Bernard had to give up his red robe to be cut into pieces for those who would go east. His helpers became tailors and stitched the pledges of the holy pilgrimage on to the cloaks of the faithful. An orgy of commitment promised another holy war. After preaching later to the people of France, Bernard was able to write to the Pope: 'The crusaders have multiplied to infinity. Villages and towns are now deserted. You will scarcely find one man for every seven women.'

St Bernard was not preaching a personal quest towards the divine, but the remission of the sins of the crusaders through the Church of Rome, which also wished to assert its authority over the warlords of Europe. The refrain of a popular crusading song offered the same benefit:

> He who leaves with Louis need not worry about Hell.
> His soul will go to Paradise with Our Lord's angels as well.

Bernard also persuaded the Pope to consecrate the future Knights of the Grail, the Templars, founded in Jerusalem in 1118 by Hugh de Payens and eight companions from Champagne and Provence. Their duty was to guard the pilgrims to the Holy Land, where they were masons as well as monks with a sword. Their strongholds and chapels would become models for many Grail castles, while their service to

God would make them examples to all chivalry, before they would be condemned as traitors to orthodoxy. In his day, Bernard of Clairvaux compared them to the early anchorites:

> They come and go at a sign from their commander; they wear the clothes which he gives them, seeking neither other garments nor other food. They are wary of all excess in food or clothing, desiring only what is needful. They live all together, without women or children . . . They are never seen combed and rarely washed, their beards are matted, they reek of dust and bear the stains of the heat and their harness.

This way of life was modelled on the questing knights of the Round Table as well as on the early Christian saints. Here the standards of chivalry met the ordinances of the Church. But these directives could not bridge the deepening chasm between Templar wisdom and the Holy See. The knights of that Military Order were a permanent standing army in Palestine, a few hundred horsemen holding the Holy City and a broken necklace of castles across the waste. They were particularly influenced by the rival Isma'ili warrior sect of the Assassins, who held fortresses and territories in the mountains near the Caspian Sea and in Syria. They were assimilating Shi'ite and Sufi doctrines of eastern mysticism and resistance to the dictates of church and state.

There had been two recognised 'Grails' in Jerusalem. One of them, described by Albert of Aix, was the golden urn hanging from the centre of the Dome of the Rock, that marvellous Muslim shrine mistaken by Christian pilgrims for the Temple of Solomon. That precious vessel was believed to hold manna from heaven and the Holy Blood of Christ. And there was the True Cross, recovered from the Orthodox Syrians in 1099, a golden and jewelled reliquary containing a little of the wood from the torture of Jesus. The rest of the Holy Cross had been taken to Constantinople, but this relic was carried into battle by the crusading knights until it was lost to Saladin at his victory at the Horns of Hattin. It was either sold to the Byzantine Emperor by Saladin's brother and successor, or it disappeared in the Islamic wars after the capture of the Kingdom of Jerusalem.

The loss of the Holy City put an end to the main purpose of the Knights Templars, who were the protectors of pilgrims to the Christian holy places, now in Muslim hands. Although they were to survive for another 120 years as a Military Order, the Templars had to find a new role. They fell back to the sea and built fortresses there, preparing for another crusade to take back Jerusalem. More and more, the Templars became merchants, bankers and administrators of their estates rather than seekers after the divine.

Their fate was foreshadowed by another crusade, now directed by Rome against its brother Christians in France. The victims – the *cathari*, or pure ones – were called heretics, as the Templars were to be in their turn. Since their foundation by Hugh de Payens, the Templars had been closely connected with the Court of Champagne, Provence and the Langue d 'Oc. The patrons of the culture of the south of France, certainly the richest and most civilised in Europe in the 12th century, supported the crusades and died while serving upon them. But the kings of France coveted these independent principalities, and the Popes distrusted the increasing power of the Cathar priests, called *perfecti*, who wanted to reform the faith by preaching a personal contact with the Light of God.

Both the Cathars and the Templars were influenced by Manichean, Sufi and Islamic doctrines, as well as by early Christianity and the Kabbalah. They believed the flesh was corrupt and life was an ascension to the spiritual, rather like the quest for the Grail. In the Merovingian crypt of the basilica of Saint-Victor at Marseilles, carvings of a descending Serpent of Wisdom and a Tree of Life and the Knowledge of Good and Evil, with its roots exposed, adorn one column in evidence of the enduring heresies of the Langue d'Oc. For the Cathars were convinced that Lucifer, or the devil, had brought about the creation of man.

Through the mystical feast, known as the *manisola*, and the *consolamentum*, the chaste kiss of reception into the faith, the *perfecti* took their initiates into the path of the Spirit. This religion was certainly more pure and personal than Catholicism at the time, for an individual was made responsible for his or her own soul by an ascetic way of life. Cathar influences were evident in the quest for the Grail and in the early crusading zeal to reach the holy city of Jerusalem. The

Albigensian Crusade was turned into a tragedy against a recruiting ground for the previous crusades to the east.

St Bernard, too, incited this perversion of a holy war. He considered the people of the south of France to be little better than heathens:

> The churches are empty, the people have no priests; the priests are not shown the respect which is their due. The Christians deny Christ and their temples resemble synagogues. The sacred character of God's sanctuaries is ignored, and the sacraments are not accounted holy.

White and black monks preached the conversion of Provence to the orthodox faith. They denounced the direct contact with God, so attractive to the south of France with its wandering knights and minstrels. The concept of the quest for self-perfection through trial, hope and fear was thought an oriental and mystic heresy, even if its philosophy had wide popular appeal in the Grail romances and the poems and love songs of the troubadours.

The lands and cities of the Langue d'Oc were as thoroughly ravaged as the Waste Land of the Fisher King. Predictably, Montségur, one of the last Cathar castles to hold out, was held to be the Grail Castle, where spiritual food and life were available to the *perfecti*. The Catholic besiegers called it the 'Synagogue of Satan', the term which the Cathars used for the Church of Rome. Indeed, there may have been a form of Mithraic worship at a temple of the sun at Montségur, which was the heart of the heresy.

A chalice and other treasures used at the *manisola* were said to have been smuggled out of the stronghold by four refugees before its fall and to be buried still – another real Grail – in the caves near that fortress. Although some of the Templars joined in the Albigensian Crusade, many of the Cathar knights who escaped the slaughter were to be received into the Military Order of the Temple of Solomon, which was itself permeated with oriental influences.

The Grail epics were always an irritant to the Catholic Church, which was prepared to order the massacre of Christians, seeking a direct approach to the divine Word and Light. In both *Perceval* and the later *Parzival* of Wolfram von Eschenbach, the way to the Grail was suggested by a holy lay hermit. Such a revelation might be reached in a castle, not of this world. The unnecessary priests of Rome had little to do with the transmission of the grace of God to humanity through a jewelled cup or a dove of the Holy Spirit.

The premier romances of the Grail diminished the role of the Church as the mediator between heaven and earth. Even if the Knights of the Grail went to Mass regularly and the Holy Spirit came to them at Camelot during the feast of Pentecost, their trials along the many ways to the Castle of the Fisher King made them able to experience or pass by the grace of God. By their deeds, not by the Latin Mass, they were chosen to view the divine.

Once the quest for the Grail had been described by Chrétien de Troyes, many actual Grails were identified within the Christian faith. Although that sacred vessel had ancient and pagan sources, it was declared to lie within the bowls, dishes, weapons and instruments that the Gospels associated with the Last Supper and the Crucifixion. Anything that was believed to have contained or touched the blood and wounds of Jesus Christ was considered to be a kind of Grail.

In the ecstatic confusion of the real and the visionary, which was the inspiration of the crusades and the early Middle Ages, sacred relics were venerated and became the advertisements of the abbeys and cathedrals that were spreading the worship of God across Europe. If the ceremony of the Mass changed bread and wine into the Body and Blood of the Son of God, His actual image, drops from His veins, or evidence of His martyrdom in Jerusalem were the literal proofs of a dominant faith. Holy relics were the medieval verdict of history in the Bible. These proved that what was believed had taken place.

The most precious Grails were the Holy Lance and the Holy Shroud, the Holy Veil given to Saint Veronica, the True Cross, the Crown of Thorns and the Cup of Joseph of Arimathea. All were surrounded by jewelled reliquaries of precious metal. As early as the 6th century, Antonius Placentinus had reported that the Holy Lance and the Chalice of the Last Supper were on show in the Church of Sion and the Basilica of the Holy Sepulchre in Jerusalem. Although these vanished with the Arab conquest of Palestine, pieces of the True Cross emerged again in Byzantium, also called Constantinople, along with the Crown of Thorns and the Holy Shroud and the Holy Veil, ransomed from the Muslims at the siege of Edessa and returned to Greek Christian ceremonies.

Three years before the Fourth Crusade seized Constantinople in 1204, the treasurer of the Pharos Chapel, Nicolas Mesarites, warned the enemies of the Byzantine Emperor not to attack the place: 'In this chapel, Christ rises again, and the Shroud with the burial linens is the clear proof . . . They still smell of myrrh and are indestructible since they once enshrouded the dead body, anointed and naked, of the Almighty after his Passion.' But a crusader, Robert de Clari, saw the Holy Shroud in the Church of Saint Mary Blachernae. Here 'was kept the Shroud in which Our Lord has been wrapped, which stood up straight every Good Friday, so that the features of Our Lord could be plainly seen there'.* When this crusader found this most precious relic – the Holy Shroud – in Constantinople, he added a description of another Grail. For the image of Christ was on a Veil imbued with the Water and Blood of Jesus, soaked with the fluids from His Body. In the Church of St Mary, the cloth with His features was contained in a rich vessel 'of gold hanging in the middle of the chapel by heavy silver chains'. To the Knights Templars, those containers of His Blood and the image of His head both signified a Grail, for the Holy Shroud certainly came into their possession after the sack of Constantinople.

The jewelled reliquaries of the Holy Shroud and Veil were said later to have reached the vaults of Rosslyn chapel, because of the close connection of the Cistercians and the Templars and the St Clair bloodline. The first of the family to reach northern Britain, Guillermus or William Saintclair, did not fight at the Battle of Hastings with his nine Norman cousins. As the later chronicler, Father Hay, wrote of him: 'He was sent by his father to Scotland, to take a view of the people's good behaviour. He was able for every game, agreeable to all company, and stiled the Seemly Saintclair.'

He arrived in the train of Queen Margaret, whose brother Edgar the Atheling had the best claim to the English Crown, and who would

* See Illusrations.

serve on a crusade. Exiled to Hungary, she had been chosen by the Scots King Malcolm Canmore as his wife. She brought with her one of the precious relics of her foreign stay, a piece of the True Cross, dark with age and enriched in a silver and gold casing, the Holy or Black Rood. In that mystical and devout age, the Rood symbolized the possession of the Blood of Christ, while the Coronation Stone of Scone or Destiny represented the keystone to the Temple of Solomon and a consecration from the kings of Judah.

As Father Hay took up the story, William Saintclair's 'qualifications came to the Queen's ears, who desired him of her husband because of his wisdom. The king made him her cupbearer, in which station he purchased to himself great favour and love of both Princes.' And so began one of two roles of the St Clair family for seven hundred years; the keepers of royal and holy treasures and the defenders of the crown. 'He got also of the King and Queen the barony of Rosline in liferent; after which, being desirous to try his fortune in warres, he obtained a company of men, underwent many dangers in resisting the Southern forces, and was appointed to defend the borders.'

As for the Cistercians and the Knights Templars, King David I was their special patron. The younger members of the St Clair branch were to serve as canons at the neighbouring abbeys of the white monks at Newbattle and Melrose, also in religious posts at Selkirk and Kelso, Dunkeld and St Andrews, Dornoch and Dunfermline. Faith and fighting went hand in fist in the age of the crusades. The St Clairs were always conscious of their duty to the royal house as the defenders of spiritual as well as secular power.

After a visit to Scotland by Hugh de Payens, King David also encouraged the Knights Templars and gave them the first of more than six hundred properties that they came to acquire in his land. Their headquarters were at Balantrodoch or Temple, a mere six miles to the east of Rosslyn. Because of this long association, the broken Templar tombstone, which I discovered, would still lie in Rosslyn chapel, a proof that the legacy of those Knights would never perish, even after their official destruction.

5

The Knights of The Stone Grail

Confounding the invasion of Europe by the Muslims, advancing from Spain over the Pyrenees in the 8th century, the knights of the Franks had defeated the light horse of the scimitar and the curved bow. Such weapons and Parthian tactics had previously destroyed the Roman legions in the Near East, but at the battle of Poitiers in 732, Charles Martel with his Austrasians announced the future supremacy of heavy armoured men, the tanks of their time. The unarmoured mobile cavalry of the Saracens charged the massed Frankish ranks and were slaughtered. As one chronicler related:

> The men of the north stood motionless as a wall; they were like a belt
> of ice frozen together, and not to be dissolved, as they slew the Arabs
> with the sword. The Austrasians, vast of limb and iron of hand, hewed
> on bravely in the thick of the fight; it was they who found and cut
> down the Saracen King.

Such an encounter between eastern and western forces was repeated time after time during the crusades and the ninety years of the Christian Kingdom of Jerusalem. The paradox was that a few thousand mailed knights operating from some fifty castles and walled cities could dominate Syria and Palestine for as long as they did. They were aided by mercenary horsemen, the Turcopoles, with equipment similar to the Sarmatian horse on Hadrian's Wall. On the Kirkwall Scroll of the 15th century, a mounted Islamic knight with his pointed helmet and scimitar can be seen riding against the invaders' camp at the siege of Damietta on the Nile, which fell on the Fifth Crusade.*

Almost impervious to all weapons except the javelin, however, the military orders such as the Knights Templars in their double-layered mail shirts on their embattled horses could be devastating, as they wielded their two-sided axes and broadswords and maces. In the hands of Genoese archers, the new cross-bow was a penetrating device, its bolts far more deadly than the arrows fired from the horn bows of the Arab cavalry. The only advantage in Muslim hands was the scimitar with its damascene blade, far superior in close-quarter combat to Frankish daggers and short swords.

Yet in Saladin's total defeat of the crusaders at the Horns of Hattin in 1187, the Knights Templars found themselves surrounded without water. The scrub around them was set on fire, and arrows fell from the sky day and night, killing the horses as well as the foot-soldiers. A series of furious cavalry charges did not reach Saladin's tent, and as at the Battle of Hastings, the doomed King of Jerusalem grouped his last knights around the True Cross, where they fought until they were overwhelmed. The only cruelty of Saladin was to have all the knights of the Military Orders beheaded, for never had so few held so much Arab land for so long.

In terms of future wars, the Knights Templars were to bring back to Europe the weapons and tactics of the Near East. They would also carry in their train the techniques of the masons who had built their castles and chapels. Yet with the fall of Jerusalem after Saladin's victory, the surviving Templars had lost their reason for existence, which was to provide guardians for the Temple of Solomon and protection for pilgrims to the Christian holy places, now in Muslim hands.

Although they were to survive for another one hundred and twenty years as a Military Order, the Templars would have to find a new role. They fell back to the sea and built fortresses there, preparing for a new assault on Jerusalem. Only the Third Crusade with King Richard I of England, who took the sea fortress of Acre, would come near to achieving this second objective; but Saladin would prove a match for the Lionheart himself.* More and more, the Templars would become merchants and bankers and administrators of their estates.

* See Illustrations.

Their downfall was caused by their wealth, their arrogance, their secrecy and their heresy. By the 13th century, they were the leading bankers, and they owned some nine thousand manors across Europe, all free of taxes. They provided security for the transport and safe-keeping of gold and silver treasure. Even the Muslims left their coins with the Templars, in case the fortunes of war should force them to ally with the Christians. The Paris Temple became the centre of the money-market of Europe.

The pride of the Grand Masters of the Order was notorious, and their secrecy evoked envy among the princes and the people. They were seen as both the poor knights of Christendom and as rich conspirators against the Papacy and royalty and public welfare. Their ceremonies and investitures and practices were hidden and gave rise to endless speculation. Yet their confessions at their trials after 1307 were extorted by threat and torture, and these should largely be discounted.

The truth was that the Templars inclined to heresy as well as independence. They were a church within the Catholic Church, a state within the royal State. Among the Military Orders, a belief in the Sophia, the divine female intelligence, appealed to their cult of chastity and the individual pursuit of truth. Officially, however, their worship was that of the Virgin Mary, who was impregnated by the divine essence to produce Christ. No man had anything to do with the birth of the Son of God. The human mind came from the Virgin womb without a father on earth.

Although King Philip the Fourth of France, in his seizure and destruction of the Knights Templars, was as efficient as Hitler's coup against Roehm and his Brownshirts, there is no record of his finding the Templar treasure in Paris or the secret archives of the Order or its fleet, based mainly at La Rochelle in Brittany. Much evidence and some tradition points to the removal of the treasure and most of the archives on ships, with refugee Templars taking these to Portugal and to the west and east coasts of Scotland, where they were welcomed.

One of the confessions, written down in Latin by the Inquisition and extorted from the French Templar Knights, was the testimony of John de Châlons of Poitiers. He stated that Gerard de Villiers, the Preceptor of the Order under the Treasurer, Hugh de Peraud, knew in advance of the mass arrests and fled the Temple in Paris with fifty knights, whom he commanded to put to sea on eighteen Templar galleys. He added that another knight, Hugh de Châlons, had fled with all the Treasurer's hoard. No Templar who knew of it had dared to confess before this admission. Certainly, Gerard de Villiers and Hugh de Châlons escaped the first arrests and were captured only after several days of freedom. Whatever they had taken with them was already gone.

Those knights who managed to sail away voyaged to Scotland and Portugal, where they proceeded to their main stronghold at Tomar. There, they were particularly well received because of their experience in navigation. In the Levant, their sailing ships had led in using the compass and the lateen sail rig, which they had adopted from Arab *dhows* and steersmen. Whatever the Templar refugees brought with them, they were incorporated into the same Order under another title, the Knights of Christ. The ships of the renamed Order sailed under the eight-pointed red cross of the Templars. The African explorer Vasco da Gama was a Knight of Christ, and Prince Henry the Navigator was to become a Grand Master of the Order.

The dualism of Gnostic thought supposed the world made by Jehovah and Satan to be dark and evil, set against the light and heaven with Jesus as the messenger. This was the ideology of the Military Orders in their struggle with the devil of Islam, a struggle in which death would mean a translation to paradise. In the more esoteric level of understanding of the Grand Masters, who might exchange knowledge with the Assassins, even Judas became a saint. The name *Iscariot* derived from the Greek word for assassin and denoted also the carved dagger worn by the extreme Jewish sect of the Zealots, who believed that the coming of the Messiah could only occur by force and self-sacrifice. This belief was shared by the members of the Military Orders, who believed that Christ had ordained them to their sanguinary role. Had He not in St John's Gospel ordered Judas to betray him: 'That thou doest, do quickly?'

As the Knights Templars grew in wealth and power, their questioning of orthodox faith became more elaborate, and they began to take issue with the conventions of society and the pretensions of the Papacy. They became less the warriors of the Holy See and of the Cistercian Order than the avenging angels of a sinful world, whose

Grand Masters spoke directly to the All Knowing, as Mary Magdalene had in her time. Their leaders looked to communicating directly with divine inspiration.

The knights of the Temple of Solomon would be particularly feared for their long tenancy of the site of the Temple. Had they discovered their arcane knowledge there? Had they discovered the sacred wealth of King David, and even the Ark of the Covenant? Although the Old Testament never declared what was the divine intelligence contained within the Holy of Holies, its treasures and those of the Temple were a matter of record.

The tabernacle erected round the Ark, and later the Temple of Solomon, was a treasure-house of precious metals and stones, some of which the Templars were meant to have excavated as the capital for their banking wealth. Architecturally, they translated to some of their chapels the two pillars, Jachin and Boaz, which held up the Temple, but they rejected its shape as a cube – similar to old Phoenician places of worship and the Ka'aba at Mecca – in favour of the sacred octagon crowned by a dome. This was the design of the Islamic Dome of the Rock, thought by Christian pilgrims to be Solomon's holy building, even though it was celebrated in Islam as the site of the stone, from which the Prophet Muhammad was held to have stepped into the seventh heaven.

In fact, the Templars seem to have acquired a foundation for their riches, when they lost their headquarters in Jerusalem. In 1185, the Patriarch Heraclius of the Church of the Holy Sepulchre had travelled to London to consecrate the Temple in that city. Two years later, when Islam conquered the Holy City of Israel, Heraclius was allowed by Saladin to depart with all his sacred treasures, many adorned with gold and jewels, for the Templar castle at Acre, which served as the strong-room of the Levantine bank of the Order. Also gathered there were the spoils of Constantinople, when it had been seized by the warlords of the Fourth Crusade.

The Holy Shroud and the Holy Veil of Veronica were meant to have passed into Templar possession along with their golden vessels, which contained the cloths of the Passion, and so were given the name of Grails. For they had held the Body and Blood of Christ. After the fall of Acre and the flight of the Templars from Palestine, these precious objects were carried overseas. In 1306, one year before the condemnation of the Military Order, the Templar treasury was moved from Cyprus by sea to Marseilles, and then on to the Temple in Paris. The Holy Shroud would surface in France, the Holy Veil in Rome, after the disappearance of the Templars on charges of heresy.

Sure of a welcome from the crusading St Clairs and other neighbouring landowners in Midlothian near their chief presbytery at Balantrodoch – now called the village of Temple – most of the seaborne French refugee Templars made their way to Scotland, probably with their treasury and the remaining archives from the Paris Temple. One French Masonic tradition declares that the records and wealth were taken on nine vessels to the Isle of May in the Firth of Forth near Rosslyn. Others believe that these vessels went to Ireland and then to the Western Isles of Scotland. When the authorities burst into the Irish Templar presbyteries, they found them stripped of ornaments, while Robert the Bruce was receiving new supplies of weapons before the Battle of Bannockburn – to the cost and complaint of King Edward II of England.

A recent inquiry discovered Templar graves near Loch Awe in Argyll by Kilmartin Church. One tombstone bore the steps of the Temple of Solomon leading up to a foliate cross before a crusader sword, as on the Sir William St Clair grave at Rosslyn. Also at the ruined chapel of Kilneuair to the east of Loch Awe were the remains of an ancient circular church and a gravestone with the Templar cross patte, as there was at neighbouring Kilmichael Glassary. And near Castle Sween lay the fallen chapel of Kilmory, where another Templar cross was carved near a sailing ship, far larger than a war galley, and near a masonic set-square – found only on the early graves of members of that Order. Eight other Templar tombstones discovered at Currie near Edinburgh and at Westkirk near Culross in Fife suggested that most of the Templars who fled to Scotland reached the Firth of Forth, where they would be safe.

At the time, the excommunicated Robert the Bruce held part of Scotland with his army, fighting against the allies and armies of the English King Edward II, who ordered his officers to arrest all the Templars and keep them safe in custody. Because English members had fought against the rebel William Wallace, and because he needed the support of the refugee Order, Bruce only put on trial in 1309 two of the Templars, both from south of the Border. They were soon released, after testifying that their colleagues had fled overseas. Another Templar in London at his interrogation declared that his brethren had fled to Scotland, where the writ of the English King was only partly enforced.

The fortunes and wealth of the St Clair Lords of Rosslyn certainly began to improve dramatically after the arrival of the refugee Templars. There was little proof that the military knights kept their treasures or communicated with the Borders, until the recent discovery of a buried treasure at the commandery at Pimprez in northern France. The hoard consisted of 12 silver ingots and 450 mint silver pennies, struck in Carlisle for the English Kings Henry I and Stephen in the 12th century. The discovery proved the role of the Templars as carriers of bullion and keepers of currency.

The question was, however, whether the Templars also brought their other treasures, such as the two Grails from Constantinople, and their architectural and esoteric eastern knowledge to the future Grail chapel at Rosslyn. They were identified as the guardians of the Grail in the most superb of the late Grail romances, *Parzival*, by Wolfram von Eschenbach, a poor knight and bard in the Germany of the Holy Roman Empire.

Wolfram claimed that Chrétien de Troyes had erred in the original legend of the Grail knight. He now asserted that the true story derived from Kyot, who had lived in Anjou with its close connections with Breton bards. If the name Kyot was invented, it would derive from the Gaelic *keo*, a cave, or *ceo*, a magical mist. But Wolfram took his source further back to Moorish Toledo, where he claimed that a Jewish mystic had recorded the tale. His name Flegetanis was the Latin version of the Persian word for astrologer.

Watching the heavens, Flegetanis discerned the mystery of the Grail, which was written in a cluster of stars. Angels had left it on earth to be guarded by the best of the knights, as *Parzival* would relate. It was identified as a green stone fallen from heaven after the battle of Lucifer with the Trinity. It was the most brilliant gem in the crown of Lucifer, whose very name meant the bearer of light. It had close affinities with the source of the sacred Islamic black stone at the centre of Mecca, a meteorite also believed to have fallen from heaven and to be a means of communication with God. Moreover, as long ago as classical times, a meteorite had been the head of the earth goddess Cybele, brought to Rome to save that city from disaster.

The Koran stated that its meteorite was given by the Angel Gabriel at the time of the building of the cubic shrine, the Ka'aba, where it was kept. The Muslim commentator, Ibn Malik, also told of a vision of the Prophet Muhammad, in which He ascended to the skies and saw a green goblet 'of such penetrating brightness that all the seven heavens are illuminated by it . . .' A voice declared, 'O Muhammad, the All Highest God has created this goblet for Your enlightenment.' Both divine stone and cup remain important in Islamic belief.

For thirteen hundred years, pilgrims on the *hajji* to Mecca have been directed to enter the Ka'aba and kiss the black stone embedded in the wall. Once it was stolen by a Shi'ite sect, but it was ransomed and returned. Religious traditions associated the sacred stone with Adam and with Abraham, as well as with Allah, stating that an angel brought it to earth to record the deeds of the faithful, to be examined on the Day of Judgement.

Worn smooth by tens of millions of lips, this heavenly blessing was the sole object from the pagan temple which the Prophet Muhammad had kept, when he converted the idolatrous shrine at Mecca into an Islamic temple. Apparently, a flash of lightning had persuaded the prophet to retain this Muslim Grail. As the poet Ikbal Ali Shah wrote, the Ka'aba was the heart of the body of the world:

> And the stone that you call the Black Stone was itself a ball of dazzling light. In ages past, the Prophet said, it shone like the crescent moon, until at last the shadows, falling from the sinful hearts of those who gazed on it, turned its surface black. And since this amber gem, that came to earth from Paradise with the Holy Spirit, has received such impressions upon itself, what should be the impressions which our hearts receive? Indeed, whoever shall touch it, being pure of conscience, is like him who has shaken hands with God.

In *Parzival*, Wolfram von Eschenbach went as far as giving his perfect Christian knight a piebald half-brother, Feirefiz, born in the Levant. The subtext of the long romance was, indeed, the reconciliation of

Christians and Muslims, and their respect for one another; also the change of nature of the Grail to a stone fallen from heaven, as at Mecca. Parzival began by defining lack of faith as dark and the Christian soul as white. And Wolfram also stressed the hidden significance of his text: 'I tell my story like the bowstring and not like the bow. The string is here a figure of speech. Now you think the bow is fast, but faster is the arrow sped by the string.'

In *Parzival*, Gamuret Angevin, a knight from the crusading French family of Fulk of Anjou, which produced the Kings of Jerusalem, took up service with the Muslim Baruch of Baghdad. Dressed in his surcoat 'green as the emerald vase', Gamuret defended a black Muslim queen's city, defeating Scots, Norse and French crusaders. He then married the queen, returned to Europe and left her with their son Feirefiz, striped like a humbug, 'dark and light, black and white . . . as a magpie the hue of his face and hair'. Feirefiz grew up to become a supreme knight, whose surcoat of precious stones, asbestos shield and cloak of salamander could defeat even the knights of fire.

As in the romance of Chrétien de Troyes, Parzival began his career in chivalry as a fool, a rapist and a robber. So when the Fisher King, with his incurable wound, whose 'life was but dying', directed him to the Grail Castle, he was tongue-tied at the wonders that he saw. A squire carried the bleeding Holy Lance through the great hall in front of the assembled knights of the Holy Grail, while the Grail Queen bore the Grail stone on a cushion of green silk. Unknown to Parzival, the Queen was his aunt. She laid the holy vessel on a pillar of jacinth, and its horn of plenty nourished all the knights and maidens in the castle.

Parzival was given a mystical sword, its hilt carved from a ruby. But he did not question the mystery of the bleeding lance, the abundant Grail or the incurable wound of the Fisher King. Simpleton that he was, he woke in the morning in a deserted castle and rode away to King Arthur's camp, where he was blamed by the sorceress Cundrie for not asking the Fisher King the question that would heal him.

Parzival left again on the quest for the Grail, and he killed a knight who was defending the Grail Castle. He was bitter against God, who had made a fool of him. But he met a hermit, Trevrizent, who had a green shrine or reliquary, and who revealed to him the origin of the Grail and the nature of its later defenders.

Parzival was told that, when Lucifer rebelled against the Lord God, some of the angels took neither side. They were sent down to earth to look after the Grail. Wavering between good and evil as Parzival in a sinful and dual world, they were recalled to heaven. The knights of the Grail were identified as *Templeise*, wearing white surcoats with red crosses, as the Templar Knights did. The Templars, of course, had many contacts with their Muslim equivalents, the Sufis, and some of their secret practices – particularly a belief in selfless obedience and purity – derived from oriental mysticism. The German romance preached religious toleration between Christianity and Islam, especially when a crusader might rule over a Muslim land or a Muslim over Christian believers.

When Parzival finally asked the Fisher King the right question and healed him, and became the Grail King, Feirefiz was baptised from a ruby font standing on a round pillar of jasper: this was filled with holy water by the Grail. Feirefiz now married the princess of the castle, who would give birth to the Christian African emperor, Prester John. The black-and-white colour of his skin could now be seen as the Templar battle flag, *Beauséant*. The reconciliation between the opposite colours was achieved, as in a stalemate in chess.

The concept of semi-divine rule on earth by a companionship of mysterious monastic Knights Templars confirmed the links between the concept of the Grail, the crusades and the Military Orders, which were influenced by Islam, because of a mutual respect bred by long diplomacy and frequent wars over the Holy Land and Jerusalem. The Knights of the Grail were the heirs of classical, oriental, Celtic and Christian tradition. They were called to their duty individually by God. Their family names appeared by a miracle on the Grail itself. Only they might benefit from its blessedness. And, most significantly, Wolfram von Eschenbach wrote of the Knights of the Grail:

By a stone they live,
And that stone is both pure and precious – Its name you have
never heard?
Men call it Lapis Exilis –

If you daily look at that stone

(If a man you are or a maiden) for a hundred years,

If you look on its power, your hair will not grow grey, your face
appears

The same as when you first saw it, your flesh and your bone will
not fail

But young you will live for ever – And this stone all men call the
Grail.

Wolfram von Eschenbach developed this description of the Grail as a
stone taken down from heaven by angels, who then returned on high
because of the sins of mankind. On Good Friday, a dove flew down
with the white host to lay on the Grail – the Body and Blood of
Christ. This fallen stone, which was all fruitfulness and gave eternal
youth, was also called *lapis exilis* by the alchemist Arnold of Villanova.
He identified it as the Philosopher's Stone, not as the Grail. It was not
made from green emerald, but was unremarkable in appearance. Such
a correspondence made commentators look for alchemy in *Parzival*
and presume that the author meant *lapis elixir*, the life-giving or
Philosopher's Stone.

Certainly, Wolfram von Eschenbach was influenced by oriental
and Cathar beliefs. The Jewish philosopher Flegetanis, whom he
declared to be the discoverer of the Grail and of the bloodline of
King Solomon, was thought to be Thabit ben Qorah, who lived in
Baghdad at the end of the 9th century and translated Greek texts
into Arabic from the legendary emerald tablet of Hermes Trisme-
gistus, the semi-mythical founder of alchemy. Moreover, the
Templars were believed to be the guardians both of the Grail
and of the Temple of Solomon, which stood upon a rock, *lapis*, at
the centre of the world, and had contained the Ark of the
Covenant, the fount of the Christian faith. The cornerstone 'which
the builders refused' in the Psalms was another symbol of Christ.
And it was also upon this *lapis* or rock that the Christian Church
was founded.

In the *Book of Revelation* of St John the Divine, the Holy Spirit as a
stone and a green gem, or fire and crystal, was also emphasised. As the
holy man saw in his vision:

Straightaway I was in the Spirit: and, behold, there was a throne set in
heaven, and one sitting upon the throne. And he that sat was to look
upon like a jasper stone and a sardius; and there was a rainbow round
the throne, like an emerald to look upon . . . There were seven lamps
of fire burning before the throne, which are the seven Spirits of God.
And before the throne there was a sea of glass like unto crystal . . .

The visions of the legendary Knights of the Grail of *Parzival* also
depicted the Holy Vessel as a sacred stone, falling in fire.

Indeed, a blessed stone was the foundation of the faith, as Bishop
William Durand de Mende made clear in the 13th century in his
manual for understanding the symbolic significance of cathedrals and
churches. Repeating from the words of Christ, 'I will liken him unto a
wise man, which built his house upon a rock', the bishop or the priest,
who had permission to conduct the ceremony, should sprinkle holy
water in order to chase from that place ghosts and demons. Then he
should sink the foundations on the first stone, engraved with the sign
of the Cross. Onyx should adorn the sanctuary, while the church
should be the replica of the human body of Christ, facing to the east.

Another source for *Parzival* was a legendary treasure of Solomon,
which was taken to Rome after the fall of Jerusalem, then seized by
the Visigoths. When Muslim armies captured Toledo, they asked after
Solomon's Table, which was meant to be able to feed all who sat
down to eat, also to be made from a gigantic emerald, the sacred green
stone of the alchemists. The Table was said to be hidden away in a
Grail Castle in the mountains of Spain. Charlemagne was also said to
have copied the Table of Solomon by having the universe made as
three circles in jewels and precious metals, then set on legs of gold as
another version of King Arthur's Round Table, for himself and twelve
knights. The Koran itself referred to a table brought down from
Heaven by Jesus to feed Him and the Apostles, but this divine gift
disappeared again because of the sins of mankind.

For his *Parzival*, Wolfram also drew on the *Alexanderlied*. In this
Latin book of the exploits of the Greek conqueror, Alexander went to
the Earthly Paradise, which some poets declared was, or was nearby,
the Grail Castle. He was presented with a stone, which gave youth to
the old. This *lapis exilis* was like a human eye, but brilliant and rare in

its colours. An ancient Jew told Alexander that it would tip the scales, heavier than any sack of gold, yet a feather would weigh more, if any dirt stained the holy stone. While human greed was insatiable, even the eye of the conqueror would be stopped by dust. 'This stone came before you, master of the world. It warns you and rebukes you. This small talisman restrains you from desire and base ambition.'

So Alexander was deterred from making the whole earth into his empire. This tale of the stone from paradise was an admirable metaphor for Wolfram's version of the Grail. It was also the fountain of life, restoring youth to the aged. Although Wolfram wrote that his stone was given its powers by a dove descending from heaven on Good Friday with a bountiful wafer in its beak, its provenance was Greek and Jewish and Islamic mythology and belief. The Host brought by the Holy Spirit was the manna on the pagan rock.

The eastern and Templar tradition and the cult of the Grail in *Parzival* was to be the inspiration behind the building of the later Rosslyn chapel, designed as a new Temple of Solomon. Carved on the stone roof at the east end of the structure, Christ the messenger still blesses among the angels and cluster of stars a dove with a wafer in its beak, descending towards the Grail.* This is a chalice or cup in the shape of a crescent moon or goblet without a stem, pouring forth not only the Holy Body and Blood, but what Wolfram promised in his poem:

> Root and blossom of Paradise garden, that which men call 'The Grail',
> The crown of all earthly wishes, fair fullness that never shall fail.

---

* See Illustrations.

6

The Matter Of Bannockburn

In two battles, the St Clairs of Rosslyn proved their worth to Scotland and the fellow Norman family of the Bruces. The first was near Rosslyn to the south. So many remains are still poking through the soil there that the fields are known as Shinbones, the Hewings, Stinking Rig, and Killburn. Sir William St Clair was supporting Bruce's claim to the Crown of Scotland against the English puppet king, John de Balliol, backed by King Edward I, called the Hammer of the Scots for his many invasions; he even removed the Holy Rood and what he believed was the Stone of Scone.

Split into three divisions, a great army of 30,000 men was sent to subdue Scotland. One division of 8,000 men opposed them, led by supporters of the fighter and martyr for independence, William Wallace. Although Sir John Comyn was no friend of Robert the Bruce, who stood against the Balliol family, he combined with Sir Simon Fraser and Sir William St Clair and his son to resist the English forces.

The first enemy division was hardly defeated, when the second one appeared. As at the later battle of Agincourt, the Scottish commanders ordered the killing of their prisoners for fear of a stab in the back. Retreating over Draidon Burn, the Scots stood in line and destroyed the second enemy advance over boggy ground. Arming even the camp followers with superior weapons taken from the English dead, they fell on their knees to beg God's mercy before the approach of the third division of the foe. As the chronicler Father Hay described the outcome:

The English thinking because they were with heads uncovered, and knees bended, that they craved mercie of them; and so without thought of any resistance to be made, they came over Draidon Burn, where, contrarie to their expectations of friends, they found foes; of men overcome, men redie to be victors, Yea, within short time, put them to flight, although the battle continued for a space with uncertain victory.

Sir William St Clair was presented with the battleground to defend in future, and also English prisoners of quality for ransom. One of them advised him to relocate his castle on the actual promontory above the North Esk, invulnerable on two sides and protected towards the north-west by marshlands called the Stanks. He began the building of the wall tower of the castle, which was to be completed by his heirs. He was also 'rewarded by King Robert with a sword, whereof the hand was set with stones, and the scarbard, velvet covered with plate of gold, bearing on the one side this inscription: "*Le roy me donne*", and on the other the following words: "*St Cler me porte*".'

On the death of his father after the barbaric hanging and drawing and quartering of William Wallace by the English, Sir Henry St Clair committed himself to the cause of Robert the Bruce against the rival claims of the Comyns, who had now sworn allegiance to the English Crown. Robert the Bruce personally stabbed John Comyn in front of the high altar of the church of the Grey Friars in Dumfries. Leaving the church, he met his brother-in-law, Christopher Seton, who cut down Comyn's uncle and asked if Bruce's victim was dead. In a notorious phrase, Bruce said he would 'mak siccar' and returned to make sure that the murder of the bleeding Comyn was completed.

If Bruce had not committed a ritual murder, he had killed in a holy place. He was excommunicated by the Pope, an act that allowed any nation to mount a crusade against him. That same year, King Edward I crushed the Scottish forces at Methven and had Christopher Seton and his brother executed along with one of Bruce's brothers and Sir Simon Fraser. Bruce was forced to flee, his supporters to lie low. There seemed to be no hope of resisting the English, particularly the dominance of their heavy cavalry. This was the age of the armoured knight, and foot-soldiers could not resist their massed charge. Without fresh resources and armaments, the cause of Scottish independence was condemned.

Three months after the Templar Grand Master, Jacques de Molay, had been burned at the stake in France, Robert the Bruce took his stand against the invading King Edward II at Bannockburn outside Stirling Castle. The battle took place on St John's Day in June, 1314, a significant date for the Military Orders. After preliminary skirmishes, in which Bruce himself on a pony shattered the head of a Norman English knight on his charger, the Scots advanced from the forests in four hedgehogs of axe-carriers and spearmen, called schiltrons. The contemporary chronicler Geoffrey Baker of Swinbroke revealed the course of the combat:

> The Scots chose a fine position, and dug ditches three feet deep and three wide along the whole of their front from right to left, covering them over with intertwined branches, that is to say, hurdles, screened by grass, across which indeed infantry might pass if they knew the trick, but which could not bear the weight of cavalry. None of the Scots were allowed to mount their horses, and arrayed in brigades as usual, they stood in a closely formed line behind the aforesaid cannily, I will not say deceitfully, constructed ditch.
>
> As the English moved from the west, the rising sun shone on their gilded shields and helmets. Such a general as Alexander would have preferred to try conclusions on some other ground or other day, or at least could have waited till midday when the sun would have been on their right. But the impetuous and headstrong obstinacy of the English preferred death to delay.
>
> In the front line were the cavalry with their heavy chargers, unaware of the concealed ditch; in the second were the infantry, including the archers who were kept ready for the enemy's flight; in the rear the King, with the bishops and other clerics . . .
>
> The front line of cavalry charged, and as the horses' legs were caught in the ditch through the hurdles, down fell the men and died before the enemy could strike; and at their fall on came the enemy, slaughtering and taking prisoners, and sparing only the rich for ransom . . .
>
> Many were killed by the archers of their own army, who were not placed in a suitable position, but stood behind the men-at-arms,

whereas at the present day the custom is to post them on the flanks. When they saw the Scots charging fiercely on the horsemen who had fallen at the ditch, some of them shot their arrows high in the air to fall feebly on the enemy's helmets, some shot ahead and hit a few Scots in the chest, and many English in the back.

Over two days and a night, these tactics were repeated, cavalry charges against ranks of spears. As the Lanercost chronicler stated: 'The two hosts came together, and the great steeds of the knights dashed into the Scottish pikes as into a thick wood; there arose a huge and horrible noise from rending lances and dying horses, and they stood locked together for a space.' The spearmen in thick leather coats and iron caps aimed at the chargers. Once the knights were dismounted, they were easily dispatched by short sword and dirk and dagger.

A flanking attack by the lethal Welsh archers with their longbows was scattered by a charge from Sir Robert Keith with five hundred light horsemen from the Borders, for the launchers of arrows had no infantry or cavalry protection. And then occurred an intervention of legend and dispute. A new Scots force appeared and charged, making a fearsome noise. The English retreat turned into a rout. These people were said to be yeomen and camp-followers, banging their pots and pans, and assisted by some of the refugee Templars in Scotland, fighting for its excommunicated leader.

No army can win a victory without its weaponry. This last body available to Robert the Bruce consisted of his armourers. Many of them had been brought over by the Templars from the Near East. By royal command, they were already under the protection of the Lords of Rosslyn, who would hold the position of law masters of the crafts and guilds of Scotland for many centuries. They would also retain the role of guardians of the royal treasures; one of them was carried by Bruce at the battle – the *Brechennoch*, the bones of St Columba enshrined in the jewelled and enamelled Monymusk reliquary.

Three of the St Clairs fought alongside Bruce at Bannockburn. One of them was the Fighting Bishop of Dunkeld, who destroyed a sea raid by the enemy the following year in Fife. 'Many of the English,' Father Hay reported, 'not getting in time enough to their boats, were cut in pieces. Others, striving to save themselves by swimming, perished in the sea. Others, who were got there, for that they were already too full, were made a prey either to the water which swallowed them up, or to the enimie, who slew them from the shore. Several of their boats sunk, as being too heavily loaded.'

Another of the St Clairs who fought at Bannockburn, the Lord of Rosslyn, was a signatory of the Scottish Declaration of Independence at Arbroath in 1320, with its defiant statement: 'So long as a hundred of us are left alive, we will never in any degree be subjected to the English. It is not for glory, riches or honour that we fight, but for liberty alone which no good man loses but with his life.' And the third St Clair in Bannockburn was Sir William, who later died with other Scottish knights in a charge against the Muslims in Spain, while taking the Heart of Bruce for burial in Jerusalem. His is the Grail and Templar gravestone in Rosslyn Chapel. If refugee Templar Knights did enter the service of Bruce before Bannockburn, Sir William St Clair would have had a strong claim to have been their leader. The evidence lies carved on his tomb, which shows the burial of a Master of that Military Order.

Whoever dispersed the English knights, the victory at Bannock-burn confirmed Scottish freedom and Robert the Bruce as King. The benefit to the St Clairs was immediate, the grant of more lands and a bishopric. For it was to the Firth of Forth that part of the Templar fleet had evidently sailed from France. The extensive Templar properties stretching between Rosslyn Castle and the Seton estate near Mus-selburgh were centred on Balantrodoch, now known simply as Temple.

The preceptory and church there had been built in the middle of the 12th century between two St Clair estates on lands under the jurisdiction of the St Clairs as Sheriffs of Midlothian. That ruined graveyard is still full of Templar and Masonic tombstones, bearing the symbols of both rites. Although Robert the Bruce confirmed by charter all the possessions of the Hospitallers in Scotland six months after his victory, he made no mention of the Templars at all, any more than he referred to them at the Battle of Bannockburn. Yet, curiously, two charters show a Seton as the Master of the Hospitallers, presiding over 'Temple Courts' at Balantrodoch, thirty-two years after the English defeat.

As Wardens of the Marches, the St Clairs and the Setons in Lothian were the main Scots defence against an English attack from the south-east, while the Douglas clan played that role in the south-west. For three hundred years, from the 13th century until the Union of the Crowns of England and Scotland under James I and VI, warlords led light cavalry raids across the shifting frontier. In their arms and their tactics, these Borderers or Steel Bonnets hailed back to the Roman soldiers on Hadrian's Wall and the legends of King Arthur.

On their sturdy fell ponies, cross-bred from stock as far away as Hungary and Poland and Spain, the Borderers used a strategy which derived from the steppes and the desert. The Parthians had defeated the Roman legions by raiding their flanks and using bows from the saddle and picking off the enemy without a charge. The Dacians and Sarmatians and Scythians had been brought over to harass the attacks of the Picts and the Scots from the north. Now once again, mobile horsemen would be able to defeat their enemies by continual sorties. In the local dialect, they were called *prickers*.

For the frontier was the breeding-ground of raiders. Across a lawless line, chieftains amassed wealth by stealing cattle and sheep. As well as meat to eat, wool meant riches, once woven into cloth. Further tactics and weapons were being brought back by returning crusaders, who had been beset in Asia Minor by light-armed archers and Turcopoles, the later models for the reivers.

Under an iron helmet, which first looked like a pudding-bowl hammered into shape by a local blacksmith, the Borderer wore a jack, a white quilted coat of stout leather, studded with metal plates. On his lower limbs were britches and leather boots. He carried a curved bow and a long lance, which could be thrown as a javelin. He had a small round shield and a slicing sword and a dagger or dirk. His supporting infantry had the long bill, which combined a cleaver with a pike, and also the Jedburgh Axe with its round cutting edge.

All these weapons may still be seen carved on medieval gravestones, mainly of Templar origin, in Cumbria, and in Argyll and Fife and Lothian. The likelihood is that some of the proscribed Knights Templars in their many commanderies in the Border region continued to prosper from their cattle and sheep herds, but now as local war leaders. Again, the symbol of the shears used by laymen Templars often appears on their tombstones.* The military knights, excommunicated after 1307, merged into the warlords of this frontier, now called 'The Debatable Land'.

Up to 30,000 horsemen could be raised in small bands from a total Border population of 5 times that number. Outside the fortified houses and small keeps and towers of the warlords, the Borderers lived almost as Plains Indians in their teepees. Makeshift crofts and shepherds' shelters sufficed, for all expected a destruction from the next raiding-party after their cattle and sheep. To the antiquarian, Camden, these frontiersmen were 'rank robbers . . . as it were the ancient nomads, a martial kind of men who, from the month of April until August, lie out scattering and summering, with their cattle, in little cottages here and there, which they call sheils and sheilings.' For them, survival was a series of continual skirmishes over the centuries, which would end in a triumph against a whole Scottish army.

The rise of the Lords of Rosslyn after Bannockburn was not only due to their prowess in battle, but to their contributions to the defences of the realm. They progressed from the age of iron and leather to the age of cannon and gunpowder. They would construct fighting ships on the Firth of Forth, capable of creating a Northern Commonwealth alongside Scandinavia and Denmark. Three of the St Clair Earls of Orkney from Rosslyn were to become Lord High Admirals of Scotland. Aided by Templar skills and wealth, they would supervise the making of artillery trains and armoured vessels, as well as creating the most curious chapel in the north of Europe.

* See Illustrations.

7

The Makers of Weapons

In front of the changes of cultures, there has been the advance of weapons. Both in their mythology and their history, the Greeks and the Romans recognized how their empires had been won, not only by war, but also by those who had made their arms. That is the question of the past, which is rarely asked and hardly answered. Behind the warrior with the sword, who forged the sword? Just as the fighter pilots of the Battle of Britain could not fly without the ground crews and mechanics repairing daily their battered Spitfires and Hurricanes, so the Knights Templars could not maintain their interminable skirmishes and sieges without the support of their armourers and metal-workers. These were the vital smiths and tinkers. And this inquiry will show how such skilled workers from the Near East came to Scotland and ended under the protection of the St Clairs, the Grand Masters of the crafts.

In legend, the classical authors described an Iron Age and a Bronze Age, followed by more luxurious Ages of Silver and Gold. The Greek smith-god Hephaestus was sickly at birth, and his disgusted mother Hera dropped him from Olympus. He grew with crippled legs, but he was so ingenious that he became close to Athena, the goddess of wisdom, and became the husband of Aphrodite, the goddess of love. The Olympians and the heroes could not conquer without his weapons and his mechanical skills. He made the first robots, seven serving maidens of beauty and the fire-breathing giant Talos of Crete, who destroyed all attackers. His Roman successor, Vulcan, was merely a fire-god, who gave his name to the volcano and lived beneath Etna and Vesuvius.

In Rome, we first hear of a unit of armourers, the *fabriciae*. They travelled with the legions all over the Mediterranean coasts and northern Europe. By the 3rd century, many of them were based in arms factories in cities, where their guilds rivalled those of the *Magistri Comacini*, the stone-masons. Indeed, the *Quatuor Coronati*, the martyred four Christians under Imperial Rome, are commemorated by Masonic Lodges to this day.

Although the original Temple of Solomon was meant to have been built by the mystical Shamir without the use of iron, certainly bronze and brasswork in sacred bulls and altars covered its interior. And all later medieval fortresses and cathedrals relied for their construction on metal as well as stone.

In the case of the Sainte-Chapelle in Paris, the Shrine of the Crown of Thorns, master masons embedded iron chains among the stone blocks. These later rusted and cracked the pillars and the walls. In his important book, *The Medieval Machine*, Jean Gimpel told of the building of the octagonal chapter house in Westminster Abbey in the 13th century, 'an iron, umbrella-like structure to prevent the walls of the chapel from falling outward'. The master mason sunk iron ties in the walls as at Sainte-Chapelle, but in this case:

> He used a series of iron bars to link the iron ties to hooks embedded in the slender central stone column of the chapel. It was remarkably ingenious, but not entirely successful, in the 14th century the bars had to be taken down and flying buttresses installed to ensure the continued stability of the chapel walls. Nevertheless, iron bars are still to be seen a few yards away in the Abbey itself, still keeping the walls parallel.

When St Bernard of Clairvaux created the Knights Templars as the armed fist of the church in order to defend his Cistercians in their monasteries, set often so close to the military commanderies, he did not forget that a trade in weapons might benefit both Holy Orders. The industrial technology of the white monks matched their agricultural expertise. To their fired pottery kilns, they added water-powered trip-hammers over the forges at the abbey of Fontenay. Clairvaux itself was situated in the heart of the best deposits of iron ore in France. Before 1330, the monks already owned a dozen factories, which produced iron ingots for sale to armourers and masons. They were the leading iron and steel producers in the Champagne region, and also significant in Cumbria and the Borders, with rich metal and coal resources.

The use of water power was the Cistercian contribution to an industrial revolution in the weapons trade. Powered by rivers and burns, stamping mills were built to break up the iron ore, while water-driven bellows could produce a draught that raised the temperature of the furnaces to 1,500 degrees Centigrade. This heat made the furnaces produce molten iron, ready for casting. In the 14th century, the first blast furnace was already in operation, although the blacksmith with his forge was still the usual metal-worker. Spanish steel had to be imported to Britain for the creation of the best sword blades, also at Portchester, 'for the hardening of the axes and other tools of the masons'.

The Knights Templars were known as those 'of the trowel and the sword'. In Palestine, they were totally dependent for their weapons and castle-building upon Semitic and Arabic craftsmen. The laymen of the Military Orders were recruited from local skilled workers. And at the time, the Saracen sword was superior to the Frankish broad-sword. After their expulsion from the Holy Land, the Templars would have taken their armourers with them, as the Roman Legions once had. These craftsmen would become known as Romanies or Egyptians or gypsies. They were accustomed to a vagrant life with a cart and a forge, camp-followers at the back of an army. Without them, the military could not sustain a campaign. The path of those Templars who fled to Scotland was recorded in gravestones near Loch Awe in Argyll, which charted a way from the Western Isles to Lothian. In Muckairn churchyard, there was a tomb with a piece of the staff of a cross, on which a sword was incised. At Taynuilt, a gravestone was carved with a crusading sword, surrounded by leaping thistles and dogs and a hare, while another showed a battle-axe and a Lombard Sword, as on the monument to William St Clair at Rosslyn.★

The most telling evidence of the arrival of the Near Eastern armourers at Loch Awe lies in their clan name. They were known as the Mac Nocairds. They arrived in Scotland at this period, and their name in Gaelic, *Clann-na-ceairde*, meant *craftsman* or *worker-in-metals*. Four hundred years later, they changed their name to Sinclair. As the

★ See Illustrations.

scholar MacBain noted, the name Sinclair, when borrowed into Gaelic, became 'Tinkler' pronounced as a Scots 'tinkler', or *caird*. And as the lords of Rosslyn were the law masters of all the crafts and guilds of Scotland, what better for the *cairds* to take their name?

A welter of resources in Cumbria also reveal that the many commanderies there were weapon factories as well as cattle and sheep farms. In fact, the look of the local Herdwick flocks still resemble those from Mesopotamia, a breed perhaps imported by the crusaders. Along the Solway Coast, iron ore is still washed up on the beaches, while old mines pepper the interior, as do ancient smelting works. A whole medieval foundry has been restored in the Duddon Valley. Carboniferous limestone was used to extract the pig iron, and it is still used in the Bessemer process at Workington to make high grade steel. Indeed, I even discovered two more Templar headstones laid away in a church there. In a poem, Norman Nicholson tells of the long tradition of the fells yielding materials for arms manufacturers:

> From one shaft at Cleator Moor
> They mined for coal and iron ore . . .
>
> But now the pits are wick with men,
> Digging like dogs dig for a bone:
> For food and life *we* dig the earth –
> In Cleator Moor they dig for death.
>
> Every wagon of cold coal
> Is fire to drive a turbine wheel;
> Every knuckle of soft ore
> A bullet in a soldier's ear.

The techniques for smelting iron were simple and effective. River water was poured down a perforated pipe which allowed oxygen to enter with the wind. The deluge fell into a covered pit with a funnel for the steam to blow out. In the pit was red-hot charcoal and the crushed and washed mineral ore. The iron melted and flowed out of a small drain, which the Catalans called the tail of the fox.*

* See Illustrations.

On the Templar stones at the parish church at St Bees, those of lay brothers depict, beside chalices and rosy crosses above the steps of the Temple of Solomon, such mundane things as shears for the sheep-herders or blocks. One tomb-marker is unique in Britain, showing an archer in a kilt firing with a curved bow a long arrow across a scabbard at a short sword – the equipment of the early Border light horse.* Above rises a cross, which quarters the circle of the sacred city of Jerusalem with its four gates. Two strange nooses or stirrups or pouches top the central cross. It is likely that the two figures sometimes seen on Templar coins or carvings represent a knight with an archer or squire armourer riding behind him on campaign.*

As early as the 12th century, a John Tinkler was recorded as living at Perth. And while Italian masons probably built Kilwinning Abbey, James, Lord Steward of Scotland, entertained in 1286 the Lords of Gloucester and Ulster at Kilwinning Lodge, the founding temple of all Scots Masonry of the Ancient Rite. That same year, the St Andrew's blue cross or saltire was being flown as the Scottish national flag. And certainly in his conflicts, Robert the Bruce had need of the rebel Knights Templars and their armourers.

In medieval times, Muslim iron-workers and doctors and dancers were called Moors or Saracens. An Arabic inscription on a Grail tombstone testifies to their presence at Corstorphine church. Excluded from Spain, a troupe in 1491 received from King James IV the sum of twenty unicorns for dancing the Moorish or Morris dance, later a staple of folklore. And before the arrival of Anthony Gaginus and boatloads of Hungarian gypsies at the port of Leith in 1504, along with the illustrious Faa family, vagabond metal craftsmen already travelled the land. Here were Irish tinklers with their Shelta language and the Highland *cairds* with their lingo based on Gaelic – *pan* for frying-pan, *pal* for friend.

Johnny Faa was so famous that his death was recorded in a Border Ballad. The travellers came to the castle gate, and there they 'sang bonnie'. And Lady Cassillis was seduced by her Gypsie Laddie and his band, and she ran away with them:

* See Illustrations.

> They wandred high, they wandred low,
> They wandred late and early . . .

But the Earl of the castle caught up with them by the wan water and put them to the sword:

> They were fifteen valiant men,
> Black, but very bonny,
> And they lost all their lives for one –
> The Earl of Cassillis' Ladie.

When King James V became the special patron of the wanderers, he was no romantic, even if credited with the ballad of the Gaberlunzie Man – a blue-cloaked bard and beggar. He was re-arming Scotland against an English assault, and he needed to favour the makers of armour and weapons. Thus the Lord High Treasurer referred to the migrants in 1505, 'to the Egyptianis be the Kingis command', while their leader Gaginus, Lord of Little Egypt, was given a safe conduct to the King of Denmark. His successor Johnny Faa was granted an even more remarkable position in 1540. Under the Great Seal, all the Sheriffs and Baillies were bidden to assist the Lord of Little Egypt to govern his people and collect his dues:

> And als charge all oure lieges that nane of thame molest, vex, inquiet, or truble the said Johnne Faw and his cumpany in doing of thair lefull besynes or uthir wayis within oure realme, and in thair passing, remanyng, or away ganging furth of the samyn under the pane abone writtin: And sicklike that ye command and charge all skipparis, maisteris, and marinaris within oure realme at all portis and havynnis quhair the said Johnne and his cumpany salhappin to resort and cum to resave him . . .

The reason why the Kings of Scotland extended this extraordinary protection to the Scottish gypsies and tinkers was their important role in the armaments industry, under their long protection by the Lords of Rosslyn. From the time of Robert the Bruce, the St Clairs had been recognized as the protectors of the early smiths and masons. Yet at Rosslyn, they were also the guardians of the royal family and its holy treasures in Edinburgh. They could not have fulfilled their role without an intense interest in weaponry and those who made the weapons. They were the chief patrons of the metal-working travellers, who tended to follow the armies.

Although their role is disputed by modern Protestant Masonic historians, it is proven by one of the few manuscripts to survive the sacking of the Rosslyn library after the Reformation. Commissioned by Earl William St Clair in 1488, the thousand pages written in longhand are the earliest surviving examples of Scottish prose. They contain Guild Laws and Forest Laws and 'The Laws and Custumis of Ye Schippis'. The Earl was then dealing extensively with the craft-masons working on Rosslyn chapel, also the carpenters and hammer-men or iron-workers, who were constructing a Scots navy on the Firth of Forth. He had to have authority over their disputes, if he was to protect the Crown by land and sea.

These military concerns were also demonstrated by a translation from René d'Anjou's writings on Battles and the Order of Knight-hood and the Government of Princes. At various times in his life, René held the title of Duke not only of Anjou, but also of Calabria and Lorraine, as well as being the King of Hungary, Naples, Sicily, Aragon, Valencia and even Jerusalem. He was a conduit to Rosslyn of Oriental, Gnostic and Kabbalistic teachings, which were spreading from Florence and Burgundy as far as Scotland. The patronage of the wandering Near Eastern iron-workers helped the St Clairs to be the suppliers of arms for the defence of the realm. With the white monks of Newbattle, they had been working on the coal seams near Dalkeith since the latter part of the 12th century, also establishing foundries nearby in Lothian and Fife. They held all the necessary resources to become makers of weapons. And through their control of the guilds, they could use the Romanies among the armourers of Scotland.

Moreover, the chief royal armaments' works in England were based on Kentish iron and oak charcoal. The leading metalworkers were the gypsy families, who took the name Smith – based on the mythical Wayland Smith, who had made the weapons of the old gods. My old Kentish friend, the master builder and marble mason, Ronald Gilbert, has even restored tombs in Westminster Abbey. We rebuilt five ruins together, ranging from riverside and Regency London and Paris to a fortified farmhouse in Normandy and a Venetian villa in Corfu. He never knew that his name was French, and that his ancestors had probably been the travelling masons from the *compagnonnages*, who had settled nearby from their temporary lodges after building Canterbury Cathedral. Certainly, he had retained all their old skills, and as for ironwork, we used the Romany families, still ranging through Greece to the South Downs.

As early as 1300, the London blacksmiths had formed a guild and prosecuted interlopers in Church courts. The smiths in Chesterfield went further and threatened 'excommunication without cavil or appeal' for anyone failing to pay craft dues. Yet craftsmen in the Middle Ages, and particularly masons and armourers, had to travel to find work. 'Only in 1356 were the London masons persuaded by the Mayor to set up a guild "as other trades do". Outside the towns the masons had their lodges, a word derived from *loggia*, the monkish name for the shelter erected by the church or castle wall during construction.' During the building of Rosslyn Chapel, for instance, a whole camp was erected in the shape of a cross for the foreign masons, later becoming Roslin burgh.

The early guilds were protected by the Church. Without them, cathedrals could not be built. Yet they were opposed by the Crown, because the masons clubbed together to force up wages, particularly after the Black Death. The Statute of Labourers of 1351 actually forbade the movement of workmen, but it could not be enforced in an economy of travellers outside the small cities. Thirty years on, the Peasants' Revolt was led by a rebel priest, John Ball, and staffed by craftsmen, who would not serve as serfs.

In fact, the period of 150 years after the beginning of the 13th century was the golden age of the wandering worker. The late medieval craft structure suppressed the old guilds and accompanied the destruction of the monasteries, which had protected the early lodges. Although the blacksmiths still were members of the fraternity of St John, as were the French *compagnonnages*, the yeomen in 1458 were made to 'search for forrens' and check that no stranger was employed in any workshop without the permission of the craft. Future bargaining over wages and practices would be between established craftsmen and their masters. By 1514, a petition was sent to Parliament from various trades complaining that the King's natural subjects were utterly decayed because of the immigration of the 'grete multitude pepyll, estrangers of dyvers nacions, Frenshemen, Galymen, Pycards, Flemynges, Keteryckis, Spuryars, Scottis, Lumbardis and dyvers hother nacions.'

'Without iron the commonalty be not sure against enemies,' Bartholomew wrote in late medieval times. 'Well-nigh no handi-work is wrought without iron: no field is cared without iron, neither tilling craft used, nor building builded without iron.' Metal-workers were highly valued and given the freedom of cities, particularly in York during the period of the Scottish wars. In 1295, a special smith's lodge was created to build a galley for the King of England. The leading smiths and cutlers and blade-makers and armourers were the cream of their trade. Although iron ingots had to be imported from Sweden and smelting works were small-scale, the guilds of iron-workers in York 'dight no swerds but workmanlike' and 'skabberds but of good stuff'. In that city, plate armour was manufactured and refurbished, while women were used in making chain-mail from iron wire and sewing it onto the leather jerkins used in Border warfare.

The makers of the ultimate weapon of the period, the longbow, were also organised in the three guilds and crafts: the bower, the stringmaker and the fletcher. Because of the Border wars, King Edward III took over the responsibility for supplies for his armies. In 1436, the sheriffs of Yorkshire were given the order to have plucked 100,000 goose-wing feathers and to find 'sufficient workers and put them to work on the said arrows'.

The bowers were the cream of their crafts. Because English yew was considered too grainy, Baltic yew with its greater give was imported. Within one century, over a hundred bowers were made free in the city of York alone. The prosperous fletchers made cross-bow bolts as well as arrows, and so they had to employ smiths for the spare parts. The arrow shafts were made from aspen and oak, ash and birch. In their carpenters' guilds, they were joined by the turners and joiners, pateners and coopers or barrel-makers. This last craft for holding drink was also vital for military operations. For an army marched, not only on its stomach, but in its throat.

Yet this urban manufacture of weapons did not answer the need for travelling armourers, who could sharpen and maintain the swords and pikes and axes needed in combat. The Tudor English protest against vagrant craftsmen did not extend to Scotland, until the rigid Protestant Reformation of the 16th century would destroy the protection given by the Catholic Church to travelling workers. The records of the early guilds and lodges under the protection of the Lords of Rosslyn would also be burned. Even the Romanies, who were not held to be Christian, had been tolerated because of their necessity. No church or cathedral could be built without their skill in ironwork. They would only be condemned by jealous Presbyterians, who wanted no elegant stoneworkers or rival makers of weapons.

Indeed, a gypsy museum is now set by Rosslyn Chapel, and the patterns on the metalwork created by the Romanies are those carved within the church. As late as the 19th century, the mysterious and untouchable *cagots* were admitted into French cathedrals for restoration work only at midnight, for they were not true believers. Yet legend made them workers at the building of the original Temple of Solomon, while their wives dealt in silk shawls and embroidery. To this day, the Romanies celebrate their chief annual fair at Les Saintes-Maries-de-la-Mer in the Camargue, using their own version of the Christian creed. Thereabouts, the Saints Mary Magdalene and Clarus had first landed in France.

With the coming of guns and cannon, itinerant metal-workers had to yield to foundries and armament factories. As for the incomparable light horsemen of the Borders, they never cared for gunpowder and shot. Although they began to use the heavy pistol called the 'dag' in Tudor times, they knew a bursting cannon had killed King James II, and as late as 1540, Lord Hertford noted that the 'Scotishe borderers . . . love no gonnes, ne will abyde withyn the hearyng of the same.' As their original weapons had made the Steel Bonnets, so the new firearms would begin the ending of their command of the Borders.

Yet in the 14th century, the Borderers proved that their raiding and harassing tactics were a better method of confronting the English than a pitched battle such as Bannockburn. Although Robert the Bruce had made peace with England before his death, the exiled Edward Balliol was backed by the new English King Edward III to assert claims to the Scottish throne. After the victory of Dupplin, when English archers laid low the larger schiltrons, even William St Clair, the fighting bishop of Dunkeld, attended Balliol's coronation, which might have been a *coup d'état*. In the words of a chronicler, all who were there 'were armed save for their helmets, since the people and the nobles inclined to Balliol more from fear than from love.'

The new king was soon ousted, but his flight led to repeated invasions by Edward III, and a second great defeat at Halidon Hill near Berwick, where the Scottish army was decimated. Learning from Bannockburn, the English forces were grouped on a slope behind a marsh, making an attack difficult. The battle was won at a distance by the longbow, which was soon to wreak havoc among the allied French knights at Crécy.

That Old Alliance was to save Scotland from too many more depredations. In pursuit of his own claims to the French throne, Edward III would begin the Hundred Years War across the Channel. Although the Scots King David II was defeated and taken prisoner in 1346 at Neville's Cross, a truce was achieved with his release on payment of a yearly ransom. If he were to die childless, his crown would pass to England and not to his Steward Robert, the son of a Bruce mother.

In 1371, King David died, and Robert Stewart took the throne, forgot the treaty with England and signed a new alliance with France. In spite of English incursions as far as Edinburgh, which the magnanimous John of Gaunt refused to sack, Robert II counter-attacked with Border raids, refusing to fight pitched battles. Although reinforced by French knights under John de Vienne, the commanders of the Scottish forces preferred to retreat and harry. The great Cistercian abbeys of Melrose and Newbattle were burned by the army of the new English King Richard II, while even Edinburgh and royal Holyrood were put to the torch. Although at Otterburn in 1388, a dying James Douglas did triumph in a formal conflict, a stupid incursion by the Scots army fourteen years later led to another crushing massacre by the longbow on Homildon Hill in Northumberland.

The lesson of the frontier wars was to slash and harry, raid and burn and never to engage on a field of battle. Otherwise, all that would remain was 'The Lament of the Border Widow', whose husband was slain by the king:

> I took his body on my back,
> And whiles I gaed, and whiles I sat;
> I digg'd a grave, and laid him in,
> And happ'd him with the sod sae green . . .
>
> Nae living man I'll love again,
> Since that my lovely knight is slain;
> Wi'ae lock of his yellow hair
> I'll chain my heart for evermair.

8

The Northern Commonwealth

The pinnacle of power achieved by the Lords of Rosslyn was under Henry St Clair. Spared as a child from the Black Death, he was left at the age of thirteen by his father, sailing from the Firth of Forth with a body of Scottish soldiers to fight for the Teutonic Knights on their crusade to extend their Prussian empire into pagan Lithuania. The resources and the sea-skills of the fleeing Templars were being absorbed by the St Clairs at Rosslyn, who had also profited from extensive land-grants given by Robert the Bruce after the victory of Bannockburn.

In Germany, the Templars had been ingested by the Teutonic Knights, while the St Clairs at Rosslyn were already involved in the Baltic timber trade in exchange for wool through the Cistercian abbeys of Melrose and Newbattle and Culross in Fife. Old alliances and commerce prompted the Scottish knights to set off on another crusade to the East. In 1358, in a skirmish in the forests towards Russia, the father of Henry St Clair was killed, and the son came into his titles.

He inherited claims, chiefly to the Earldom of Orkney. His mother Isabella was the daughter of Earl Malise II of Orkney, Caithness and Stratherne, whose previous marriage and other children had produced more pretenders to the title. One of these, Alexander de Ard, intervened and took over the earldom, since its rightful heir, Henry St Clair, was still an adolescent, who would have to assert his claims at the Scandinavian royal courts as soon as he had come to manhood.

His chance came in 1363, when he had reached the age of eighteen.

Haakon VI had become King of Norway and also King of Sweden. He was to marry Princess Margaret, the daughter of King Waldemar of Denmark, in Copenhagen. Because of his Norse family connection, Henry St Clair was knighted and appointed as the Scottish ambassador to the wedding, and he sailed across the North Sea. Most of the Scandinavian royalty and nobility would be at the ceremony. Although the bride was only ten years old, she was to become the ruler of all three kingdoms, united in her person.

At Copenhagen, Sir Henry had the lands left by Earl Malise in Orkney confirmed as his right, but he was not yet granted the title of Earl by the King of Norway. He would first have to prove that he could assert royal authority in Orkney and be a faithful servant of the Norse Crown, which disliked having an over-mighty subject or a rebel on its Northern Isles. He was also said to have concluded a marriage to a daughter of King Magnus, Princess Florentia: but if he did, she died young, probably before the age of puberty, and she bore no children.

On his return to Scotland, Henry St Clair did marry Janet Halyburton, the daughter of the Lord of Dirleton Castle, twenty miles from Rosslyn. She was to bear him four sons and nine daughters. The parents were reputed to be the most handsome couple in the region, except perhaps for Henry's cousin, Margaret Stewart, who was the ward and then the mistress of the First Earl of Douglas, who sometimes lived in his sea-fortress of Tantallon on its promontory. Along with Castle Pilgrim, it would serve as a model for Henry's own sea-fortresses on Orkney and off Shetland.

He followed the crusading example of his father and his Templar ancestors. He was recruited with other Scottish knights to join the crusade of Peter I, the Lusignan King of Cyprus. In 1365, he visited his Norman relations on the way south through France before embarking at Venice. There he would have seen the shipbuilding yards of the Arsenale enclosed within its fortifications. And he would have noted the lateen rigs of the merchantmen and the mounted cannon on the war galleys, which were to take him and other Scottish knights to attack Egypt.

When the crusaders reached the Nile, they succeeded in occupying and sacking Alexandria. They could not hold the position and were forced to withdraw with their booty, while Henry St Clair proceeded to Palestine, now held by Muslim forces. He went to Acre and Jerusalem under a safe-conduct for pilgrims, previously negotiated by the Holy Roman Emperor Frederick II. This second crusade by the St Clairs was recorded by their chronicler Father Hay, who wrote in a lay that their 'Predecessors by their val'rous hand/Wonne endless fame twice in the Holyland/Where in that Christian warre their blood been lost.'

Certainly, this pilgrimage gave a nickname to Earl: 'Henry the Holy'. His behaviour testified to his reputation. As Father Hay also noted:

> Att this time the Prince of Orknay had all his victualls brought by sea from the north in great abundance, for his house was free for all men, so that there was no indigent that were his friends but receaved food and rayment, no tennents sore oppressed, but had sufficient to maintain them and, in a word, he was a pattern of piety to all his posterity; for his zeal was so great, that before all things, he preferred God's service.

When he was to die, Earl Henry would look after the future of his soul. He was to leave tithes to the Abbey of Holyrood, consisting of land enough to feed 7,000 sheep, also 'gold and silver, and silkes'. And as the *Obitarium Sanctae Mariae* of Newbattle Abbey was to state: 'There died on the first of February Henry Earl of Orkney, who, among other things, loving our church, has conferred many benefits on us: we have held of his property many flocks, one silver cross worth 50 pounds or there about, on the sides of which stand Mary and John, books and other items for which we must be indebted to him for ever.'

Earl Henry had become powerful at court. He was appointed to hold many state offices, including Lord Chief Justice of Scotland and Lord High Admiral. The Scottish Queen was Euphemia Ross, his great-aunt, who had married the new King Robert Stewart of that dynasty. This close relationship with the Scottish throne disturbed the King of Norway, but Henry St Clair was appointed Earl of Orkney. The assent of powerful Scottish nobles would be procured to confirm Henry's title. No lands or rights of the King of Norway on Orkney would be touched. And any breach of any of the terms of the Deed would result in the loss of the earldom.

The stringent conditions of the Deed of Investiture confirmed the new Earl of Orkney as the vassal of the King of Norway. He would have to go there in person and establish his authority against all rivals, especially the Bishop of Orkney. He would have to build a fleet and recruit forces to control the 170 Orcadian Isles of the Far North, where he would effectively be a Norwegian Prince.

'He was more honoured than any of his ancestors,' Father Hay wrote. 'For he had power to cause stamp coine within his dominions, to make laws, to remitt crimes; he had his sword of honour carried before him wheresover he went; he had a crowne in his armes, bore a crowne on his head when he constituted laws, and, in a word, was subject to none, save only he held his lands of the King of Danemarke, Sweden, and Norway . . . In all those parts he was esteemed a second person next to the King.' His coat of arms was, indeed, in the shape of a sea-beast or dragon, reminiscent of the prow of a Viking ship. It bore a coronet above the engrailed Cross, the symbol of the keepers of the Holy Rood and other royal treasures.

Henry St Clair had inherited considerable resources to enforce his rights and to make himself a sea-power in the north. The Register of the Great Seal of Scotland shows Bruce and Stewart grants of land to Henry St Clair, 'our chosen defender and faithful to us,' the guardian of the Crown Prince. In addition, he had absorbed many of the Templar lands and treasures from their headquarters at Balantrodoch near Rosslyn castle.

His power and state, also that of his son Henry, were considerable. 'There were very few but were some way bound to him,' Father Hay wrote. 'He had continually in his house three hundred Riding Gentlemen, and his Princess, fifty-five Gentlewomen, whereof thirty-five were Ladies. He had his dainties tasted before him: he had meeting him, when he went to Orknay, three hundred men with red scarlet gownes and coats of black velvet.'

He was hardly going to a new dominion. The St Clairs were a Norse and Norman and Scottish family, which had held the name of Møre or Moray and had changed it long ago on the borders of Normandy. The diplomacy of Henry St Clair had persuaded King Haakon VI to invest him as the Earl. He certainly had legitimacy, not only through his mother, but through his Møre ancestors. But the new Stewart Kings were never easy about one of their subjects also being a subject of another sovereign power. Orkney and the Shetlands should be Scottish. This was a factor in foreign policy long before it was achieved.

Before he could secure the Orcadian Isles, Earl Henry had to build a fleet. And here he would be invaluable to the Crown of Scotland and become the first of three successive St Clair Lord High Admirals. He had the iron and coal resources for foundries in Lothian, and he could import Baltic timber for the deep-keeled ships developed by the Vikings. He controlled the guilds of the carpenters and the hammermen, also the Romany iron-workers and makers of weapons. He had inherited Templar skills in seafaring and navigation, particularly the use of the lodestone and mariner's compass. And he was given the factor which would change frontier wars on land and sea – gunpowder.

The invention of cannon is usually credited to a Franciscan monk in 1313 in Germany; previously, another monk of that Order, the philosopher Roger Bacon, had made known a formula for using saltpetre to make gunpowder. Fourteen years later, the English King Edward III first used muzzle-loading *pots de fer* at the siege of Berwick, where the chroniclers told of such cracks of war that never were heard before. Indeed, Shakespeare in his play *Macbeth* told of 'cannon overcharged with double cracks'.

At the naval battle of Sluys against the French, Welsh archers won the struggle with their arrows, but small cannon were mounted on the English ships. And although the longbow again triumphed against the French cavalry charge in the succeeding land battle at Crécy, a few breech-loading guns firing iron or stone or leaden-case balls caused some damage to the enemy chivalry.★ These longer guns were now looped to prevent the explosion of the barrel, and they would serve in the Venetian and Scottish navies, also on the Zeno voyage of Henry St Clair from Orkney to the New World. One of these early *petriera* remains in the sea-fortress of Louisburg in Nova Scotia until this day, as evidence of that transatlantic passage.

★ See Illustrations.

There was not only the building of a fleet, but the provisioning and the maintenance of the ships, that were necessary. Here Earl Henry was aided by his connections at Melrose and Newbattle Abbeys, where the Cistercians were famous for moving into a wilderness and creating within a decade a paradise of the arts and crafts. In his history, *The Irish*, Seán O'Faolain told of the effect of an early foundation of the white monks by William Marshal on a village in Kilkenny. The people were taught every needful occupation, 'boat-building, nail-making, weaving, boot-making, bacon-curing, the making of salt, starch and candles, tanning, a small foundry, wheelwrights, carpenters, joiners, tinsmiths, bakers, coopers, quilters, and so on.'

Without this command of the means of production, Earl Henry could never have constructed and provided for the fleet of thirteen ships, which would encounter a Venetian trading vessel, after his conquest of Orkney. Yet where did he find his sudden wealth? He did not secure it from his revenues or the Crown. The only likely source was the laundering of Templar money through the St Clair family, the secure keepers of royal treasures in times of riot and invasion, the very role which the Military Order had before its dissolution.

The first requisite for the new Earl of Orkney was a secure base for his knights and his fleet. He had seen the Arsenale in Venice and the Templar sea castles at Acre and Castle Pilgrim, and he knew of the Douglas fortress at Tantallon, where a huge wall guarded a rocky promontory, enabling ships to sail into a defended harbour beneath the cliffs. Although his Deed of Investiture precluded him from building a strongpoint, he did so with the help of masons imported from Lothian, who had already set up the massive red walls of Rosslyn Castle. He put up a monumental fortress on the site of an old Norse emplacement in Kirkwall, which afforded sanctuary for ships dragged ashore. So thick were its ashlar blocks that two centuries later, one of its besiegers with cannon protested 'to God the house has never been biggit without the consent of the Devil, for it is one of the strongest holds in Britain – without fellow.'

The death of King Olaf after a short reign confirmed Prince Henry's estimation as 'a second person next to the King'. As Earl of Orkney, he was an elector to the three kingdoms of Norway, Sweden and Denmark. So he sailed across the North Sea to confirm

King Olaf's mother, the Princess Margaret, whose wedding he had attended in Copenhagen, as Queen of Norway and Sweden and as Regent of Denmark. She adopted as her heir a five-year-old boy, her grand-nephew Eric of Pomerania, and so sustained her power during his minority.

Earl Henry's presence in Scandinavia caused him to miss the Battle of Otterburn against the English, but the peace of 1389 between England and the old allies, Scotland and France, allowed him to consider extending his power to the Faroes and the Shetlands. Evidently, his assertion of royal authority on Orkney had been so effective that he was now asked to do the same on the neighbouring outcrops of the north.

Before he could begin the reduction of these far islanders, who resented paying church tithes almost as much as royal taxes, Earl Henry had to pay homage at Scone to the new Stewart King of Scotland, Robert III. He was truly a catalyst between all the nations of the north, allied by blood and trust to the ruling families of four kingdoms. His ambitions were also expanding, for he intended to aid the foundation of a Commonwealth of the North Atlantic, fuelled by the trade of Scotland and Scandinavia, and stretching as far as America and Venice.

The trade routes of the North Sea had been contested for many centuries. As far back as 1297, William Wallace had written, after his victory at Stirling Bridge, to the Mayor of Lubeck. He had invited the German merchants of the Hanseatic League to begin trading directly with the Scots, as the English no longer blocked the coasts of his country. His offer did not survive his defeat and execution.

The chief power in the Baltic Sea remained the Hanseatic League. The fleets of these Germanic trading ports, under the protection of the Teutonic Knights, were powerful enough to burn Bergen and force commercial concessions on Norway, Denmark and Sweden. Although Queen Margaret united the three Scandinavian countries by the Treaty of Kalmar of 1397, she was not in command of the ocean. Not only had the armed Hansa ships destroyed much of the old Viking merchant marine, the *knorrs*, but piracy was rife in the North Sea. In response to her need, Earl Henry had travelled in 1392 under a safe conduct to London to take delivery of three ships, which he would sail to Bergen. The Queen had written to King Richard II, who had given his reluctant permission.

The usual English strategy was to combine with the Hansa to cut off Scottish trade with France and the Baltic. But now that Venice was excluded by the fleets of Islam from trading with the Near East, the Italian maritime power was looking for expansion beyond the cloth marts of Flanders up to the rich trade in salt fish and furs, timber and resin, of the North Sea. That was the reason for the probing voyage of Captain Nicolò Zeno, who was shipwrecked, probably on Fair Isle between Orkney and the Shetlands. There he was rescued by Earl Henry, who had a fleet of two galleys, ten trading vessels and a large warship.

The expedition for the expansion of commerce in a Northern Commonwealth followed the old Viking routes past Iceland and Greenland and the colony of L'Anse aux Meadows in Newfoundland to anchor off Estotilandia, which now bears the name of Nova Scotia. Earl Henry wanted to found a city there, but many of his crew wished to return under their Captain Antonio, the brother of Nicolò Zeno, who had died. The Earl sent them home and wintered near Louisburg, where his Venetian ship's cannon was found, before proceeding to Rhode Island to build a fortified beacon tower at Newport, later identified by Verrazano, the first European explorer to reach those coasts, as a 'Norman Villa'.

Although Earl Henry had been far from home for two years, he had timber and pine tar and fibre for ropes in abundance in the New World. He had also brought with him iron, weapons and tools for the use of the shipwrights, taken from the Firth of Forth. In 1400, he returned to Orkney, but his survival was short.

That August, King Henry IV of England invaded Scotland and reached Edinburgh, for Earl Henry was not at Rosslyn to hold the southern road from London against an English incursion. Marine raiders from East Anglia beat off a counter-attack and captured the Scottish commander, Sir Robert Logan. They then proceeded up to Orkney to challenge the new sea-power of the North.

The marauders pillaged several of the islands and made a surprise attack on Kirkwall. In his description of the family, Father Hay wrote of Earl Henry's death in Orkney: 'Resisting them with his forces, through his too great negligence and contempt of his ound friendly forces [he was] left breathless, by blows battered so fast upon him, that no man was able to resist.' An account of 1446 stated tersely that he 'deit Eirle of Orchadie and for the defence of the countrie was sclane thair crowellie be his innimiis.'

With his death, the dream of a trading link across the Atlantic passed away. And the Northern Commonwealth itself was ended by continued assaults from the Hansa and the pirates. Queen Margaret died in 1412, and eleven years later the Kalmar Union broke up once more into three separate kingdoms. Although Earl Henry's heir and successor, Earl William of Orkney, was considered a future King of Norway because of his noble Møre bloodline, he was discarded under pressure from the Hansa in favour of a Prince Christian of Denmark. And so the great adventure of the Lords of Rosslyn beyond the seas sank with little trace.

9

Renaissance and Defeat

The dying of weak kings always leads to intrigue. The end of the reign of the Stewart King, Robert III, saw him in 1406 sending to France his heir James, still a child, under the protection of the Lord High Admiral, Earl William St Clair of Orkney and Rosslyn. The boy's life would not have been spared, any more than those of the Princes in the Tower were to be by their uncle, Richard III of England. If the boy Prince James were also to die young, the throne of Scotland would pass to the king's brother Robert, the Duke of Albany, who was already the Regent of the realm.

Whether or not information was passed on to the English, Prince James and Earl William were captured. This was the Earl's second imprisonment, for the English had already taken him at Homildon Hill, before releasing him. As Father Hay recorded, the Earl and the royal child had cast themselves 'to the sea's mercie; but when they had sailed a little space, Prince James not being able to abide the smell of the waters, desired to be att land, where when they were come (for they landed att his request upon the coast of England) upon their journey to the King [of France] they were taken and imprisoned.'

While the pair were held in England, the Duke of Albany acted as king of the realm. In a letter of 1410 to the gaoler King Henry IV, Albany referred to his subjects in Scotland. He shrewdly allied himself with the powerful Earls of Douglas, the major power on the south-western Borders. When the grown Stewart King James I was finally released in 1423, he found that the interregnum under the Albany clan had beggared Scotland, although the puritan doctrines of the Lollards, the heralds of the Reformation, had been suppressed through the new University of St Andrews. Yet King James was determined to rearm his country, and also to live in some style.

Unfortunately, he had lost his fellow prisoner and Lord High Admiral, William St Clair of Rosslyn. He had soon been released and had gone with his brother John and his brother-in-law Lord Douglas to fight for the Dauphin before the disaster at Agincourt. He had to return to defend Scotland against furious English counter-attacks, which ended in the burning of Penrith. Between the politics of Scandinavia and France, the St Clairs were best placed in the defence of their homeland.

Father Hay called Earl William 'a man of sharp wit [who] projected great matters, when he breathed out his life'. The *Book of Cowper* recorded his passing in 1422: 'there also died Henry de Sinclair, second Earl of Orkney . . . as a result of a pestilential disease, which was commonly known as the quhew.' There was further testimony to his gifts as a commander, for he was 'a man who was very experienced indeed in military knowledge by land and by sea, who from his youth had gained glory and authority in the eyes of all for the great deeds he had achieved with the utmost bravery and success'.

His legacy as the defender of the Stewarts could not yet be achieved by his child heir, William St Clair of Rosslyn, whose authority in Orkney was assigned by the Norse king to Thomas, the Bishop there. Not until twelve years after his father's death did William receive the title. According to Pontanus, quoted by Father Hay, 'King Eric proclaimed William de Sancto Claro, commonly called Sinclair, a noble Scot, Earl of Orkney, and in addition the services which belong there.' These services were chiefly military. 'Whenever he was asked, he would serve in the army abroad with one hundred armed men for the advantage and use of the King [of Norway] . . . He also, if any people by chance tried to make hostile invasion of Orkney and the Shetlands, having gathered together all the island troops and forces, would use them and defend his territories.'

William was to be the third and last St Clair Earl of Orkney. His position was untenable, caught between his duties to the Norse and Scottish Crowns. Anyway, his earldom ceased with his life, for he pledged that he would build no more 'citadels or defences', and that 'on his demise he would return to the King and his heirs and the Kingdom of Norway, without contradiction, the islands and citadel of Kirkwall'. Just as the formidable Rosslyn castle was the strongpoint holding back an attack on Edinburgh from the south, so the Kirkwall fortress was the dominant factor in the control of the Orcadian Isles and the trade routes of the North Sea.

The young Earl Henry inherited a position of considerable wealth and power. Among his many titles were to be Lord High Admiral, Lord Chief Justice, Lord Warden of three Marches, Knight of the French Order of the Cockle, and Knight of the Golden Fleece. He shared with King James I a liking for extravagant building in the flamboyant Gothic style, and for the new armaments. He was also large in manner and person. 'He was a very fair man,' in the words of Father Hay, 'of great stature, broad bodied, yellow haired, straight, well proportioned, humble, courteous, and given to policy, as building Castles, Palaces and Churches'. So was the Stewart King, who spent his revenues on Flemish bombards, which failed to reduce Roxburgh castle. He also began to rebuild Linlithgow palace, and he maintained an extravagant court, as did the Earl of Orkney, when sent on a mission to France with a train that incurred the royal envy.

He was sailing with the King's sister to marry her to the Dauphin. He was accompanied by a hundred gentlemen, 'twinty in white and black velvet, signifieing his armes, which is a ragged cross in a silver field; twinty cloathed with gold and blew coloured velvet, which signified the armes of Orknay, which is a ship of gold with a double tressure, and flower de luces goeing round about it in a blew field'. After the disaster of the Battle of Neville's Cross in 1446, he pushed back another English invasion two years later and was ordered on diplomatic missions to London to secure peace at the end of the Hundred Years War. He supported King James II in a struggle with the Douglas family and was made Lord Chancellor of the kingdom. The Black Douglas had actually been stabbed by a royal dirk, as Robert the Bruce had killed John de Comyn, and both murderers had needed St Clair support against clan revenge.

King James II was so enthralled by artillery that he brought over from Flanders the greatest cannon in Britain, Mons Meg. And in 1456, his Council or early parliament insisted that it was 'speedful that the king make request to certain of the great barons of the land that are of any might to make carts of war, and in each cart two guns, and each of them to have two chambers, with the rest of the gear that pertains thereto, and a cunning man to shoot them'.

With his command over the Scottish hammermen and the means of production, Earl William of Rosslyn would have been a good manufacturer of armaments. But four years later, the King was killed at another siege of Roxburgh castle. One of his own cannon 'brak in the fyring'. He was only thirty years old, and left another boy heir to the throne, although he did fulfil a prophecy that the castle would be won from the English only by a dead monarch. And the fortress did surrender in the end.

Although Earl William became the Regent of the new King during his minority, he had affected his country's diplomacy. In 1456, the governor of Iceland and his treasure had been seized while sheltering from a storm in Orkney – an incident that sabotaged the efforts of the Stewarts to come to good terms with the King of Norway. Ten years later, Earl William's eldest son was to throw Bishop William Tulloch of Orkney into prison in another effort to break Scottish–Norse relationships and put a stop to talk of a marriage between the two royal families, by which the Orcadian Isles would go to the young King James III. In fact, the king's eventual marriage with the daughter of King Christian of Denmark would mean that the Isles were handed over to Scotland as a pledge for the payment of the Princess's dowry of 60,000 gold florins.

This pledge would be followed by the removal of the title of Earl of Orkney from William St Clair. He was also required to exchange Kirkwall castle for Ravenscraig castle, built to withstand artillery attacks and admirable for defending his lands in Fife. In exchange for his lands in Nithsdale, he had already been made Earl of Caithness. And as his Scottish properties were now far more valuable than the royal domains he had controlled in Orkney and the Shetlands, he was pleased to resolve the problem of his dual allegiance to two Crowns in favour of Scotland.

Earl William and his heir Oliver St Clair were an inspiration for the young rebel Prince James, who became the fourth King of that name in 1488; he was to be the architect of the Scottish Renaissance. Like

King Henry VIII in England, he would serve as the creator of the first powerful national navy in his country. In 1511, when he lost two ships in a firefight with the Lords Howard, the *Lion* and the *Jenny Pirwin*, he demanded their return, only to be told that they were pirates.

Both by land and sea, cannon were the new weapons. Those who made and serviced and moved them demanded payment in coin. The St Clairs remained in control of the necessary guilds of gunners, smiths, hammermen, ship- and wheel-wrights, coopers, miners and masons. Early trials of carting cannon were made at Stirling before going to Edinburgh castle, which also manufactured powder and shot. The costs of maintenance and movement were high. In a raiding expedition of 1497, King James IV had to engage nearly 400 road-builders, quarrymen and masons to smooth the way for the gun-carts, and also more than 100 drivers and 30 smiths and armourers.

Before this reign, the Scottish navy had merely consisted of armed cogs or merchantmen. The first new warship was the *Margaret*, which boasted 21 guns. Yet the pride of the new fleet was the great *Michael*, which rivalled Mons Meg as the largest weapon in existence. Some 80 yards long, she sported 6 cannon on either side with 3 basilisks at stern and prow, and 300 smaller guns, 'falcons, slangs, pestilent serpentines, and double dogs, with hackbutts and culverines'. She also needed 300 sailors and 120 gunners for her use, while she carried 1,000 men-at-arms. Unfortunately, *Michael* hardly saw action and was sold to King Louis XII of France; she rotted away in the harbour of Brest.

This vast exercise in shipbuilding was under the supervision of the Lord High Admiral, Earl William St Clair, also the lawgiver to the guilds, as recorded in his 'Lawis and Costumis of Ye Schippis' from the Rosslyn Library. He was made Chancellor and Lord Chamberlain to supervise these works. He also co-operated with the king in rebuilding palaces, castles and cathedrals, as well as designing his spectacular church and chapel at Rosslyn, which would be completed by his heir Oliver, before King James IV marched to his terminal disaster on Flodden field.

Some of his artillery there had been supplied from St Clair sources. Lord Henry St Clair served the King as 'Master of all our Machines and Artyllerie' and sold to his royal leader eight great 'serpentynis' for a hundred pounds, paid to his widow after both of their deaths at

Flodden. St Clair had gone down with three hundred members of his clan wearing green jackets: that colour would hardly be worn again.

The battle began in 1513 with a flanking movement by the English forces under the Earl of Surrey, and an artillery duel. With their superior cannon placed high on Branxton Hill, the Scottish gunners could not lower their muzzles enough to strafe the English ranks, while the enemy bombards made hay among the schiltrons. Broken into disorder, the advancing men with pikes came into contact with the dismounted English Borderers with their eight-foot shafts and battle-axes. As the Bishop of Durham later wrote: 'Our bills quit them very well . . . for they shortly disappointed the Scots of their long spears wherein was their greatest trust.' However well the Scots then fought with their short swords, large and strong men had to fall 'when four or five bills struck on them at once'.

Weapons and tactics remained the masters of battles. King James IV had been supplied by the King of France with 400 muskets, 600 hand-guns, and 6,000 each of pikes, spears and maces. Sergeants had been sent over to instruct raw troops in the use of these three arms. Moreover, 2 cannon and 40 cartloads of gunpowder had been contributed to add to the 15 Scottish big brass guns, some made by the Master Gunner, Robert, Lord Borthwick, a neighbour and steward of the St Clairs at Rosslyn. A mobile workshop of armourers accompanied the cannon train, which had a complement of smiths with cranes and tools, anvils, iron ingots and coals.

During the opening barrage, many of the Border light horse under Lord Dacre fled the field, terrified by the noise. This loss to the Earl of Surrey's side was compensated, when Dacre still held onto some two thousand of the cavalry behind his divisions of two main bodies, flanked by two wings. This force came mainly from Cumbria and Westmoreland and was true to Dacre, who was the Warden of the English Middle and West Marches. They rescued Lord Edmund Howard, when he was beset alongside his billmen: but then they deserted the field to rob the slain and to steal horses.

King James IV fought in the van with a pike. He was killed, perhaps as King Harold had been at Hastings, by enemy archers. Many of the Scots threw down their useless overlong prickers and took to lead maces or stabbing swords. The arrows won the day against a final charge of the heavy Scots knights, with their leader Bothwell dying, pierced with a grey-goose-feathered shaft. The vultures of the English soldiers acquired all the Scots munitions of war, including 17 cannon and 2,000 pikes, while the sword and body armour of King James IV were hung with the Scots standard in St Cuthbert's shrine at Durham cathedral.

The Scots monarch had married Margaret Tudor, who became the Queen Dowager and Regent of the kingdom. Her 'pet' and 'trusty and true servant' was Patrick Sinclair of Draidon, who was often sent by her as an ambassador to England. Cardinal Wolsey denounced him as a double agent for both countries, while King Henry VIII blew hot and cold over his policy across the Borders. No word remains of Patrick Sinclair's many private conversations with the English king, although these may have covered the royal divorces and the repudiation of the authority of the Pope of Rome. Curiously enough, at this time, a prebendary at Catholic Rosslyn chapel was accused of heresy.

Another Duke of Albany, who had been reared in France and was the heir to the throne if the young King James V were to die, became Regent of Scotland. When he was old enough, the King tried to bring some order to the Highlands and Western Isles. With the large armed fleet which he had inherited, he sailed from the Firth of Forth to Orkney, where he met his future favourite, the handsome Oliver Sinclair of Pitcairn. King James made him the lessor of Orkney and the Shetlands, as well as the keeper of Kirkwall Castle. Deposed were Lord William and Margaret, Lady Sinclair, in favour of this ambitious cousin. On another voyage to the Isles in 1540, James took a fleet of sixteen vessels, including the French warship *Salamander*. The expedition was victualled at Leith and armed from Edinburgh castle. As an English chronicler noted, 'In all Scottlande was not leffte 10 peces of ordenance besides that wyche the Kynge dothe take with Hym.' He was well defended, even on his travels.

On the Borders, James V once again proceeded to destroy the powerful Douglas family, which had forfeited its estates under King James II. The important fortress of Tantallon on the Firth of Forth was now assigned to Oliver Sinclair of Pitcairn, the second son of the Sir Oliver Sinclair who completed the building of Rosslyn chapel, and the brother of the inheritor of that place, Sir William. This Oliver of

Pitcairn had entered the royal Household, where he became the keeper of the king's purse and his cup bearer, the role of William 'the Seemly' Saintclair to Queen Margaret five centuries before. He was later accused of abusing the King's bedchamber and becoming his 'familiar'.

With King Henry VIII to the south threatening an invasion, if James did not repudiate the authority of the Pope, and with the reformer John Knox trying to lead the people of Edinburgh in a Protestant revolution, the Scottish King stuck to the Old Alliance with France and the Catholic faith. He married two French ladies with large dowries; the second was Mary of Guise, who turned down King Henry's advances, when he was looking for his fourth wife. As for Oliver Sinclair, he was denounced by the radical reformer, John Knox, as a 'pensioner of the priests', and he was prominent on a list of heretical nobles. To the English Earl of Hertford, he was 'the mooste secrete man, leving with the said King of Scottis'.

Various border and sea raids were the prelude to a military disaster. The rebellious nobility had turned against their royal master and his upstart favourites, as had happened in England with King Richard II and his minions. A large Scottish army under its feudal Lords was assembled in November, 1542, to pre-empt an English attack. Against them stood the old Border warrior, Sir Thomas Wharton, who described his strategy as 'fighting the battle as he saw it, with a reiver's eye and a reiver's tactics'.

A force of some 10,000 men advanced from Scotland, burning their path through Cumbria between the Esk river and the marshland of Solway Moss. A force of 300 enemy light horse or 'prickers' drew them forward by retreating at speed. The Scots found themselves enmeshed and leaderless. In the words of Father Hay, the angry aristocracy could not stomach the elevation of the King's familiar, Oliver Sinclair:

> Oliver thought time to shew his glory, and so incontinent was displayed the King's banner, and he holden up by two spears lift up upon men's shoulders, there, with sound of trumpet, was declared Generall Lieutenant, and all men commanded to obey him as the King's person, under the highest pains, so soon a great noise and

confusion was heard. The enimie, perceaveing the disorder, rushed on, the Scots fled, some passed the water, but escaping that danger, not well acquainted with the ground, fell into the slimy mosse; happy was he that might get a taker. Stout Oliver was without stroke taken, flying full manfully, and so was his glory suddenly turn'd to confusion and shame.

This was the finest and final victory of the Border cavalry. As with the Parthians and the later Apaches, mounted archers with javelins and tomahawks or axes could harass and defeat armoured ranks, which outnumbered them ten times over. If the morale and strategy of the foe failed, as at Solway Moss, the light horse could harry the legions and the schiltrons and the heavy knights into the wet ground. That was the military lesson of this frontier over the four hundred years of its fighting times.

'Oh fled Oliver!' King James V of Scotland cried, when he heard that Oliver Sinclair had lost the battle of Solway Moss. 'Is Oliver tane? Fie fled Oliver! All is lost!' Soon afterwards, he took to his deathbed at the age of thirty, stricken by the 'pest' or cholera. When he heard the news that his wife, Marie of Guise, had borne him a daughter, he said of his kingdom, 'Adieu, fare well, it came with a lass, it will pass with a lass.'

The independent kingdom had come to the Stewarts through their marriage with a Bruce princess, and it would pass with James's child, Mary, Queen of Scots. Although the Stewarts would inherit the English throne as well as that of Scotland, the twinning of the Crowns would mean the lessening of Scottish liberty and the fall of the Sinclairs of Rosslyn from power in their country.

10

The Sacred Shape of the Stones

After the battle of Bannockburn, the St Clairs had become powerful in Scotland as the defenders of the realm, the royal sacred treasures and the fledgling masons, who were beginning to build the Gothic cathedrals of northern Europe. The purpose of all sacred architecture was to reconcile the circle to the square. The Romans had achieved the Great Dome at the Pantheon. And when the Emperor Constantine was converted to Christianity, he told his architects to construct the greatest basilica in the world – the Sancta Sophia, named after the sacred goddess of wisdom – by putting the circle on the square. The result was a future model of holy architecture, the octagon holding up the dome. When the Emperor Justinian completed Sancta Sophia, he exclaimed that he had outdone King Solomon himself in the original Jewish Temple.

In the 1st century, when Sanctus Clarus was crossing the Mediterranean to Rome, two other disciples of Saint Paul, Jason and Sosipatros, had reached Corfu, bringing the Gospel there from the East. The island was the strategic maritime base between Italy and Greece and Asia Minor. A thousand years ago, on stone blocks taken from the Greek and Roman fortress of Kerkira, and in memory of the two blessed preachers, a perfect and unique Byzantine cruciform church was built on the model of Sancta Sophia – octagonal points within a circle set around an eight-sided central tower.★ This small and elegant church on Corfu survived a Roman Catholic invasion, which

★ See Illustrations.

sailed on to crush Constantinople on the Fourth Crusade; neither was it desecrated under four hundred years of Venetian occupation. Restored to the Greek Orthodox rite, its slender arched windows serve as a memorial to the original style of the Resurrection in architecture.

In his *Laws*, Plato had asked for a city to be built in the centre of any country, as Madrid would later be built in Spain. Within a ring wall, it should have an acropolis or temple, and be divided into twelve equal parts. When the Greek philosopher described his legendary Atlantis, he dreamt of a temple mount, encircled by five areas of land and water, also a moated palace enclosed in round walls on a plain of 60,000 square plots of land, a concept probably derived from the first town planner, Hippodamus of Miletus. This ideal would become the basis of all sacred architecture, the circle and the square, and their meeting together.

In addition, Plato taught that numbers and the ratios of geometry and music, interpreted by priests and builders, ensured a polyphony of society. In ancient Egypt, particularly, these proportions had resulted in the pyramids. The biblical Book of Revelation is full of the exact measurement of the New Jerusalem, usually related to the twelve months of the year. Its shape is the squared circle. Later Gnostic writers believed in a holy science of numbers, in which Greek letters were an arithmetic. This Platonic and Christian ideal of harmonious architecture would later be reconstructed in Rosslyn chapel.

Through early Christian fathers and mystics, Jesus was given 888 as his symbol, while the octahedron signified the air, and the octave would become the basis of European music. And indeed, the great Dome of the Rock, designed by Byzantine architects for their new Muslim rulers and built on the Temple Mount in Jerusalem, would have eight sides, supporting a great Dome and enclosing the 'ομφάλος, the stone that was considered the navel of the world as well as the Prophet Muhammad's step to paradise. For the Jews, it had been the sacrifice stone of Isaac, and the place where King David had prayed for the forgiveness of his sins, and the altar of Solomon.

Although drawn by later artists, the armed camps of the twelve tribes of Israel, and the later Temple on the Mount, appeared to fit the Platonic model. The tabernacle was set up in the middle of the fortified square bivouac, while the Temple was surrounded by the circular walls of the city. While the inner sanctuary and Jerusalem were described in Ezekiel and the Book of Revelation as a cube and a Messianic city built as a circle with four gates, the earthly Temple was depicted as an oblong behind two great pillars supporting an arched roof or dome, which would also serve as the design of Rosslyn chapel.

Moreover, the Essene 'Temple Scrolls' from Qumran had described a perfect Third Temple, which the Messiah would enter. This should be built in the form of a walled rectangle with four gates, containing an oblong Temple, fronted by two pillars: within its recesses would lie the square Holy of Holies. 'It shall be a House of Perfection and Truth in Israel' was its description, although it was never built any more than St Augustine's City of God would ever be.

For the Roman historian Varro, the augurs or soothsayers determined the shape of the camp or city, which was generally a quartered circle with four gates: the tents of the general and the diviner were placed in the middle. Pliny recommended a division of the circle into eight segments according to the blowing of the breezes – the shape of the Tower of the Winds in Athens as well as much of holy architecture in the Christian era to come.

From classical times, only ten volumes on architecture, the work of the Roman Vitruvius, have survived. For him, the octagon was sacred, both in the making of towns and temples, for it was the shape, which could include squares and be contained within a circle, but also could sustain a dome above. He would be a major influence on the Renaissance in Italy, particularly in the works of Leonardo da Vinci. The first fully planned city of the period, Sforzinda, was drawn about 1460 by Filarete. Its design showed a perfect eight-pointed star within a circular wall, another stimulus for Leonardo in his military and architectural plans.

The writer of the most important manual explaining the designs and symbols of medieval churches was Bishop Guillaume Durand de Mende. He studied at Paris and in Italy; he became a Professor of Law at Bologna and Modena; and in 1265 he was called to be a chaplain to Pope Clement IV. At the time of the crusades, he saw the tabernacle in the armed camp of Israel as an early version of the Church Militant. With victory, a Temple or a cathedral could be built. The foundations and doors and cornerstones were Christ; the shape was the Cross and the human body; the dome represented the perfection and inviolability of the Catholic faith; the arch was the testament to the afterlife; the cloister with its paradise garden had many chambers off its walks because heaven had many rooms; the golden chalice signified the wisdom hidden in the sacrifice of Christ, while a silver communion cup was the symbol of the purification of sin.

So we may still read medieval architecture, when we understand its many meanings. Even the cube of the sanctuary at Mecca, the Ka'aba, was the only pagan shrine preserved by the Prophet as a Holy of Holies, while the Emperor Charlemagne ordered the capital chapel at Aachen to be constructed with eight sides, holding up a dome. These prototypes would spread over the medieval cathedrals and baptisteries of Europe.

There were many notable churches built after the model of Aachen, where the circle of the dome was held up by the extended square. The most celebrated round churches lay within Charlemagne's empire at Neuvy-Saint Sepulchre and Sainte-Croix à Quimperlé and even as far away as Sainte-Marie-de-Vyscherat at Prague. The pillars which supported the domes could be sixteen, the four-by-four number of the multiplied gospels; or there could be twelve pillars, as the disciples were counted; or there were often eight, indicating divine harmony or the beatitudes.

Such forms were particularly holy in architecture. As Hermann Kern declared in his definitive *Through the Labyrinth*:

> The number eight and the octagon were associated with the resurrection and consummate perfection, with new beginnings, and with spiritual rebirth, which explains the octagonal shape of numerous baptisteries and baptismal fonts. In the Renaissance, the octagon also featured in the work of such virtuoso Italian artists as Leonardo da Vinci . . . The basic concept of the labyrinth representing an initiation process – spiritual death and rebirth – was expanded to include Christian ideas surrounding baptism, which also embrace the notion of death, sinning, and birth.

Associated with the travelling masons under their patronage, the Knights Templars were the designers of many abbeys and cathedrals from Chartres to Melrose. Very probably they brought to Europe Byzantine designs from the Near East. For most of the ninety years of the kingdom of Jerusalem, the Military Order had occupied as its headquarters the al-Aqsa mosque on the Temple Mount, beside the octagonal Dome of the Rock, which the knights called the Temple of Solomon – the design of the major surviving Templar chapels. The one at Laon has an apse and a nave protruding from the central structure supporting the roof.

At Eunate beside the pilgrim route to Santiago de Compostela, the eight sides of the church are plain, and only surrounded by an arcade.★ And at La Vera Cruz de Segovia, the shape in the middle spawns little round chapels with a square bell-tower at the end. In resolving the circle and the square, the Templar masters relied on the sacred octagon, which would become the master plan of Rosslyn Chapel. Its profile would be the eight-pointed Templar Cross, while each of its fourteen pillars would be set on a plinth with eight faces.★ And, most probably, three octagonal mazes, in the manner of Leonardo da Vinci, would decorate its original floor above the altar.

There was no absolute proof of the role of the Knights Templars as architects, until I visited the Church of St Mary and St Bega in Cumbria. There I found the evidence carved on a Templar grave-stone. The slab of the tomb is surmounted by the round plan of the Holy City of God with its four gates and the inrushing rivers of life, making an octagon of points within a circle, and enclosing a square or tabernacle, containing the six-petalled rose of the Virgin Mary. Below are the mason's tools of the plumbline and the dividers and the spread compasses, sometimes shown in medieval manuscripts in the hand of God as He measures the world. These carvings are the missing link for those who have long sought to show that the Templars were the guiding forces of the building workers in their pay, later known by the French names of their medieval guilds or *compagnonnages* as the *Enfants de Salomon* and the *Fratres Solomonis*. These masons were associated with the Cistercian white monks, while another guild of the *Maître de Saint Jacques* generally toiled for the Benedictines, the black monks.

★ See Illustrations.

Moreover, in Cumbria outside Bridekirk church, we made the first discovery that the Templars believed themselves to be the heirs of Prince Zerubbabel of Judah, the knights of 'the sword and the trowel'. Against the outer wall, six Templar burial stones are still ranged, one with shears beside the stem of the rosy cross, another with a curved mattock or trowel opposite a crusading sword.★ These were more proofs of the practical role of the knights in constructing their thousands of castles, chapels and commanderies from the Near East to Scotland. They always tried to build another Temple after the example of Zerubbabel, who was told by the biblical prophet Haggai of the words of the Lord God:

> And I will shake all nations, and the desire of all nations shall come: and I will fill this house with glory, saith the Lord of Hosts.
>
> The silver is mine, and the gold is mine, saith the Lord of Hosts.
>
> The glory of this latter house shall be greater than of the former, saith the Lord of Hosts: and in this place will I give peace.

In this construction of a Second Temple on the Mount in Jerusalem, there had been strife and discord. As the apocryphal Book of Esdras testified, many attacks made the builders use a trowel, while wearing a sword. The dream of its foundation would be carved in stone in Rosslyn chapel beside the 'Apprentice' Pillar. With two other imperial guards, Prince Zerubbabel had interpreted the dream of the Persian ruler Darius.

'Wine is strong,' was the first statement.

'The Emperor is stronger,' was the second statement.

'Women are the strongest,' Zerubbabel declared, 'but above all things, Truth bears the victory.'

So pleased was Darius at this answer that the Prince of Judah was given permission to rear high the Second Temple, accompanied by masons and carpenters, whom he paid and fed and put in lodges. He also brought a musical tradition with him, as his imitator Earl William St Clair would do in his chapel. For the Prince reached Jerusalem with the notes of 'tabrets and flutes'.

★ See Illustrations.

There is little doubt that the architect and designer of Rosslyn, Earl William, would try to put up a Third Temple, heralding the coming of the Messiah in Jewish tradition. Herod had already built another Second Temple, enclosing that of Zerubabbel; but, as the killer of St John the Baptist, the despot could hardly claim his Temple on the Mount to be the forerunner of the coming of the Saviour of mankind.

Earl William knew of the significance of the holy name of St Clair as well as that of St Matthew. This was to be a messianic church and chapel, which appealed directly to the divine light. The rough design of the west end of the sacred building would be that of the Temple of Solomon. Two flanking pillars, Joachin and Boaz, would support a carved stone roof.* And twenty small Temples of Solomon would be carved within, so that the message might never be lost.

In the more modern Masonic legacy, few high degrees were to be more desired than that of the Holy Royal Arch of Jerusalem. Its mysteries devolved from the Ancient Scottish Rite, which would be taken to France by the Jacobites in the early 18th century, when Freemasonry would become the enemy of church and state.

In the *Parfait Maçon* of 1744, the reconstruction of the Second Temple by Zerubabbel would be a part of the ceremony of induction, which asked of the initiate whether he was a Scottish Master. His reply was that he was brought from the captivity in Babylon. He was granted his degree by 'Prince Zerubabbel of the line of David and Solomon', after the destruction of the First Temple. He then testified that the Scottish Masons were still occupied in rebuilding the Temple of God.

The Knights Templars and the architect of Rosslyn chapel had long been trying to do that very thing. The ground plan and façade of this unfinished Collegiate Church of St Matthew would be a Temple of Solomon, although it was originally intended to become a cruciform cathedral, five times its present size. The surviving structure was built over an original Benedictine foundation, created at the time of the early crusades. The *compagnonnages* involved in its construction were those associated with the black monks and named after the *Maître de Saint Jacques*, or St John the Baptist, who came to be linked with the

* See Frontispiece.

martyrdom of the last Templar Grand Master, the condemned Jacques de Molay.

St Matthew had been deliberately chosen as the guardian of Rosslyn. He had written of the genealogy of Jesus, with three times fourteen generations passing from Abraham to Christ. This was an inspired heredity for the Holy Blood, which would be discovered in the St Clair bloodline in too many modern chronicles with far too little proof.

St Matthew's Day is held on 21 September. That date is the autumn equinox, when dawn is to the east and sundown to the west. Such a direction would serve as the alignment of Rosslyn chapel. Furthermore, the Gospel of the saint had spoken of 'the stone which builders rejected has become the headstone of the corner'. So it was the archstone of Rosslyn and of all medieval churches and cathedrals. And so it would become one of the highest degrees of the later Masons, the Royal Arch of the Temple of Solomon.

The Royal Arch, so important to the Knights Templars in their buildings and later to the Freemasons in their symbols and ceremonies, was meant to have covered the Holy of Holies, the cube of darkness within the Temple of Solomon, containing the Ark of the Covenant. There is no biblical evidence of this arch; as in the case of the early Phoenician temples, the Tabernacle probably had a flat roof. The Ark was overlooked only by a Mercy Seat and two winged cherubim of gold. No arches were mentioned in any description of the construction of the First Temple. Yet in Ezekiel's vision of the Second Temple, arches were frequently cited, spanning the pillars round the various courts. As the Templars particularly identified with Zerubbabel's warrior masons, and as the arch was fundamental to their sacred architecture, they probably used it as a symbol in their rituals.

In Templar tradition and later Masonic practice, the Royal Arch represented four concepts: the arch said to have spanned the Tabernacle in the Temple of Solomon, shielding the altar and the Ark below; the arch over a hidden cellar in the Temple of Solomon, where the Ark is still preserved; the crown of the human head, under which divine intelligence is implanted by the Architect of the Universe; and the vault of the firmament, separating heaven from earth. These were the symbolic meanings of the Royal Arch to the higher degrees of the Military Orders and the later lodges. Flanked by twin Templar strip maps of the route of the Fifth Crusade to the Nile, two symbolic Royal Arches still appear on the huge Kirkwall Scroll of the 15th century, the period when Earl William of Orkney was designing his sacred chapel at Rosslyn.

The only surviving illuminated psalter from the fall of Acre and the end of the Kingdom of Jerusalem was carried off by the Grand Master of the Knights Hospitallers of St John, the fellow Military Order of the Templars. The saint is shown holding the Agnus Dei, the Lamb of God, on a green Grail platter, signifying the Blood of Christ. Below him in miniature, a tiny Grand Master kneels in prayer.* The Agnus Dei was also carved in Rosslyn chapel, now bearing on its back a cross with a banner. This symbol was used by Templar high officers as a seal on their rings.

Another frieze at Rosslyn links the Templars to the Grail vessels containing the Holy Blood, which they may have brought to the vaults there from Constantinople. Although headless now, probably due to the fury of the Protestant Reformation, St Veronica holds up her veil, imprinted with the Mandylion, the true image of the face and beard of Christ. In legend, she wiped His sweat and wounds during the Passion. Beside her are Templar and Masonic marks on the bearded warrior figure of Pontius Pilate, washing his hands near his guard of armoured knights, carrying battle-axes. This head of Jesus is much the same as on the Holy Shroud of Turin, and its likeness is also painted in the 13th-century presbytery at Temple Combe near Shaftesbury.

An actual carving of a mailed Templar knight with his lance also graces the Rosslyn chapel. He does not ride alone. Behind his saddle is an angel, carrying the Cross of the Church militant. Traditionally, the knights were said to carry a poor man or a pilgrim on the horses. Such charity was part of their Rule. In fact, as they were usually fighting, their fellow rider was another warrior, an archer or a squire or a man-at-arms. In his celebrated works, the chronicler from St Albans, Matthew Paris, showed two Templar knights riding on a single steed

* See Illustrations.

behind their black and white standard, an image which also appeared on their minted coins.★

More arcane is the carving in the chapel of the horned Moses, an interpretation that the stone mason Michelangelo himself made into a sculpture.★ These horns referred to the ancient bull cult of Cybele and Mithras, as well as Leah, the first wife of Jacob: in Hebrew, her name signified 'wild cow', and so an earth mother. Yet the Templars at their trials were often accused of worshipping a Satanic horned head in their heretical rituals, some of which derived from the ancient practices of the Near East. This particular Masonic carving, as that of Michelangelo, also refers to guild practices in the 15th century, when the Lords of Rosslyn regulated the Scottish crafts.

Even more Gnostic and significant in the chapel is the carving of the fallen angel, its hands and body bound by ropes. Traditionally, the work is identified as Lucifer, the carrier of the light of divine intelligence, the castaway from heaven for his rebellion against God. The cult of Sanctus Clarus and the Templars, whose Masters could even give absolution and communion as did the Cathar 'Perfect Ones', believed in the direct approach of the faithful to the Holy Spirit without the need of papal or royal intervention. This was also an inspiration to the early Masonic guilds and lodges.

The celebrated gashed head of the Apprentice, who was said to have made the pillar in Rosslyn during his master's absence in Rome, again points to a revolt against religious authority.★ While later Masonic lodges also associated the wounded bust with the death of Hiram, the builder of the first Temple of Solomon, such a legend also indicated some resistance to state power in the name of secrecy. Certainly, the Freemasons after the Enlightenment would attack kings and churches, while venerating their early martyrs in search of the divine light.

Yet the most telling of the carvings at Rosslyn was that of Melchizedek, one of the highest grades and Priestly Orders of later Masonry. He was the priest-king of Salem at the time of Abraham, and the ancestor of Jesus Christ through the House of David. He became the symbol for the early Byzantine emperors, who wanted to

★ See Illustrations.

assert their dominance, not only over their own imperial Greek church, but over the See of Rome. Their buildings and images at Ravenna would influence Charlemagne and later German rulers, as well as the French kings, in their assertion of their divine right against the Papacy.

Beside the sea at Sant' Apollinaire-in-Classe at Ravenna, two key mosaics of the royal and holy Melchizedek are to be found. In the first, a gold chalice is set before the Old Testament ruler on a table altar or Ark covered by a white cloth; Abel offers to his sacred majesty and to Almighty God a sacrificial white lamb. On the altar are a pair of round loaves in the shape of sun discs and a paten, two misaligned squares making up an octagon within a circle – the sacred building shape of the Baptisteries at Ravenna, both of which have exquisite and naturalistic mosaics of Jesus being baptized in Jordan with the Holy Spirit as a dove descending upon Him.

Opposite the mosaic stands the bearded Byzantine Emperor Con- stantine IV, granting privileges while holding a bowl. The first imperial Constantine had turned Byzantium towards Christ: he and his heirs were the rulers of state and church: that was the message of the Melchizedek mosaics. Their significance was repeated in the statues of the biblical priest and sovereign made for the benefit of the Merovingian and early Capetian kings of France; these were placed by them in the cathedrals of Reims and Chartres. As the Byzantine emperors, they needed to show that their succession was blessed by God. To be of the blood royal was to rule by divine right, whatever the Church had to say on the matter.

This was no message for the later Popes of Rome, who not only opposed the Greek rite and eventually sent out their crusaders to take Constantinople, but also found themselves in frequent conflict with the German Holy Roman Emperors, contesting their claim to be supreme in religion as well as politics. In Byzantine Ravenna, no potentate went on his knees to Canossa to seek papal forgiveness. The churches were intended to celebrate the glory of the imperial family.

The second mosaic of Melchizedek is in San Vitale, a huge octagonal church consecrated in 547 by the great Archbishop Max- imian along with Sant' Apollinaire-in-Classe. At the head of the court, the Empress Theodora, dripping with pearls, is shown as a priestess holding a golden chalice studded with gems: on her robe are embroidered the three Magi, who appear time and again in mosaic and marble, pressing their generosity on Christ, as the Byzantines did. Theodora faces her husband, the emperor Justinian, who holds a large gold paten – the monarch here usurping the role of Archbishop Maximian, whose last resting place is there.

The building remains an encyclopaedia of early signs of the Holy Vessel. On the archbishop's sarcophagus are two doves drinking from a flowing Grail; on his ivory throne is carved the feast at Cana and the miracle of the loaves and fishes, while the four Evangelists surround the Virgin Mary, two of them bearing a dish, one with little loaves and one with the Lamb.

The link from Melchizedek at Ravenna is forged at Notre-Dame in Reims. There, in the most sacred royal cathedral in France, is a highly significant representation of the early ruler of Israel, presenting a wafer of bread and a cup of wine to the Patriarch Abraham as he returns from victory over the enemies of the King of Sodom. As Genesis tells the story:

> And Melchizedek king of Salem brought forth bread and wine and he was priest of God Most High.

> And he blessed him, and said, Blessed be Abraham of God Most High, possessor of heaven and earth:

> And blessed be God Most High, which hath delivered thine enemies into thy hand.

In the carvings, the bearded Melchizedek in his long robes offers a wafer with his right hand, holding a large chalice in his left. Behind him, a cloth covers a table altar. Standing before him is Abraham in medieval chain-mail armour and helmet, with surcoat and swordbelt and spear, and his hands joined in prayer. Another knight faces us, holding up his right arm, broken off at the wrist, perhaps representing the King of Sodom. His armour consists of dragon-like scales, his round ridged shield resembles the sun, its rays spiking from the boss.* This ensemble is remarkable for the 13th century in its portrayal of the

* See Illustrations.

knight receiving communion directly from the priest-king without the benefit of the Church, which did not yet exist.

Such an ancient assertion by the Kings of France of a primordial divine sanction was transposed to the age of chivalry and crusade and expanding royal power. The gravest accusation against the Templars at their trials would be that, like Melchizedek, their leaders gave communion to their knights after battle. Indeed, Melchizedek had been praised in a Psalm of David for his prowess in holy war:

> The Lord hath sworn, and will not repent. Thou art a priest for ever, after the order of Melchizedek.
>
> The Lord at thy right hand shall strike through kings in the day of His wrath.
>
> He shall judge among the nations. He shall fill the places with dead bodies; He shall strike through the head in many countries.

Nearby in the small rose window of the litanies of the Virgin Mary, the Ark of the Covenant is displayed as one of her attributes. Shown as a brown pouch with a red diamond in its middle, it hangs from two carrying poles. On its golden top sit two brown and yellow birds – owls, phoenixes or eagles – representing wisdom. A blue sun encompasses it, the light of heaven.

At the rival cathedral of Chartres, there is another carving of Melchizedek, holding a chalice with a stone inside its rim. Also to be found there are two reliefs of the Ark of the Covenant, this time carried on spoked wheels and not on the prescribed staves. A mysterious Latin inscription, *Archa cederis*, may be translated, 'You are to work through the Ark'. The Templar architects of Reims and Chartres and the *compagnonnages* they directed appear to have taken this ancient wisdom to heart, for both French cathedrals have been constructed on many of the principles of the lost art of sacred geometry.

The importance of Melchizedek was also recognized in the New Testament. As King of Salem (an early name of Jerusalem), and thus the heir of Aaron, who first wore the sacred breastplate of the High Priest studded with twelve gems, on which were inscribed the names of the Twelve Tribes of Israel, he was declared to be a divine source.

St Paul himself wrote of Christ that He was 'called of God, an high priest after the order of Melchizedek'. According to the early Jewish historian Josephus, Melchizedek built the first Temple and served there as a priest. One of the Dead Sea Scrolls extolled Melchizedek as a heavenly figure at the right hand of the Almighty, who judged the guilty and the innocent in the manner of another archangel Michael.

Through Jewish interpretation, Melchizedek thus became for the Templars a forerunner of Christ: the bread and wine given to Abraham was an early Eucharist without a church. In the *Epistle to the Hebrews*, he was described as 'without father, without mother, without descent, having neither beginning of days, nor end of life; but made like unto the Son of God; abideth a priest continually'. This biblical emphasis on his importance would enhance his significance to those who opposed the later Christian orthodox establishment, unable to condemn the example of Melchizedek because of his holy provenance.

Before the Knights Templar were instituted, their first Master, Hugh de Payens, visited Constantinople, where he met the imperial Chancellor, Michael Psellos, also the Master of the Byzantine Order of Melchizedek. Possibly, the customs and organization of this Military Order were passed on to the Knights Templars, and through them to the Freemasons. Whatever the truth of this secret history, the bust of Melchizedek at Rosslyn is a testament to the Gnostic wisdom of its creator and his masons.

11

The Chapel of the Grail

Any understanding of the mysteries of Rosslyn chapel lies in the character and learning of its creator, William, Earl of Orkney, and the European influences of his time. Although he was the designer of his Temple of Solomon and Grail chapel, his masons with their own creative carvings were messengers of the later lodges of the crafts and guilds. For, as Father Hay attested, Earl William 'caused artificers to be brought from other regions and forraigne kingdoms, and caused dayly to be in abundance of all kinde of workemen present, as masons, carpenters, smiths, barrowmen, and quarriers, with others.' And 'for the space of thirty-four years before, he never wanted great numbers of such workmen.'

A carved shield supported by two kneeling men in the chapel testifies to the two splendid marriages of William St Clair. The first and third quarters bear a ship and an engrailed cross for Orkney and Rosslyn, while the second has a lion passant and the last, a bleeding heart, the arms of the Earl's first wife, Lady Elizabeth Douglas. The second wife of the widower was Margaret Sutherland, who bore him a son and heir, Oliver, who would complete the work on the chapel. A second son William would become the Earl of Caithness and die on Flodden field.

The masons were also used to strengthen the castle as well as the chapel. Over the 'great dungeon' of five stories built by his father along the cliff face confronting the Esk river, Earl William erected another chapel within the walls and the two towers, called Robin Hood and Little John, where the gypsy armourers could hold their summer fairs and practise their archery. He also had built the bridge into the castle and many 'French features', such as galleries and projecting chambers and turrets. These ornaments were fit for his second wife, who was known as 'the Princess' and was held 'in great reverence, both for her birth, and for the estate she was in'. Indeed, 'none matched her in all the countrey, save the Queen's Majesty.'

More rebuilding had to be done after 1447, when part of the castle burned down because of a bedroom fire. The Earl's chaplain managed to save four great trunks of his papers by throwing them down. The Earl 'was sorry for nothing but the loss of his charters and other writings', but he became cheerful when he knew they were spared. This fire was the first of many destructions of the records of the St Clairs on land and by sea. The savaging of the writs and manuscripts by shipwreck and English armies and Protestant mobs has obscured the history of Rosslyn and its founders.

Above all, as a latter-day King Solomon, Earl William concerned himself with justice and mercy. These qualities were rarely displayed in that rough age, but as Father Hay witnessed:

> Earle William was a man of rare parts, haveing in him a mind of most noble composition, a perceing witt, fitt for managing great affairs; he was famous not only for moral virtue and piety, but also for military discipline, in high favour with his Prince, and raised to the greatest dignitys that in those times a subject had. He was averss from putting criminels to the rack, the tortures whereof make many ane innocent person confess himself guilty, and then with seeming justice be executed, or if he prove so stoute as in torments to deny the fact, yet he comes off with disjoynted bones, and such weaknes as rendres himself and his life a burthen ever after.

Earl William frequently visited France and Burgundy. He was a member of their two most prestigious orders, the Knights of the Cockle and the Knights of the Golden Fleece. Both were dedicated to a final crusade to recapture Constantinople and Jerusalem, although this sacred adventure would never take place. The insignia of the Cockle referred to the clamshell, which pilgrims wore on the road to Santiago de Compostela: it is reproduced in Rosslyn chapel. Earl

William also wore the medals of the militant St Michael and St James, for the Knights of Santiago had fought alongside the Knights Templars in many crusades from northern Spain to clear the country of the Moors and the Jews, an ethnic and religious cleansing achieved at the end of the 15th century by the conquest of Granada.

The Knights of the Golden Fleece were the invention of the remarkable Philip the Good, the Duke of Burgundy, the rival to the French Crown at that time. Above all, he was the mellow swansong of his age. As Huizinga wrote in his masterpiece, *The Waning of the Middle Ages*:

> 'The choice lay, in principle, only between God and the world, between contempt or eager acceptance, at the peril of one's soul, of all that makes up the beauty and the charm of earthly life. All terrestrial beauty bore the stain of sin . . . All aristocratic life in the later Middle Ages is a wholesale attempt to act the vision of a dream. In cloaking itself in the fanciful brilliance of the heroism and probity of a past age, the life of the nobles elevated itself towards the sublime.'

In this sumptuous decline of a period, every ideal demanded a concrete shape. Each vision sought expression in an image, which would make it solid. This changed the stark definition of forms in Norman architecture to the flamboyant Gothic styles of the end of the Middle Ages. Simplicity was replaced by a luxuriant imagination, although still in the pursuit of saintliness. And William, Earl of Orkney, was the rich embodiment of those mystical beliefs and extravagances.

As a whole, the Collegiate Church of St Matthew resembles the Burgundian churches of the Cistercian Order and the neighbouring abbey at Melrose. As well as ribbed vaults above the altar, the barrel vaulting supports the only stone carved roof in all of northern Europe. The ornate decorations also appear to derive from the Church of Rome near Abbeville, the Porch at Louviers in Normandy, and the Savoy Mausoleum in Bresse, where Flemish sculptors worked, some of whom may have progressed to Rosslyn.

Certainly at Melrose Abbey, the contemporary master builder Jean Morow brought along his *compagnonnages* of European masons. Still carved into the stone there is his Masonic epitaph:

SA YE CVMPAS GAYS EVYN ABOVTE S VA TROVTH AND LAVTE SALL DO BVT
DIVTE BE HALDE TO YE HENDE Q° IOHNE MORVO. [As the compass goes
evenly about, so truth and loyalty shall do without doubt. Look to the
end quoth John Morow.]

Morow also left another inscription, declaring that he was in charge of
the Masons' work in six major Scottish ecclesiastical buildings, and he
prayed to 'GOD AND MARI BATHE & SWETE SANCT: IOHNE TO KEPE THIS
HALY KYRK FRA SKATHE.' Mary and St John were also venerated by the
Military Orders as the protectors of holy places from harm. The
exuberance of some of the carvings in the ruined chapel at Melrose,
poppies and roses and a Moor's head along with devil's masks and
Green Men, also suggests the influence of Morow on Rosslyn Chapel
with its profusion of stone ornaments. Certainly, the crusading St
Clairs and the Cistercians always kept in close touch.

Most significant are the decorated tiles in the museum at Melrose in
the Commendator's house, which survived in 1544 the pillage of the
abbey by an English army. The penultimate holder of that office was
the Catholic Cardinal of Guise, but he could not rebuild the
destruction of that marvellous monument with its ornamented floors.
Fortunately, modern archaeologists have excavated fragments of
whole tile pavements at Melrose and its sister Cistercian abbey at
Newbattle, so close to Rosslyn. Outside Melrose too, tombs with
skull-and-crossbones between the twin pillars of the Temple of
Solomon still front the rose-red ruins.*

Both holy places were founded by King David I of Scotland, who
introduced a thousand Norman nobles to his country along with the
St Clairs, but also supported the building of cathedrals and churches in
the most lavish of styles. At Melrose, indeed, the floor designs were
exuberant. Some showed the fleurs-de-lys alongside stars with six
points: some were roses spreading with the five petals of the Virgin
Mary, as on the roof of Rosslyn chapel; some are the four devices of
the Rosy Cross.

Melrose possessed a kiln for this work, which dated from the 13th
century. These ornate designs only developed in the late and exuberant end of the medieval period, when luxury was overtaking earlier

* See Illustrations.

austerity. The main pattern was the cosmos or the wheel, containing other whirling and still circles. But most significant, at the great founding of the Cistercian abbey at Rievaulx, a maze pattern is evoked as a puzzle in the museum, which also displays an original green-and-yellow glazed wheel of fortune. These tiles also depicted griffons and eagles, showing how the baronial houses of the time were infiltrating the old seclusion of the White Monks.

The builder of the Collegiate Church of St Matthew, Earl William St Clair, would have been aware of the building at Melrose and Newbattle. Among his 'foreign masons', many would have come from the construction of those abbeys. And he would have known of the favourite sung Mass of the time, developed in Burgundy and France. That rite of the Armed Man, which processed over the decorated tiles of the cathedrals of northern Europe, most probably was danced in the Rosslyn church and chapel.

The flagstones behind the altar all date from the 18th century. There is no knowledge of what lay there before, except in the remarkable ceiling. There Earl William commanded, behind his three supporting Masonic pillars of a Temple of Solomon, a series of four sacred octagons within four squares. Arcs of stone ribs lead to an ornamented central boss. On each curve, nine musical notes protrude, mainly in the carvings of stars and lozenges. They seem to show a head view of a ritual dance, once marked on the lost floor tiles beneath.

In his remarkable book, *The Maze and the Warrior*, the professor of Music at Yale, Craig Wright, insisted that Guillaume de Marchaut's Mass of the Armed Man was performed in Scotland until 1550 and the Reformation. Thus it is highly likely that Earl William laid down a maze-like pavement in a wheel or an octagon under three of the four spoked roof vaultings behind the altar – the last one was set over the stone stairs, leading down to the old crypt. These tiled floors may well have resembled the remarkable maze in Amiens Cathedral and the octagonal labyrinth at Reims Cathedral.* In the tradition of maze dances, then flowering across Scandinavia, the priest or laird would have led the believers from the maze to their final capering. At Rosslyn, this was probably the later Scottish folk dances over crossed

* See Illustrations.

swords, three of these performed under the central bosses behind the altar.* Such a ritual would have corresponded with the Morris or Moorish dances, brought by the immigrant gypsy armourers to the royal Court and to Roslin, where they were welcomed at their annual fairs.

What is certain is that the Sinclairs of Lothian remained the lords of the French dance. Killed at Flodden along with the King, the Earl of Caithness and three hundred other clan members was the Queen's knight, Sir John Sinclair. As the poet Dunbar wrote of him:

> Sir John Sinclair begouth to dance,
> For he was new come out of France:
> For any thing that he do micht,
> The ane foot gaed aye unricht,
>   And to the tother wald not gree.
> Quoth ane. Tak up the Queen's knicht:
> A merrier dance micht na man see.

Given the small size of its population, Catholic Scotland outdid the rest of Europe in its construction of medieval sacred buildings. Through royal and aristocratic patronage, thirteen cathedrals were raised on high, while in England, with six times more people, only twenty-six were built. Castles and abbeys also made necklaces across the Lowlands. The arts of their construction often arrived with operative masons from overseas. The very founding of the original Scots lodge of Kilwinning Abbey in the 12th century was traditionally connected with the *comacini* of imported Italian masons, while later lodges developed with the French *compagnonnages* and the Scottish crafts and guilds under the protection of the Lords of Rosslyn.

William, Earl of Orkney, certainly had need of the best masons and stone-workers of his time. They were trained in sophisticated continental methods of construction and carving, based on sacred geometry. In the extraordinary album of Vilart de Honnecourt, two men wrestling with their feet planted on the ground show the principle of the solid base needed for the circle and the square, while another

* See Illustrations.

couple grasping each other demonstrates the firm foundations of the barrel-vault ceiling, as at Rosslyn. Other models for the foreign lodges were Byzantine and Classical architecture, particularly that of the Roman Vitruvius. In his famous picture, Leonardo da Vinci drew 'Vitruvian Man' with eight limbs and a head as a cornerstone within a circle – the principle of sacred architecture, expressed as the Golden Mean of the human frame.

The plans for Rosslyn chapel show a profound knowledge of stress in building, and the strong support and buttresses necessary for a stone structure. The masonry itself was cop crag, a local red-and-yellow abrasive sandstone. At this time, the differences were growing in the crafts and guilds between operative and speculative masons, and their semi-skilled workers. Aided by carpenters and smiths, also slaves and serfs, stonemasons had been organized under their Masters since the building of the pyramids and the Temple of Solomon. The operative masons were the quarriers and carriers, pavers and carvers, wallers and slaters and tilers. The glaziers and plumbers were also important, for making the stained-glass windows and binding the blocks in the cathedrals. Through many years of learning and labour, a craftsman might become a 'free' mason, registered as a guild member by a city or an institution. They put their special marks on their works, many of which survive at Rosslyn.* From their ranks rose the speculative Master Masons, versed in the study of architecture.

Because of his position and esoteric knowledge, William St Clair served as his own director of works. Father Hay wrote that the Earl 'caused the draughts to be drawn upon Eastland boards, and made the carpenters to carve them according to the draughts thereon, and then gave them for patterns to the masons, that they might thereby cut the like in stone.'* Very good wages were also paid with the Master Mason receiving forty pounds yearly, the other 'free' masons ten pounds yearly, and the Earl rewarding by their degree, 'the smiths and the carpenters with others'.

The name of that Master Mason at Rosslyn is unknown, unlike that of John Morow at Melrose. As well as a Temple of Solomon, the Earl intended to plan his chapel from the ideas suggested by medieval

* See Illustrations.

romances. As Lewis Spence wrote, 'Nothing can shake my conviction that Rosslyn was built according to the pattern of the Chapel of the Grail as pictured in Norman romance, and that William St Clair had in his poet's mind a vision of the Chapel Perilous when he set hand to the work.'

The many signs of the Knights Templars, the keepers of the Grail in both the *Queste of the Holy Grail* and *Parzival*, and the symbol of the stone dove flying down to the crescent Grail on the chapel roof, were augmented by the famous 'Apprentice' Pillar.* The barley-sugar and twined column was Byzantine and Near-Eastern in design with a sister at the Templar church at Tomar in Portugal. This inspired creation was as pagan and Masonic as it was Christian. At its base, eight octagonal winged serpents surrounded an apparent stone tree-trunk, which supported the roof. The concept referred to the Tree of Life, as well as to the Tree of Knowledge of Good and Evil in the Garden of Eden; the winged serpent was not only Lucifer, but also part of the secret wisdom of the Cathars and the Templars. The 'Apprentice' Pillar derived from Gnostic myth in spite of the four strands of stone as close as hemp rope about it, probably a posy to the Four Gospels.

There was further symbolism on the 'Apprentice' Pillar. By Rabbinic and Arabic legend, King Solomon built his Temple by means of the Shamir, a fiery Great Worm or Serpent of Wisdom; its touch split and shaped stone. For *Deuteronomy* in the Old Testament had stated that the Temple should be built without the use of tools made of iron. In Masonic tradition, the martyr Hiram, the architect of the Temple, refused to surrender the secret of the Shamir, which remained one of the Grand Secrets for Freemasons in higher degrees.

Eight Great Worms or Shamirs were grouped in a rough octagon round the base of the Pillar. These comprised the number of points and the shape of the Cross of the Knights of the Order of the Temple of Solomon, who knew of the Shamir when they named the Dome of the Rock as the Temple on its original site in Jerusalem, before its tradition and its symbolism were brought to Scotland.

In his expert study of the stonework of Rosslyn chapel, the monolithic sculptor and Knight Templar, Shawn Williamson, found

* See Illustrations.

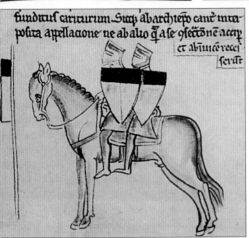

TOP. The crusaders take Constantinople, 1204.

MIDDLE LEFT. The crusaders besiege Acre, 1189.

MIDDLE RIGHT. The Mameluke knight by the crusader camp above Damietta, from the Kirkwall Scroll, 15th Century.

ABOVE LEFT. Matthew Paris showed two Knights Templars riding on one horse with their black-and-white shields and banner.

ABOVE RIGHT. The crusaders capture Damietta on the Fifth Crusade, 1219.

TOP. Mithras Altar in a cave, from Jayce, Bosnia.

BELOW LEFT. The Church of St Mary and St Bega at St Bees, Cumbria. Archer on Templar Tombstone.

BELOW RIGHT. The Bridekirk Stones and Font. On the etching of the 10th-century Saxon font we see the earliest carving of a stone-manson's mallet and long chisel chipping out scrolls, while outside the church on Templar tombstones we see their swords along with a compass and a mattock or long trowel. (All © Jim Davis)

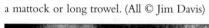

TOP LEFT. The maze-fired tiles of the old pavement in Melrose Abbey, dating from the 13th century.

TOP RIGHT. The carving of the murdered St Magnus, also called Hiram or the 'Apprentice', in Rosslyn Chapel.

ABOVE LEFT. The eight-pointed roof boss in the centre of the octagonal rib vaulting behind the Rosslyn altar, probably above maze-fired tiles for a processional mass.

ABOVE RIGHT. A horned Moses carrying the tables of the law.

LEFT. A Knight Templar with a militant angel or pilgrim riding behind him on his horse.

TOP. A Relief from Reims Cathedral. Melchizedek offers bread and wine from an altar to Abraham, dressed as a medieval knight, after winning a victory for the King of Sodom.

MIDDLE LEFT. The winged serpents at the base of the 'Apprentice' or Prince's Pillar, each clutching the ends of four hemp ropes in its jaws.

MIDDLE RIGHT. The Octagonal Templar church of the 12th century at Eunate beside the pilgrim route to Compostela.

LEFT. The octagonal crusading Chapelle Saint-Clair below the Chapelle Saint-Michel on its lava pinnacle at Le Puy-en-Velay.

RIGHT. The Ulster Boyne Society Wall Chart dating from the 1690s, and containing the serpent on the Tau Cross and the crusading Paschal Lamb with banner and the Royal Arch above the Ark of the Covenant.

Map showing
Followers of
Valentinus and
their enemies
AD 50–600.

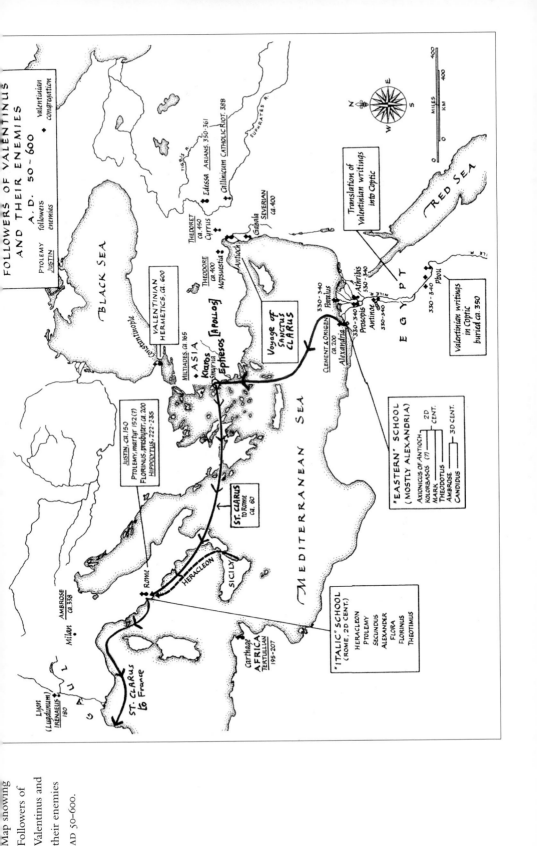

FOLLOWERS OF VALENTINUS
AND THEIR ENEMIES
A.D. 50–600

PTOLEMY   Valentinian
           congregation
JUSTIN   followers
           enemies

VALENTINIAN
HERMETICS. ca. 600

Translation of
Valentinian writings
into Coptic

Valentinian writings
in Coptic
buried ca. 350

Edessa   ARIANS 350–361
Callinicum CATHOLIC RIOT 388

THEODORET
ca. 450
Cyrrhus
Gabala   SEVERIAN
          ca. 400
THEODORE   Antioch
ca. 400
Mopsuestia

BLACK SEA

Constantinople

MILTIADES. ca. 165
Klaros [APOLLO]
Smyrna
Ephesos [APOLLO]
ASIA

Voyage of
SANCTUS
CLARUS

CLEMENT & ORIGEN
ca. 200
Alexandria

Pamlus 330–340
Prosopis 330–340
         Athribis 350–340
Antinöe 350–340
         330–340
         330–340

E G Y P T

330–340
330–340   Pboii

RED SEA

JUSTIN, ca. 150
PTOLEMY, martyr 152 (?)
FLORINUS, presbyter, ca. 200
HIPPOLYTUS, 222–235

ST. CLARUS
to Rome
ca. 60

HERACLEON

Rome

SICILY

MEDITERRANEAN SEA

"EASTERN" SCHOOL
(MOSTLY ALEXANDRIA)

AXIONICUS OF ANTIOCH
KOLORBASOS (?)   2D
MARK   CENT.
THEODOTUS
AMBROSE   3D CENT.
CANDIDUS

Milan AMBROSE
       ca. 358

Lyon
(Lugdunum)
IRENAEUS
180

ST. CLARUS
to France

ST. CLARUS to France

G   A   U   L

Carthage
AFRICA
TERTULLIAN
195–207

"ITALIC" SCHOOL
(ROME, 2D CENT.)

HERACLEON
PTOLEMY
SECUNDUS
ALEXANDER
FLORA
FLORINUS
THEOTIMUS

N
W   E
S

MILES
0   400
KM   400

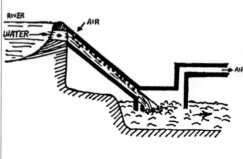

TOP LEFT. A Sarmatian steppe cavalryman with dragon banner, 2nd Century AD, Chester.

TOP RIGHT. A model of the ringed cannon, fired as early as the battle of Crécy, 1346.

MIDDLE RIGHT. A model of a Catalan smelter for iron ore in the 13th century.

ABOVE LEFT. The Maze at Reims Cathedral.

ABOVE RIGHT. The Maze in Amiens Cathedral.

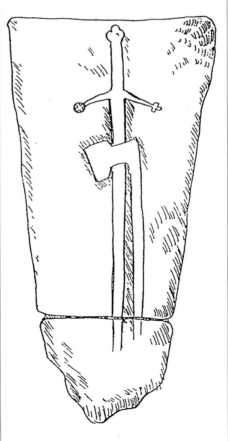

ABOVE. The octagonal Byzantine Church of Saints Jason and Sosipatros, Corfu, 10th century.

LEFT. Two Templar Gravestones from Taynuilt.

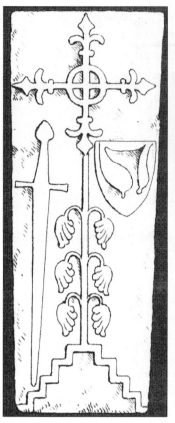

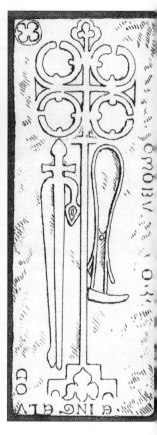

Three Cumbrian Templar Gravestones:

LEFT. Saddle bags adorn the shield of this Templar knight. Beside his sword, leaves cluster around the Stem of Jesse, leading to the fleur-de-lys of French and Scottish chivalry.

CENTRE. Shears or compasses and a pilgrim Bible flank this flowering chalice enclosing the Templar cross and sacred octagon within the circle.

RIGHT. The wise serpent hangs over the crusading sword, a claw hammer is on its loop, while the four broken circles around the central cross represent the four gates and the four rivers of life flowing into Jerusalem.

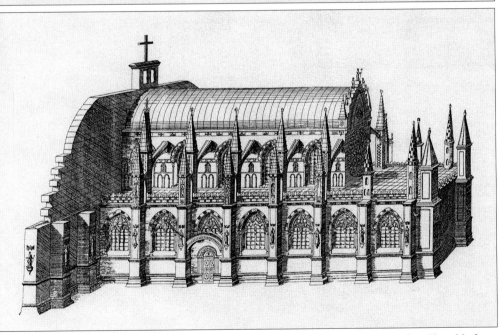

TOP. Rosslyn Chapel before
1700, showing the two pillars
of the Temple of Solomon,
supporting the stone roof.
ABOVE. Rosslyn Chapel
before 1700, showing its
ornate carving.

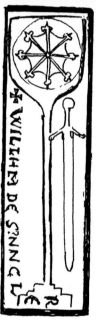

TOP. The ruins of Rosslyn castle.

ABOVE LEFT. The Grail tombstone of Sir William St Clair,
d.1328, Rosslyn Chapel.

ABOVE CENTRE TOP. Bull drawn in relief on stone slab
from Burghead, Moray.

ABOVE CENTRE BELOW. The dream of Alexander the Great.

ABOVE RIGHT. The ornate 'Apprentice' Pillar, Rosslyn
Chapel.

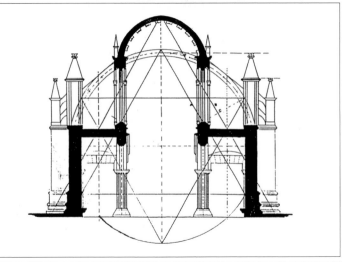

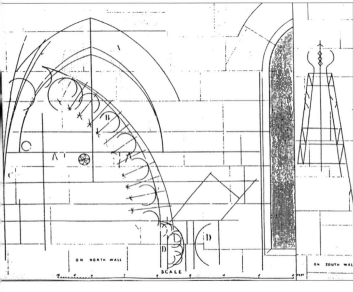

TOP. Jesus Christ blesses the Grail, carved on the roof of Rosslyn Chapel.
MIDDLE AND LEFT. Working Drawings of the Building of Rosslyn Chapel.

RIGHT AND BELOW. Mason Marks and
Templar Crosses, Rosslyn Chapel.
BOTTOM. Tombstone of Knight by
Altar, Rosslyn Chapel.

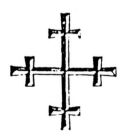

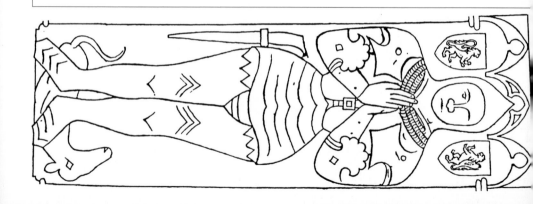

that the celebrated Pillar was built of seven solid sandstone cubes, set at angles so that the squares could be shaped into a rough cylinder. Then four helical ropes of hemp, each with three strands, were carved on the rough Pillar, already supporting the stoned roof. Eight of these strands ended in the mouths of the winged Accursed Worms at the base. The ropes twisted up the main body, based on the design of a square with rounded corners. Their trajectory was dictated by spherical geometry, although they climbed from four different points and ended in the diametrically opposite corner. For Williamson, it was 'the nearest thing to viewing nature in stone I have ever seen. The geometry of the great cathedrals is based on natural forms.'

A similar accretion of Christianity overlaid the carvings in the rest of the chapel. The representation of a man with a wound in his forehead was always associated with the legendary Apprentice, who was said to have carved the pillar and was killed by his Master Mason. In fact, he may have represented Hiram, the martyred builder of the Temple of Solomon. The legend of the murdered Apprentice was probably a Christian cover story for an apocryphal saint and founder of the Order of the Temple of Solomon and of all Masonry with its symbols of the sword and the trowel, the compasses and the maul. And the gash on the stone head may well have been caused by a lead bullet or a pike stroke from one of the Puritan cavalrymen, quartered in the chapel and bent on defacing its Catholic monuments after the Civil War.

Moreover, the split brow on the wall could represent the beheaded St John the Baptist or even the original Sanctus Clarus. Yet the most likely candidate is a St Clair ancestor, Earl and St Magnus of Orkney, martyred and buried in the cathedral there, dying of a blow to the head, his death a re-enactment of the murder of Hiram. He, too, was known to the Templar Earls of Orkney, who had their Norse predecessor beatified. And when the original name of the carved column was discovered to be the Prince's Pillar, the legend of the murdered Apprentice or Hiram clearly became a later Masonic myth. A more likely candidate was a Prince of the Orcadian Isles, perhaps even 'Henry the Holy' St Clair, struck down in combat, and the grandfather of the builder of the chapel.

The question was whether Earl William built his Grail chapel because of his wide reading from the best library in Scotland at

Rosslyn, or whether, as the keeper of royal and Templar treasures, he stored in the vaults some jewelled reliquaries, which had held the Body and Blood of Christ. These would have been the Holy Rood and the precious vessels containing the Holy Shroud and the Holy Veil, seized at the sack of Constantinople. Furthermore, many still believe that the Templars excavated their Stables of Solomon below the Temple Mount in Jerusalem, where they may have found the Ark of the Covenant and the Holy of Holies, secreted there by the ancient priests of Israel.

Fortunately, I was allowed to lift flagstones and reach a side vault within the chapel. I found the remnants of three wooden coffins, but the way to the lower ground was blocked by heavy masonry. A description of the vaults in 1693 declared that they were built of polished ashlar, divided into compartments and arched from east to west with a supporting wall down the middle. The twenty St Clair knights, buried in full armour down there, were later celebrated by Sir Walter Scott, and a previous witness declared the dead men lay 'in a vault so dry that their bodies have been found entire after four-score years, and as fresh as when they were buried.'

Father Hay backed this account. Sir William St Clair was the last mailed knight to be consigned below, on the same day as the Scottish defeat at the Battle of Dunbar. His corpse seemed entire at an 'opening of the cave, but when they came to touch his body it fell into dust; he was lying in his armour, with a red velvet cap on his head, on a flat stone; nothing was spoiled except a piece of white furring that went round the cap, and answered to the hinder part of the head.' Hay later saw his St Clair stepfather interred in a coffin beneath Rosslyn chapel; the widow was reproached by King James VII and II of England for not burying him in full armour, but she thought such an old custom was beggarly.

Yet if the holy treasures were secreted in the vaults of Rosslyn, they must have already been walled out of reach during the full fury and pillage of the Reformation. That was the reason that the greatest medieval illuminated scroll in Scotland was sent from Earl William's scriptorium and library to his castle at Kirkwall in Orkney. Between two strip maps of the Fifth Crusade to Egypt, a ground plan of Rosslyn chapel and the Temple of Solomon shows the Ark of the Covenant and the Holy of Holies in the underground chambers at Rosslyn. This huge parchment appears to be more of a wish-fulfilment by Earl William than a treasure map. And yet, as the Kirkwall Scroll is also covered with biblical and Templar and Masonic symbols, it proves that the planner of Rosslyn did intend to build another Temple and Grail chapel, a model and a mystery for the future Masonic movement.

When I viewed the top of the Kirkwall Scroll, I found the Garden of Eden, painted in faded pastel colours. From the sky shone a six-pointed sun and a moon with a face, surrounded by seven stars. On the ground below were three doves or cocks and a swan, a ewe and a ram and a pair of horses, a single serpent and a maned lion, and three other beasts, which rang the changes from black cattle to a dromedary. They stood in front of a pink hermaphrodite, an Adam confused with an Eve under the shade of a Tree of Life. This strange human being with long hair and thin legs beckoned towards an answer.

I was seeing the Sophia, the Gnostic principle of masculine merged with feminine, the ancient wisdom through which divine intelligence solved the problems of gender. That understanding from the Near East had attracted the Knights Templars, who had passed it through their writings to the creator of Rosslyn with its many esoteric symbols. Indeed, on the back of the central pillar, which begins the series of friezes around the whole chapel, we may still watch the Fall of Man and the expulsion from Eden. Two figures approach a tree and leave it to veer towards a huge beast with a chain collar and a cord bridle, a man lying on its back. So Adam and Eve received wisdom, but it pushed them towards the Satanic Beast of Revelation, never to be ridden or restrained.

Such were the guides and the interpretations which led me in my inquiry to the third meaning of the chapel of Earl William, for he had also built a paradise in stone.

12

An Eden of Stone

The Director of Works at Rosslyn had Norse and Norman as well as Scottish roots. Through his family and inheritance in Orkney and the Shetlands, he was exposed to Nordic culture, which had infiltrated the Gothic cathedrals of Europe with ancient fertility cults. The many Green Men within the chapel were associated with several archetypes, particularly the serpent or dragon of wisdom and rebirth; the sacred Tree of Life, which held up Heaven from the earth; and the cycle of life and death through mortality.

The famed 'Apprentice' Pillar in Rosslyn Chapel also bore witness to Norse myth. Eight winged serpents encircled its base, a tribute to the great snake that girdled the earth nine times to bind together the roots of Yggdrasil, the Norse ash tree, which was the prop between the Underworld and the gods in the sky. Their divine leader Odin had himself sacrificed on the Tree of Life, hanging in the storm for nine days and nights, in order to learn the secrets of wisdom and creation from the severed head of another god called Mimir, kept forever murmuring and alive with herbs and spring water – the primal Green Man.

These masks of the earth-force were carved only in the churches and the civilisations of the Mediterranean and of north-western Europe. In the seminal Gothic cathedral at Chartres, some remain, particularly on the portal of the south transept. There, three Green Men gobble and disgorge leaves of oak and vine and acanthus. All green and growing things had their symbolism in the Middle Ages. The oak was associated with a pagan past, the Druids and their sacred groves, the forest culture before the Roman invasions. The vine signified Bacchus and Orphic celebrations before the serving of the Blood of Christ in the communion cup. And the acanthus was the herb of rebirth, the synthesis between the tree of the woods and the cultivated grape.

Each of the plants and leaves that proliferate from the mouths of the seventy or more Green Men carved inside and outside Rosslyn Chapel has its own significance and meaning. In the discovery of these secrets lies the meaning of the Garden of Paradise and the Tree of Life in the Middle Ages. For Rosslyn Chapel is an Herbal in stone. It displays the monastic physic garden of the late Middle Ages, which was largely forgotten with the Renaissance. It is the lost green medicine of its time.

When Rome conquered Greece, its botany and medicine emigrated to a language and a mentality that were less scrupulous and original. Pliny the Elder's voluminous *Natural History* became the gardener's guide of the Middle Ages and was published after the discovery of printing in 200 editions within 350 years. His encyclopaedia was not a good guide to ancient science, but he did invent the syntax of botanical Latin: some 200 of his terms are still in use, roughly in the sense he meant them. The word 'botany' itself came from the Greek word for 'herb' and was established by Pliny's follower, Isidore of Seville, who wrote another major source book for medieval times.

When the Dark Ages descended on Europe, Greek practice fled to the Second Rome of Byzantium. From there, it became the inheritance of the Islamic world. For 400 years after the 8th century, Arab thinkers enriched Greek studies of botany and medicine. In the Eastern Caliphate, Rhazes and the Zoroastrian experimenter on animals, Haly Abbas, and Avicenna added to learning. The Western Caliphate at Córdoba benefited from the studies of Albucasis and Algalzel and Avenzoar, and the Jewish Moses Maimonides. Jewish doctors, who had studied Islamic medicine, would develop the first secular European medical school at Salerno, the generator of European healing.

With the conquest of Sicily by the enlightened Normans and the translation of Greek and Arabic texts into Latin by Constantinus

Africanus from the cloisters of Monte Cassino, Greek and Islamic learning lit up the darkness of early Christian Europe. When Rufinus wrote in 1290 his *De virtutis herbarium*, he advanced, by his own observations, the botanical studies which he had inherited from the classical and Islamic world. He provided the first details of flower and leaf and stem. Strangely enough, the carving of vegetables and plants on the capitals and friezes of medieval cloisters in the late 13th century was far more accurate than most of the illustrations which accompanied these early Latin Herbals.

The Greeks had chiefly valued two of the Alexandrian imports from Asia – saffron from the wild crocus and the rose. Many other novelties were to follow the spices and the herbs, which were to become the drugs and medicines of the Middle Ages. And in the Islamic Gardens of Paradise, the trees and fruit and flowers had a figurative meaning as well as a medical use. The almond meant the eye, the quince and the apple were the chin, the pomegranate and the lemon were the breasts, the rose was the cheek, the plane-tree leaf was the hand, the date palm was the figure and the mandrake was the down on the skin.

Nowhere in the Bible was there a description of the fruits and flowers and herbs of Eden. The names in translation from Hebrew and Greek and Latin told of anemones and aniseed, bulrushes and coriander, cumin and dill, flag and flax, mallow and mint, the Resurrection Flower and the Rose of Jericho, rue and wormwood. Among the vegetables hallowed by Holy Writ were beans and cucumbers, garlic and gourds, leeks and lentils, mustard and onions. As for the trees which were sacred in meaning, there was the acacia (or Burning Bush) and the ash, the bay tree and black mulberry, the chestnut and the cypress, the elm and the fir, the myrtle and the oak, and the sycamore and the willow.

More exotic were the aloe and ebony, the juniper and mastic, and the olive and the sandalwood and the tamarisk trees from the Near East. The early medieval historian Rhabanus Maurus excluded from the cloister garden any plant which was not mentioned in the Bible. To him, the garden had been the Church, which bore the fruits of the Holy Spirit and was nourished by the sacred founts of healing, until it would be a new Eden.

Of the many influences of Islam on Christianity through the crusades, the rose was perhaps the most significant, for it became a symbol of the Virgin Mary. Avicenna recommended the Syrian one for its rosewater and its use in medical compounds. The Persian poet Nizami told of a duel between two rival doctors: the one who used poison was foiled by the other taking an antidote, while the first was killed by the scent of the blameless rose, so corrupt was he. The same death would be ascribed to the famous Rabbi Loëw of Prague, the maker of the clay monster, the Golem: death would reach him only in rose-petals, for it could not overcome him except by that sweet odour.

Ironically, as scientific salvation came from the Near East, the crusaders began to attack the sources of their new education. Ignorance and faith assaulted a superior culture and another faith. But in Spain, where the Moors were established in Córdoba and Seville and Toledo, and in the Norman Kingdom of Sicily, Greek and Arabic scholars continued to bring the knowledge of the East to the morass of the West.

The School of Salerno produced the first European medical and herbal text, *Regimen Sanitatis Salernitum*, which eventually ran through 240 editions in prose and verse. An illuminated copy of it still exists in the British Library, displaying perfect pictures of early medieval fruit and vegetables. After the sack of Salerno in the 12th century, the School was superseded by the new medical establishments at Naples and Palermo, Bologna and Padua and Montpellier. Through them, the medical literature of Islam began to heal the superstitions of the Latin world.

Aristotle was rediscovered through his Arabic translation by Averroës, and his methods of observation and experimentation were passed on to such original scientists as Roger Bacon, who began to investigate phenomena directly and not receive truths through the wisdom of the Christian Fathers. The encyclopaedia of Albertus Magnus with its sections on *De Animalibus* and *De Vegetabilibus et Plantis*, was based on Aristotle and on primary scrutiny. These were the leading scientific works of the 13th century, when the crusaders were already being driven from the Holy Land. They returned, however, with some Islamic learning and techniques, including the process of embalming the bodies of knights or of dissecting and boiling parts to remove the skull and bones for burial at home, as happened to Sir William St Clair, before he was laid to rest at Rosslyn beneath his small Grail tombstone.

Travelling Jewish doctors cared for the sick. Otherwise, the monasteries were the infirmaries of the Middle Ages, aided by those of the Military Orders, especially the Knights of St John as well as the Teutonic Knights. The care of the ill had always been a duty of the Holy Orders. Before Charlemagne, there had been herb gardens attached to nunneries, as the one made by St Radegonde, when she fled the dissolute Merovingian Court to a nunnery near Poitiers and was praised for the green peace she had created. She even had garlands hanging on the walls of the refectory, as if she were giving holy feasts in classical times.

By the 12th century, the *Physica* of St Hildegard listed for the infirmary garden several hundred plants and nearly a hundred trees. And Alexander Neckham, the Abbot of Cirencester, who died in 1217, was specific about monastic horticulture in his *De naturis rerum*:

> The garden should be adorned with roses and lilies, turnsole (*heliotrope*) and violets and mandrake; there you should have parsley and cost and fennel, and southernwood, and coriander, sage, savory, hyssop, mint, rue, dittany, smallage, pellitory, lettuce, garden cress, peonies. There should also be planted beds with onions, leeks, garlick, pumpkins and shallots; the cucumber growing in its lap, the drowsy poppy, the daffodil and brank-ursine (*acanthus*) ennoble a garden. There should also be pottage herbs, such as beets, herb-mercury, orache, sorrel and mallows. Anise, mustard, white pepper and wormwood do good service to the small garden.

The first use of the Latin word *paradisus* in Middle English was in 1175 as a sentence in the Bible, 'God ha hine brohte into paradis'. By the time that Chaucer wrote the *Franklin's Tale*, the term was generally used to describe a flowering garden:

> May had painted with his soft showers
> This garden full of leaves and of flowers;
> And craft of man's hand so curiously

Arrayed had this garden truly
That never was there garden of such price,
But if it were the very Paradise.

Indeed, the words 'yard' and 'garden' may be traced back to the Old English word for a wattle fence, *geard*. They were also enclosed.

The crusaders had brought back from the east the simplest of all the plans for a Garden of Paradise and Eden, divided in quarters by four rivers flowing from a central fountain. This design was shown in the Hindu Vedas, the carpets of Persia, and on Templar tombstones. In the *Mappa Mundi*, however, at Hereford Cathedral, the four rivers flowed from a circular Garden of Eden ringed with fire, while Adam and Eve ate the forbidden fruit.

The severed square would become the primary design for the green space within the medieval cloister. The channels or paths within the rectangle also reflected the cross within the cosmos. Inside the four segments would be planted herbs or roses, vines or fruit trees. 'Truly,' St Bernard declared, 'the cloister is a paradise, a region protected by the rampart of discipline, in which may be found an abundant plenty of precious riches.'

The basic element of the medieval garden was the divided quadrangle. It also became the symbol for perfect love, which resisted the outside world. Its function, however, was changed by the monks, who healed as well as prayed. Through their herbs and spices, they sought to repeat the cures and miracles of Christ.

The excavations of the rubbish dump of the old Augustinian hospital at Soutra, south of Rosslyn on the Lammermuir Hills, revealed 79 varieties of pollen or spores. Most of these were mentioned in the *Capitulare* of Charlemagne or in the work of Abbot Neckham, who was held to be a major influence on Soutra's horticulture, as was the mysterious Macer, praised by the poet John Gower for his knowledge of 'the strength of herbes'. The four chief crops cultivated at Soutra were opium poppies, hemp, flax and tormentil. Two of these produced powerful drugs for anaesthesia. A sponge soaked in opium or hashish was placed over a patient's nose during an operation: he was then revived by having vinegar rubbed onto his teeth.

Drugs for surgery seemed to have been licensed in Genesis: 'And the Lord God caused a deep sleep to fall upon Adam, and he slept: and He took one of his ribs, and closed up the flesh instead thereof.' Christ Himself was meant to have been revived upon the Cross by being given a sponge soaked in vinegar. Two more of the main crops at Soutra, hemp again and flax, produced fibres for cloth and canvas and rope instead of sweet dreams. The Eastern spices excavated there were imported from Montpellier and were compounded in the medicines of the time as well as used on the food.

The Benedictines had established the prototype of the physic garden at Monte Cassino. The earliest design of one in the British Isles was drawn on the plan of the Christ Church monastic buildings at Canterbury, where a large herbal garden was shown covering half the space between the infirmary and the dormitory. At Westminster Abbey, the present College garden was part of the old infirmary garden, while Vine Street nearby still records the site of the old vineyard.

The *hortulanus* in the monastic community supplied the larder and the pharmacy. The abbey gardens both fed and healed. In the green spaces at Clairvaux, where St Bernard founded the Cistercian Order, a contemporary described how the song of the birds from the orchards delighted those who were recovering from illness. 'Where the orchard leaves off, the garden begins, divided into several beds, or (still better) cut up by little canals, which, though standing water, do actually flow more or less . . . The water fulfils the double purpose of nourishing the fish and watering the vegetables.' In the Gregorian chant the third 'O' of the seven announcing the advent of Christ was '*O Radix Jesse*' and was always sung by the Keeper of the Gardens, who was thought to have in his care the Stem of Jesse, from which sprang the House of Judah.

In using his medieval herbals to make Rosslyn Chapel into a stone Garden of Eden, William St Clair was particularly influenced by the *Lilium* of the Scottish physician Bernard of Gordon, who himself was strongly influenced by Arabic medicine. Earl William was also creating a carved Garden of Paradise, a Persian or Islamic Garden as well as a Biblical Garden. To him, Rosslyn Chapel stood on a hill or Mountain of Salvation. Its two wrought pillars represented the Tree of Life and the Tree of the Knowledge of Good and Evil. Among its carvings were the story of Genesis and the exclusion of Adam and Eve from Eden, as well as an angel with the fiery sword and another bearing palm leaves.

The walled chapel of Rosslyn was like the walled garden, 'a secret place, enclosing the mysteries of the Old and New Testaments'. So William St Clair believed when he asked his masons to carve the flowers and plants within it. Most of the carvings – if not all of them – illustrated some part of the Christian faith, a virtue or a divine lesson. The stone lily in the chapel represented the purity of the Virgin Mary and was often depicted in paintings of the Annunciation and the Assumption. The iris or fleur-de-lys recalled the spear which pierced Christ's side on the Cross. It was the symbol taken by the Kings of France and also a sign of the St Clairs, for it implied Christ's descent from the royal line of David, and perhaps that of the Capets and the family of Sanctus Clarus with its French blood. The trefoil plants of the strawberry and clover reminded the viewer of the Trinity. Wild pinks or dianthus signified the nails driven into Jesus at His Passion.

Thus each carving of herb and plant had its esoteric meaning. As a medieval physic garden or Herbal, Rosslyn chapel was a graven guide to the Bible through a walled paradise in stone. Its designer in the 15th century, Earl William, was the recorder of the divine garden before the advent of the Renaissance and the discovery of the plants of the Americas – although two of these were carved in the chapel, Indian corn and the aloe cactus. They served as another proof that his grandfather, Earl Henry St Clair, did try to found a colony in the Eden of the New World and brought back specimens from that continent. More puzzling are carvings of animals from Africa, an elephant and a gazelle and even a crocodile, apparently being suckled by a wolf.

To interpret the chapel in general is to read a carved Herbal. And the woodcuts on the pages of the great *Hortus Sanitatus*, printed in so many editions by Gutenberg's pupil Peter Schoeffer, were contemporary with the plant carvings at Rosslyn and were startling in their correspondences. The walls of the St Clair chapel are the healing garden of the end of the Middle Ages. They are botany before the Tudors, remedy before the beginning of modern medicine.

What is even more rewarding is to recognize the wildflowers of our time in their old names, hart's tongue ferns and curly kail, trefoil and oak leaves, and everywhere, sunflowers and roses. This profusion of nature suggested to William Wordsworth his fine lines, when he was to view Rosslyn, then leaking and covered in moss and lichen:

> From what bank
> Came those live herbs? By what hand were they sown
> Where dew falls not, where rain-drops seem unknown?
> Yet in the Temple they a friendly niche
> Share with their sculptured fellows, that, green-grown,
> Copy their beauty more and more, and preach,
> Though mute, of all things blending into one.

When Dorothy Wordsworth, the sister of the poet, also went to visit the sacred site, she wrote in her diary:

> Went to view the inside of the Chapel of Rosslyn, which is kept locked up, and so preserved from the injuries it might otherwise receive from idle boys; but, as nothing is done to keep it together, it must, in the end, fall. The architecture within is exquisitely beautiful. The stone, both of the roof and walls, is sculptured with leaves and flowers, so delicately wrought that I could have admired them for hours, and the whole of their groundwork is stained by time, with the softest colours. Some of those leaves and flowers were tinged perfectly green, and at one part the effect was most exquisite – three or four leaves of a small fern, resembling that which we call Adder's Tongue, grew round a cluster of them at the top of a pillar, and the natural product and the artificial were so intermingled, that, at first, it was not easy to distinguish the living plant from the other, they being of an equally determined green, though the fern was of a deeper shade.

And when Queen Victoria herself was shown the chapel in 1842, she was 'so much impressed with the beauty of the building, that she expressed a desire that so unique a gem should be preserved to the country.'

The ruin of Rosslyn chapel and castle began with John Knox and the Scottish Reformation. How many battles and wars would start in the search for the peace of God? How many people would be condemned for heresy in the personal reach towards divine intelligence and the Holy Spirit?

13

A Loyal Downfall

The two marriages of William, the third and last St Clair Earl of Orkney, would lead to a split in his titles and estates. His son Henry, by his first wife, would become Lord St Clair of Dysart and Ravensheugh and receive the lands in Fife. His second son William, by his second wife, would be given all the estates in the Far North and the new title of his father, the Earl of Caithness. His elder brother, Sir Oliver, would inherit 'the lands of the Baronie of Roslin, with the castle, parkis, woodis, stanks, millis of Roslyne, and the town of Roslin, in burgh in barony, with advocation of the Colledge of Roslyne and Chapel of Saint Matho'. This Crown charter of 1476 came at a huge price, paid by one of the wealthiest families in Scotland. 'The soume of 5,000 pounds of usual money of Scotland to be payt' to the King and his successors 'in the Abbey of Holyroodhouse of Edinburgh, upon the hie Altare of that ilk, upon a day betwix the uprising of the sun, and the downsetting of the samen.'

Earl William's first son Henry would maintain the shipbuilding enterprises of his forebears with the Baltic trade. He established his bloodline in Denmark and Norway, where many Sinclairs would fight in the Swedish wars, while one would become commander of Bergen Castle. His crest was on my own father's signet ring, 'a Phenix in a flame of fire, and for motto the word *Feight*'. His quartered shield bore four ships, two reefed and two under sail, within the St Clair Engrailed Cross. After many enterprises, he died of his gall-bladder. 'Lord Sinclair was discovered a stone approaching a nutmeg in shape and size; for he suffered his fate . . . when the stone, being too circular for it to be washed down his inner passages, had caused an obstruction.'

The new Earl William of Caithness would die in battle at Flodden. His shield of the Engrailed Cross contained two Lions Rampant as well as the two ships; it was supported by Griffons, the old Norse dragons. Above the helm was the future emblem of the Sinclairs of Caithness, the sacred Pelican feeding her chicks with her own blood, and the motto, *Commit Thy Work to God*. As the family chronicler Father Hay wrote of him:

> A man of quick and violent anger, but in other respects a good man, skilled equally in the arts of peace and war, who was vigorous in his advice in public administration for following the path of law rather than the wishes of others. His grandfather and great-grandfather were outstanding in matters conducted very well in war and peace. He himself on his very entry into youth displayed the hope of outstanding statesmanship . . . In addition, he would not show friendship to foreign princes, or make any treaty without consulting the King; within a few years, enriched by the deaths of his wives and new marriages, he became by far the most powerful man in the Kingdom after the Kings, and indeed the rest of the nobility gave precedence to him in wealth and statesmanship. He was given many kindnesses by the King, and established in himself a great model for military skill.

This Earl William of Orkney was buried at Rosslyn chapel, where his tomb would be defaced by Protestant iconoclasts in 1688 after the Glorious Revolution, along with the monument to Sir Oliver St Clair. As Father Hay recorded, he lost at that time many of the family manuscripts, because the castle would also be invaded. The major carvings, which were not destroyed, were the frieze of the dream of Darius, solved by Prince Zerubbabel of Judah, and, by the altar, 'a man in armour graven on a flat rough stone; att his head two scutcheons haveing each a lyon contourned; no supporters nor ornaments'. This existing brass tombstone appears to bear the arms of the Earls of Caithness.★

★ See Illustrations.

The extent of the rights granted to sons and heirs may be seen in Earl William's further Charter in favour of Sir Oliver Sinclair, concerning the estates in Herbertshire. These were given:

In fee and inheritance for ever, along with all their right boundaries and ancient borders, just as they lie in length and breadth, in woods, plains, moors, marshes, roads, paths, waters, lakes, pools, streams, meadows, pastures, and rights of pasture, mills, farms, multures, and their sequels, fowlings, fishings, hunts, quarries, turf-pits, charcoal pits, stone cuttings, workings in stone and chalk, brew-houses, breweries, and broomlands . . . orchards, parks, woodlands, forests, groves, doves, dovecotes, rabbits, rabbit warrens, towers, fortresses, mansions and manors, with their services, dues, and rights of the freeholdings and tenancies of the said Barony; also with the courts, and their revenues, blood-wites, heriots, and women's merchets, with fork and ditch, sok, sak, tol, them, infangantheof, and outfagantheof, pit and gallows, and with all other individual liberties, produce and easements and whatever lawful appurtenances, both named and non-named, both under the earth and above the earth, both far and near, belonging to the said lands of the Barony of Herbertshire.

King James V depended heavily on the Lords of Rosslyn for his Treasury. In a Charter of 1533 he renewed their rights, because of the destruction of their writs by shipwreck and fire:

One part of their evidence is damaged, and because of the age of its elements is with difficulty to be read clearly, and with the passage of time its seals have almost perished, so much so that it is on the point of disintegration [so for] the use of the said William, etc., we have ordained that a certain sound and complete charter [be] made by our ancestor Robert, the second of that name, for Henry Earl of Orkney, an ancestor of the said William.

King James was evidently influenced in this decision by his favourite, Oliver of Pitcairn, 'brother-german of the said William Sinclair of Roslin, Knight', as that cousin was named as one of the heirs of Rosslyn, should there be no issue. Then the lands would go 'if all of these – God forbid – are lacking, to the lawful and nearest male heirs bearing the arms and name of Sinclair, whoever they are, of us and our successors, in fee and inheritance, free barony and free forest, where there are woods and trees'.

Yet King James was equally obliged to the Lords of Rosslyn for their aid in armaments and to the Exchequer. In the royal Charter of 1542, which confirmed all the St Clair southern possessions, 'William Sinclair of Roslin, Knight,' was praised 'for good, loyal and free service . . . and for certain huge sums of money, and payment by him to us, spent and delivered to our treasury in our name'. That same good and loyal and free service to King James's daughter Mary would lead to the downfall of the St Clairs of Rosslyn.

After 1544, there was open war between England and Scotland for four years. King Henry VIII wanted his heir, Prince Edward, to marry Mary, the child Queen of Scots. Thus the Crowns of England and Scotland would be united. When a Scottish parliament renewed the Old Alliance with France and defended the Catholic faith, Henry decided on 'a rough wooing'. The instructions of the Privy Council to the English commander, Edward Seymour, Earl of Hertford, were explicit. Over the Borders, he was to pursue a scorched-earth policy.

> Put all to fire and sword, burn Edinburgh town, so razed and defaced when you have sacked and gotten what ye can of it as there may remain forever a perpetual memory of the vengeance of God lighted upon them for their falsehood and disloyalty. Do what ye can out of hand and without long tarrying to beat down and overthrow the Castle, sack Holyrood House and burn and subvert it and all the rest, putting man, woman, and child to fire and sword without exception, where any resistance shall be made against you; and this done, pass over to the Fifeland, and extend like extremity and destruction in all towns and villages whereunto ye may reach conveniently, not forgetting among all the rest so to spoil the cardinal's town of St Andrews as the upper stone may be the nether, and not one stick stand by another, sparing no creature alive within the same.

Lord Hertford with his army and fleet landed on the Firth of Forth in 1544, while another column struck across the Borders. He slashed and burned Edinburgh and Holyrood, Leith and Rosslyn Castle. The next year, he put to the torch 7 monasteries, including Dryburgh and Kelso and Melrose, along with 16 forts, 5 market towns, and 243 villages. Although the tombs of the Kings and Queens of Scotland were desecrated, and an eagle lectern and a solid brass font given by the Bishop of Dunkeld were stolen from Holyrood, the English raiders failed to seize the religious regalia and treasure there. The reason was that William Sinclair, whose family had endowed the Abbey, had removed the reliquaries and rich chalices, and he refused to restore them.

For the Sinclairs of Rosslyn had been great benefactors to the Monastic Orders. Henry, the Earl of Orkney, had given the Abbey of Holyrood sufficient land to graze 7,000 sheep, vestments of gold and silver, and 'a number of rich, embroidered cups' or chalices 'for the more honourable celebration of divine worship'. The charters of the Cistercian abbey of Newbattle – also sacked during the English invasion – further praised his generosity, including the gift of missals and a silver cross worth 50 pounds, flanked by the figures of the Virgin Mary and temporarily stolen by the English after the Battle of Neville's Cross. Many of the treasures of the Scottish Church before the Reformation were the donation of the Sinclairs of Rosslyn, who felt it their duty to keep these safe from harm.

In March 1545, the Lords in Council ordered William Sinclair to return all jewels, vestments and ornaments of 'the abbay and place of Holyrudhouse . . . put and reservit within his place'. But he would not yield them. They were part of the blessed hoard hidden in the vaults of Rosslyn chapel beside the shrine. Most probably, these also included the piece of the True Cross in its reliquary of silver and gold and jewels, the Holy or Black Rood of Scotland, which had been guarded by St Margaret's cupbearer and the St Clair family for five centuries as Scotland's most precious sacred relic. The Reformation in England had already destroyed almost all the shrines and precious relics of the old Catholic faith, and Holyrood Abbey would be defaced forever. Scotland would become even more zealous in extirpating the treasures of the Middle Ages.

This protection of sacred Catholic remains made the Regent of Scotland, Mary of Guise, issue in 1546 an extraordinary Bond to the Lord of Rosslyn, because of their shared secret, held in the spaces below the chapel. She wrote that she was bound and obliged to her well-beloved Sir William Sinclair for his special service. He would go and ride with her for all the days of his life, and take part with all his friends and kinsmen against everyone who denied his allegiance to the Crown of Scotland.

In return, Mary of Guise promised to be a loyal and true mistress to him. 'His counsel and secret shewen to us we sall keip secret, and in all mattres gif to him the best and trewest counsell we can, as we sall be requirt thereto, and sall not witt his skaith nor damnage, but we sall stop it att our power.' Sir William was further to receive for 'his gud, faithfull, trew and thankfull service . . . ane yearlie pensioun of the soume of three hundredth markis, usual money of Scotland'.

The retainers were now being retained. The Crown was paying the beggared St Clairs of Rosslyn, rather than the other way round. That year, there was no invasion, but there was a Protestant revolt. With the assistance of Mary of Guise, Cardinal Beaton had defended the old Catholic faith against the militant Reformers. The rebels murdered the Cardinal in the castle of St Andrews, for he was, in the words of the aggressive minister John Knox, 'an obstinate enemy of Christ Jesus'. Under threat himself, Knox took off to St Andrews, only to be seized in an assault by the French fleet and sent off to row in their galleys. This treatment hardly endeared that foreign country to him.

Although Henry VIII died, Lord Hertford, now the Duke of Somerset, became the Protector of Edward, the nine-year-old King of England, and he pursued the previous royal policy. In September 1547, he met the Scottish pikemen on Edmonstone Edge above the town of Musselburgh. Under cannon-fire from guns on land and offshore on the English fleet, the spear wall of the knights and the Borderers broke ranks and charged Somerset's cavalry and artillery at Pinkie Cleugh.

The slaughter ended in a rout. As the chronicler William Patten noted, the dead bodies of the Scots lay about as a herd of cattle, grazing on the pasture. Ten thousand died in that pitched battle, which was the beginning of the end of the old ways of war. The musket and the culverin could now deal with massed infantry and a Highland charge. Even the raiding days of the reivers for four centuries would be numbered, for gunpowder and the bayonet were mightier than horse fodder and the sword.

Fortunately, the sacred treasures of Scotland were still hidden at Rosslyn, for the English invaders again sacked Holyrood Abbey, where they only found lead. They stripped the roof of that last base metal. The destruction was so complete that the most ornate church in Scotland became a stone quarry for looters after the Reformation. The four-year-old Mary, Queen of Scots, was separated from her mother, Mary of Guise, and bundled off to an Augustinian island priory. Then, after the arrival of French troops, and under the care of Sir William Sinclair, Mary was carried away in a royal galley, pledged to marry the Dauphin when she came of age.

So the bold Tudor plan of uniting the Crowns of England and Scotland would come to an end for the time being. Protector Somerset considered making a strip of wasteland twelve miles wide through the Debatable Land to separate the two nations, while a proposal would later be put to Queen Elizabeth I to rebuild Hadrian's Wall, this time to be defended by 'greate gonners . . . in an arteficiall fortyficacion, consystinge for the most parte onlye of mayne earthe, raysed with trenche and rampyour, and flaunched with bulwarkes'.

By a Right of Passage in 1556, the Regent had to send her trusted Sir William Sinclair again to France to ask for more support. During his year's absence, he was excused from his judicial duties, and Mary of Guise swore to defend the hidden treasures at Rosslyn, for the religious wars in Scotland intensified with the death in 1558 of the childless Catholic Queen of England, Mary Tudor, and the accession to the throne of her Protestant half-sister Elizabeth. By this time, Mary, Queen of Scots, was married to the Dauphin, and his father, King Henry II of France, immediately had her proclaimed Queen of England and Ireland as well as Scotland. The poet Ronsard wrote that Jupiter had decreed that she should govern England for three months, Scotland for three and France for half the year.

The following year, Sir William Sinclair was made Lord Justice General. He had succeeded to all of his estates on the death of Sir Oliver, whose son George had died without issue. Now the head of Rosslyn was empowered to proceed against the Protestant Lords and Border raiders into Lothian. A Charter of Justice from Mary of Guise granted:

Our beloved William Sinclair of Roslin our Justice in this party, giving, granting and entrusting to him our full power, charge and special mandate, that the said thieves and those harbourers, likewise, wherever they can be found, should be pursued, captured and apprehended within the boundaries of Laudonia and Tweeddale, and that in this way they should be punished in accordance with the quality and quantity of their crimes and misdeeds.

To achieve this, Sir William needed weapons, and these were available from his wandering armourers, who met yearly by his castle. As Sir Walter Scott later noted in his *Provincial Antiquities*, the gypsies were always welcomed in Rosslyn Glen for their skills. Indeed, in 1559, according to Father Hay, Sir William saved a Romany from execution. 'He delivered once ane Egyptian from the gibbet in the Burrow Moore, ready to be strangled; upon which accoumpt the whole body of gypsies were, of old, accustomed to gather in the Stanks of Rosslyn every year, where they acted severall plays during the moneth of May and June.'

These travelling iron-workers were behaving in the manner of the medieval crafts and guilds of hammermen and bowmen in putting on performances, if not Miracle plays. And certainly, the weapons they manufactured were being put to use by the Sinclairs against the revolution of the Reformation. As Sir Walter Scott noted:

This was not allowed to continue long. For the Privy Council had their attention called to this Patmos of the outlawed race. They remarked that while the laws enjoined all persons in authority to 'execute to the deid the counterfeit thieves and limmers, the Egyptians,' it was nevertheless reported that a number of them were within the bounds of Rosslyn, 'where they have a peaceable receipt and abode, as if they were lawful subjects, committing stowths and reifs in all parts where they may find occasion.' The Council, therefore, issued an order to the Sheriff of the district, who happened to be Sinclair the younger of Rosslyn, commanding him 'to pass, search, seek, hunt, follow, and pursue the said vagabonds and thieves and limmers,' and bring them to the Tolbooth at Edinburgh for due punishment. This was probably done; for an order for the execution of a number of Egyptians was issued on the ensuing 27th January, 1561.

Known supporters of the Stewart and Catholic cause, the Sinclairs of Rosslyn were doomed by the Reformation. The Scottish Parliament instituted a Protestant confession of faith, abolishing the jurisdiction of the Pope and prohibiting the celebration of the Mass under sentence of death for the third offence. These acts should have received the assent of Mary, Queen of Scots, but they never did. Yet they ensured that the Reformation would succeed in Scotland, and that the Lords of Rosslyn would be condemned for their faith and their loyalty to the Crown.

Another Henry Sinclair, 'a son of Roslin', was created the Bishop of Ross and President of the Court of Session. He was described by a contemporary as 'the reformer of the law and the patron of literature of his country'. Yet the situation had deteriorated so badly by 1562 that the Bishop could not go to visit the Papal Legate, Nicolas de Gouda. 'My visiting him,' the Bishop wrote, 'would bring about the sacking and plundering of his house within twenty-four hours, and would involve himself and all his household in peril of his lives.' Bishop Henry only survived another two years himself before dying in Paris, unable to help his Queen any more.

After the death of her mother and her young husband, now King of France, Mary had sailed in 1561 to Scotland to assume the Crown. She was a tall woman, given to sports, such as hunting and hawking, archery and even golf. She rode with her troops in male costume, saying that she wished she were a man, so that she could lie out in the fields all night. One of her admirers wrote of her 'goodly personage, alluring grace, a pretty Scotch accent, and a searching wit, clouded with mildness'. Her mistakes lay in her choice of her next two husbands, although she did her best to conciliate the Protestant lords and the Kirk ministers, who saw their futures in taking over the estates of the Catholic church, as King Henry VIII had done with the English abbeys, cathedrals and monasteries.

In her preliminary encounters with the formidable John Knox, now returned to Scotland, the Queen displayed her intelligence and faith. Knox claimed that the Kirk with its *Book of Discipline* was the only true faith, and that its believers were subject to its doctrines, preached by the ministers. To this assertion Mary replied, 'I perceive that my subjects shall obey you, and not me; and shall do what they list and not what I command.' When Knox replied that only the Reformed Church could take her to everlasting glory, she countered with the words: 'I will defend the Kirk of Rome, for, I think, it is the true Kirk of God.'

The Queen's second husband, Henry, Lord Darnley, was a Lennox with a Catholic mother. A vain and foolish youth, he trimmed over his religion, attending sermons by John Knox at St Giles, and refusing to join Mary in the nuptial Mass after their wedding. This was conducted in 1565 by John Sinclair, the Bishop of Brechin, who was true to the Old Faith, as were the Earl of Caithness and Sir William Sinclair of Roslin. With the abdication and flight of Mary three years later, the latter would be arrested and the future of his estates put in jeopardy.

Darnley conspired against his own wife. He joined the Protestant lords in having her confidant and secretary Riccio murdered, also a Dominican friar, kept in Holyrood Palace. He did, however, give her a son, the future James VI of Scotland and James I of England, baptised by Catholic ceremonial. After Darnley was himself garrotted at Kirk o' Field, which was blown up, the Queen was abducted by a force led by Lord Bothwell, and she was taken to his castle at Dunbar.

Within three months of Darnley's death, Mary married her kidnapper, the man accused of her late husband's murder. Even the Pope now had to cut off all communication with the Queen 'unless, indeed, in times to come she shall see some better sign of her life and religion'. Taking on the opposition in an engagement at Carberry, Mary found her army melting away and her third husband in flight over the Border. Imprisoned in Loch Leven castle, she was forced to abdicate the throne in favour of her infant son. Escaping, she raised another force, only to be defeated at Langside in 1568, before fleeing over the Border to be held and finally executed two decades later by Queen Elizabeth I, as a danger to the realm.

Sir William Sinclair of Roslin was the Queen's Man in Midlothian. He was a staunch Catholic, although he had sat in the Protestant parliament of 1560, which had condemned the Mass and had abolished the authority of the Pope. For his support of Queen Mary, he had to wait six years for a royal pardon from the child King and his Council for 'nefarious conspiracies against us and our authority, and in plain and open war, with raised banners, and coming on to the field at Langside'. That same year, Sir William resigned his Barony and lands to his son Edward, who would repeat the act of withdrawal in 1582, in favour of his cousin William Sinclair 'near the gatehouse to the Castle of Roslin'.

There, the Collegiate Church of St Matthew had been endowed with many bequests, including 'four acres of meadow . . . with the Kips, and eight sowms grass, in the town of Pentland'. The revenues were to support a Provost, six Prebendaries, and two singing boys. Yet by 1571, such was the pressure of the Reformation that all the Catholic clerics were 'resigning, as by force and violence, all and everyone of the several donations into secular hands inalienably; and withal complaining that, for many years before, their revenues had been violently detained from them'. To this deed of resignation, 'the seal of the Chapter of this Collegiate Church was appended, being St Matthew in a Kirk, red upon white wax; as also the seal of the then Sir William St Clair of Roslin, being a ragged cross, red upon white wax.' This charter of acquiescence under menace was also signed by the Provost and the Vicar of Pentland, and a Prebendary, another Henry Sinclair.

During the various Regencies until the child monarch James VI was of age, the power of the Reformed Church of Scotland grew, while the Border raids did not cease. Although by 1572 the 'Concordat of Leith' allowed Protestant ministers to take over parish churches and lands, when these became vacant, a second *Book of Discipline* within another two years demanded the whole patrimony of the Catholic church, also the right to appoint all of the clergy.

Moreover, the *Book* also declared that the Kirk 'has a certain power granted by God', and its only head was Christ, not the King. This had been the claim of Thomas à Becket on behalf of the Pope to King Henry II of England before that Archbishop of Canterbury was murdered. John Knox had tried this assertion against the refusal of Mary, Queen of Scots. And her son and his Council would deny this usurpation of royal authority with the axiom, 'No bishop, no king'. In his opinion, King James would declare that the Presbyterianism of his country agreed 'as well with monarchy as God and the Devil'.

Mob attacks from Edinburgh were to devastate Rosslyn chapel in

1592, although many of the sacred treasures were already hidden. The empty brackets still there once held up religious statues of the Apostles and the Virgin Mary with her child Jesus in her arms. The four altars in the Lady Chapel, dedicated to the Blessed Virgin and the Saints Andrew and Matthew and Peter, were also pillaged, although the Lords of Rosslyn fought for their preservation. In 1589, William, the brother of John Knox, was censured by his Presbytery for baptizing a St Clair infant in the chapel, which was 'ane house and monument of idolatrie, and not ane place appointit for teiching the word and ministratioun of ye sacramentis'.

The following year, George Ramsay, the minister of Lasswade, was forbidden to bury the wife of Sir Oliver St Clair in the chapel. When the minister later 'enterit ye Kirk [he] fand sax alteris standing haill undemolishit, and some broken images. The Laird being informed how wicked the intertening of thame was, and thairfor exhorted to demolish thame, refusit altogether, sayand he wald defend them as he might. The breither, heiring this report, judgit the Laird not sound in his religion.'

A secret Catholic as his ancestors, the Lord of Rosslyn was summoned before the local Presbytery and ordered to 'subscribe to the heids of religione, and also to have him injoined to destroy the monuments of idolatrie'. He refused, saying, 'he was of the same mynd as befoir, neither wald he destroy the said alteris . . . he will not demolish thame, nouther gif King nor Kirk command him.' Threatened with excommunication, the Lord began to comply. The Presbytery was told that 'the upmost stones of every ane of the alteris were removit, but that the bodies of the alteris were still standing undemolishit.'

This action did not satisfy the brethren. The Master of the chapel had delayed for two years, and his avoidances were too much. He would be 'summarlie excommunicat in ye Kirk of Dalkeith'. Faced with total ruin, but left with his private conscience, he yielded. On the 31 August 1592, George Ramsay reported 'that the alteris of Roslene were haillie demolishit till ane stane or twa hight, and yt the Acts of the Generall, Provinciall and Presbyteriall Assemblies were fully satisfiet. For the quilk the breither praysit God.'

From that time on, the chapel was rarely used for prayer. The Lords of Rosslyn, who remained secret and devout Catholics, hid priests in the castle, such as their future chronicler, Father Hay. Mass was held in the private chapel behind the walls of their fortification, and not disclosed.

For two reasons, the ornate Collegiate Church of St Matthew, so full of idols and Green Men, was not wholly destroyed. The first was that the Sinclairs remained the hereditary Grand Masters of the Crafts and Guilds and Masons of Scotland, even though many of these trade organizations were leaving the Catholic faith and becoming Protestant. The second reason was the *Secret shewn* to Mary of Guise, which she did keep secret. This was the location of the shrine below the altar at Rosslyn, while the vaults there kept other Catholic religious treasures and relics, some from Holyrood Abbey or from the downfall of the Templars, all in the safe-keeping of the Sinclairs. The knowledge that Rosslyn chapel was a holy place, which was revered by Masons as well as Catholics, stayed most of the hammers and axes of the religious radicals.

The great irony was that the name of Sanctus Clarus or Seekers for the Holy Light was now being assumed by the Protestant revolutionaries, who claimed that Christ was the true king, 'and his Kingdom the Kirk, whose subject King James the Sixth is, and of whose kingdom not a king, nor a laird, nor a head, but a member'. Although the 'Black Acts' of 1584 had totally affirmed royal authority over the Kirk, the Presbyterian rebellion would continue until the Civil War of the next century. And by forsaking their long past of desiring a direct approach to the divine intelligence, and by their loyalty to the Stewart cause and the old Catholic faith, the reactionary Sinclairs would now be condemned for the heretics they once had been, and no longer were.

14

Faith and Penury

With the death of Queen Elizabeth I in 1603, the old desire of
Edward I and Henry VIII was achieved. There was a Union of the
Crowns of England and Scotland, even if it was the wrong way round.
The King of the Scots, James VI, crossed the Borders, travelling down
to London, surrounded by a host of greedy courtiers. Not for the first
time would the southern shires and cities be looted by peaceful
northern intruders, now in power. The new monarch, also James I
in Westminster, even considered calling his combined estate by the
names of North and South Britain, while the previous frontier would
become the Middle Shires. Certainly, he meant to put an end to the
incessant skirmishes and raids of the reivers and their ilk, who had even
held an 'Ill Week' of arson and mayhem, when the royal progress had
passed through the Debatable Land.

As the ruler of both nations declared, he had a 'special regard to the
Marchis and the Bordouris . . . the verie hart of the cuntrey sall not be
left in ane uncertaintie.' Within seven years, his nobles and lieutenants
had pacified the whole region by the gallows and the sword and fire,
by deportation and armed service abroad. The purge was led by Lord
Hume with a special armed guard; 32 Elliots and Armstrongs and
other raiders were hanged, another 150 were outlawed or banished,
while 2,000 men under Walter Scott of Buccleuch crossed over to the
Low Countries to help the Dutch Reformers fight against Catholic
Spain. A diplomatic complaint to King James provoked the answer
that he was not 'displeased that this rabble should be taken out of the
kingdom'.

A draconian regime followed. The iron gates of castles and swords were literally to be beaten into ploughshares, all weapons were prohibited and only heavy work-horses might be kept. Paid informers and tracker dogs would betray and pursue fugitives. The chief offenders, the Grahams of Esk, had their lands forfeited, and hundreds were deported to serve in British garrisons in Dutch ports or to settlements in Roscommon in Ireland. Forbearance was thought to breed greater insolence, and so 'Jeddart justice' was meted out – a trial after the noose. The new overlord of the Border Commission, the Earl of Dunbar, was hailed as another Hercules cleansing the Augean Stables, for he had 'purgit the Borders of all the chiefest malefactors, robbers and brigands'.

Yet the other emetic for the troubles in Scotland would be the opportunity to be purged as mercenaries in the Thirty Years War on the Continent. A Scottish brigade of up to 10,000 men fought with distinction for both the Swedish and the French Kings, who had long had the protection of the royal *Garde ecossaise*. The reverse side of this exodus was that many exiled Scotsmen became military experts in warfare and the procurement of weapons. These seasoned warriors would be recalled home with their supplies to fight for both sides, when the Reformers, called the Covenanters, were ready to take on the Stewart monarchs and their detested bishops.

By patient negotiation, King James I and VI had managed to rein in the militant Kirk of Scotland. His triumph was to create with the English bishops a vernacular Bible, which still bears his name and has had an even greater influence on the language than the works of William Shakespeare. This was despite the Moderator of the Kirk of Scotland, in 1591, declaring against 'the belly-god bishops in England [who] by all moyen and money were seeking conformity of our Kirk with theirs'.

In Scotland, King James had wisely held the line between little rebellions by Catholic lords in Caithness and Protestant mobs in Edinburgh. The Huntleys had their northern castles burnt and were forced to flee to France. Yet in 1592, during a riot of the workers, the King was saved in the Tolbooth by a sturdy blacksmith, John Watt, who was the Convenor of the Trades. He surrounded the monarch with his fellow masons, who 'offered to die all in one moment for His Majesty'.

The old craft guilds had also been religious fraternities. The best-known one in Edinburgh was that of the Holy Blood, and it had once had King James IV as a member in its scarlet livery. Thirteen other guilds were given their own altars and chaplains in St Giles before the Reformation. In 1558, John Knox had denounced one of their many processions on Saints' Days as corrupt and full of 'priests, friars, canons, and rotten Papists, with tubors and trumpets, banners and bagpipes, and who was there to lead the ring, but the Queen Regent [Mary of Guise] herself, with all her shavelings'.

The command of the crafts and guilds would soon be confirmed by the King's Catholic Master of Works, William Schaw, to the Sinclair Lords of Rosslyn. For it was vital that control of the shipwrights and armourers remained in a family which was loyal to the Stewart cause. Indeed, at the fortress port of Haddington, on Corpus Christi Day, the hammermen marched with two banners, while the masons and the wrights carried only one apiece. A continuing preoccupation of the Reformers was that they could not take over the lodges of the Catholic crafts and guilds, although gradually these would give up the Old Faith and expunge its records and rituals as a kind of treason to God, if not to the King.

Neither could the Reformers take over the masses. As late as 1618, on Christmas Day, St Giles was half-filled, while 'dogs were playing in the midst of the flour of the Little Kirk for rarity of people.' And the next year at Easter, hundreds of thousands of citizens streamed out to St Cuthbert's, to the Abbey church, and to one at Leith, 'where communion was dispensed in the old style; and when the ministers of these churches had been suspended, many, to avoid kneeling, went as far as Dunfermline. In some cases, the minister found himself deserted by his entire flock; in others, there was unseemly wrangling between the minister and the people'.

William Schaw of Sauchie came from a family which was habitually the keeper of the royal wine cellar. A page at the court of Mary of Guise, he stayed near King James VI, and signed with him under pressure in 1583 the Negative Confession, a denunciation of Roman Catholic influences. That same year, he was made Master of the King's Works for life, responsible for the building of royal castles and palaces. He was later summoned by the presbytery of Edinburgh to appear before its jurisdiction as a 'papist or apostate', while an English agent informed on him as 'a suspected Jesuit'.

The other powerful supporter of William Schaw was Alexander, Lord Seton, openly a Catholic Lord Chancellor and ambassador, who held with the Lords of Rosslyn the southern approaches to Edinburgh. As Earl William of Orkney had been, Lord Seton was 'a great humanist in prose and verse, Greek and Latin, and well versed in the mathematics and had great skill in architecture'. And as at the building of Rosslyn chapel, Seton continued the ancient Templar tradition.

Long before, his ancestor Christopher Seton had married the sister of Robert the Bruce, and the family had been prominent in royal affairs for 400 years. Although the Knights Hospitallers of St John had officially absorbed all Templar properties, a certain James Sandilands entered the Order, so that he might become the Prior of its Scottish headquarters at Torphichen. Trimming with the wind, both Protestant and Catholic according to the breezes of the day, he opposed Mary of Guise, but when the Scottish Parliament declared that all papal lands were now Crown property, Sandilands leased the Hospitaller centre, and had himself created Baron Torpichen.

Thus he became the possessor of a place which he said had been subject only to 'the Knights of Jerusalem and the Temple of Solomon'. According to *A History of the Family of Seton*, this usurpation led to the withdrawal of the remaining Knights Templars from the Knights of St John under their Grand Prior in Scotland, a David Seton. A poem of the time, *Haly kirk and her theeves*, castigated Sandilands for being as greedy as 'the knave Judas':

> Fye upon the churle quhat solde
> Haly erthe for heavie golde;
> Bot the tempel felt na loss,
> Quhan David Setoune bore the crosse.

His cousin Lord Alexander, however, went with William Schaw on an embassy to France in 1584, and then employed him on reconstructing the family's monuments. For 'he was one of the greatest builders in that age; and at the tyme had the king's master of worke at Seatoune, building that large quarter of his palace towards the north-east.' Schaw was also taken by King James VI to Norway and Denmark in 1589 to collect his bride, Princess Anne, who would not make the stormy crossing. Sent home early, he completed repair work at Holyroodhouse, which now boasted a Double Helix staircase, copied from the one Leonardo da Vinci had constructed at the *château* of Chambord by the Loire. Queen Anne made Schaw her Master of Ceremonies as well as Works, and until his death, in 1602, he held both Offices of State.

Another scheme of the Master of Works was his effort to give laws to the masons of Scotland. As their general warden, he wanted a settled order '(as the privileges of the craft requyris) tane at this time'. In fourteen separate statutes, he ordered Edinburgh to become the principal lodge of Scotland, but Kilwinning to be the second lodge as 'in all tyme cuming, as of befoir' Edinburgh, this being 'manifest in our awld antient writtis'.

At the same time, Schaw issued a Charter to Sir William Sinclair of Rosslyn. Perhaps in view of impending conflicts, the baron there had increased the fortifications of the castle. 'He built the vaults and great turnpike of Roslin . . . He builded one of the arches of the Draw-bridge, a fine house near the Milne, and the Tower of the Dungeon where the clock was kept.' Significantly, Schaw confirmed Sinclair's authority over the deacons, masters and freemen of the masons in Scotland. From age to age, the Charter declared, it had been observed that the Rosslyn Lords had 'ever bene patrones and protectors of us and our privileges, like as our predecessors has obeyed and acknowl-edged them'.

For some time, however, the office had fallen out of use because of sloth and negligence. But in their disputes, the masons and craftsmen demanded an arbiter and a judge. Therefore, Schaw had agreed with the lodges that King James should reaffirm the jurisdiction of the Sinclairs of Rosslyn. Of the five lodges which signed the Charter alongside Schaw, the most significant were from the Seton stronghold of Dunfermline, alongside St Andrews and Edinburgh and Haddington, all important in the building of the royal navy.

Sir William Sinclair was a fellow Catholic with Schaw and Lord Seton, and had long been in conflict with his local presbytery, even on charges of fornication, and having illegitimate children. He 'was a leud man', as Father Hay wrote. 'He kept a miller's daughter, with whom it is alledged he went to Ireland; yet I think the cause of his retreat was rather occasioned by the Presbyterians, who vexd him sadly because of his religion, being Roman Catholic.' Schaw's Charter was not confirmed by King James because of the death of his esteemed Master of Works, and perhaps because of the reputation of the bad Sir William, who was soon succeeded by a far more politic and respectable son and heir.

The new Sir William married the daughter of John Spottiswood, Archbishop of Glasgow and later of St Andrews. The bishop played an important role in overseeing a moderate Kirk of Scotland during the rest of the long reign of King James VI. The Assembly of Presbyterians rejected the monarch's Five Articles about kneeling at communion, private communion and baptism, the royal confirmation of bishops, and the observance of Christmas, Good Friday, Easter, Ascension Day and Trinity Sunday. Yet Spottiswood preached that the Articles should be accepted, as they were the King's 'own motions', not against the Scriptures. The fact was that James VI was so good a theologian that he knew 'what is fit for a Church to have, and what not, better than we do all'.

If the King, in his early address to the House of Commons, had hoped to leave at his death 'one worship of God, one kingdom entirely governed, one uniformity of law', he would be sorely disappointed. As for the Sinclairs in Caithness, they would be in the same mess as those left at Rosslyn. The Orkney branch of the family had already had a bloody encounter with other Sinclairs in Caithness, but when a bastard Stewart son was granted the fee of Orkney, things went from black to pitch. Mary, Queen of Scots, had granted her crown lands in the Orcadian Isles to her half-brother Robert. He and his son Patrick became predators there, although their taste in architecture was excellent. Leaving behind them the most accomplished piece of Renaissance architecture in Scotland, the palace of Kirkwall, a *château* from the Loire set by the North Sea, their depredations ended in their executions. Earl Patrick was imprisoned, while his son Robert seized Kirkwall castle, until he was betrayed. He was hanged at Market Cross in Edinburgh, where his father was beheaded five weeks later. The castle was razed, putting an end to an old St Clair dream of a Northern Commonwealth.

Meanwhile, the new Sir William Sinclair lived peaceably enough at Rosslyn, until the coming of the Scottish Revolution and the Covenant. After that, there would be nothing but strife, for, on the death of King James, his son Charles I had succeeded to the throne of both countries. Unfortunately, Charles did not inherit his father's ambiguity about the Kirk of Scotland, but only his intransigence. On his coronation ceremony in Edinburgh, the five officiating bishops in rich vestments were 'becking and bowing as they passed the embroidered crucifix'. On the following Sunday, two royal chaplains read the English Prayer Book. King Charles refused to address a petition that asked for the Kirk to be granted more of the old church lands, which remained in royal hands. The accommodating Bishop Spottiswood was then made Lord Chancellor, although no cleric had held that post since the Reformation. He would hardly oppose the powerful English Archbishop Laud in supporting the divine right of the King in appointing to high rank such prelates as himself.

To the Presbyters and many of the people, the whole idea of an intermediary higher priesthood was anathema. There should be an individual intercourse between the soul and God. This was the essence of the Protestant attack on Rome, as it had been for the original heresies of Sanctus Clarus and the Gnostics, the Cathars and the Knights Templars. Now shrieking mobs of inspired women, the precursors of the *tricoteuses* knitting under the French guillotine, would rage against this new Popishness. And a Covenant would be pronounced by a fresh Puritan tendency in accordance with many Members of Parliament in England. These would demand the cleansing of all Catholic influences, and even the overthrow of the King and his bishops, should they seek to oppose the reform.

The Covenanters had begun to import armaments and experienced commanders from the conflicts of the Thirty Years War. Only in this context may the second Masonic Charter to the Sinclairs be interpreted. Three times the length of the first Charter, the petitioners were now the deacons, masters and freemen of the masons and hammermen. Those who signed the Charter included Hew Dudk, deacon of the mason craft and wrights of Ayr, and George Lydall, deacon of squaremen, 'and was quarter master'. The signatories of 1630 came from leading ports and military bases, where ships and troops were armed and victualled, Edinburgh and Dundee and Glasgow, Stirling and Dunfermline and St Andrews and Ayr. And the reason for the issue of this second Charter was another Protestant attack on Rosslyn, where the writs were 'consumed in ane flame of fire, within the castle . . . the consumation and burning thereof being clerely known to us and our predecessors'.

Sir William Sinclair had his protector in his wife, the daughter of the promoted Bishop Spottiswood of Glasgow and St Andrews; lodges in both of these towns signed the second Charter. The Lord and the bishop were loyal to the Stewarts, and they were perfectly aware of the need to pick up armaments against any threat from the Reformers, who would become the Covenanters. And while the first Charter did not mention that the Kings of Scotland used the Sinclair family to control the crafts and guilds, the second Charter was more specific on behalf of its signatories:

> Forasmeikle as, from adge, to adge, it has been observed amongst us and our predecessors that the Lairds of Roslin has ever been patrons and protectors of us and our priviledges, likeas our predecessors has obeyed, reverenced, and acknowledged them as patrons and protectors, whereof they had lettres of protection and other rights granted be his Majestie's most noble progenitors of worthy memories . . .

The reason for the second Charter also reflected the religious conflicts in Scotland, which threatened royal authority. Since the departure of Sir William of Rosslyn's father to Ireland, 'there are very many corruptions and imperfections risen and ingenerit, both amongst our selfs, and in our said vocations, in defect of ane patrone and overseer over us . . . for reparation of the ruins and manifold and enormitys done be unskillful persons . . .'. The fact was that the remaining Catholic lodges were in conflict with their Protestant brethren, and the burning issue was control of the means of production of weapons.

Unlike his father, King Charles I signed the second Charter, expressly 'out of our princelie care to obviat any disordour in tymes comeing'. The Scottish Privy Councillors, however, were aware of future disorders on the way, and they ordered Sir William Sinclair to show the 'patents', by which he sought to become the judge and controller of 'the trade of maissonis hammermen'. His claims were contested by his rivals, Sir James Murray and Anthony Alexander, who were now the joint Masters of the King's Works in Scotland. They claimed jurisdiction over all crafts, including not only masons, but the makers of weapons and supplies – shipwrights, pike and spear armourers, coopers, hammermen and smiths. With the death of Murray, Alexander became the sole Master of Works, and he took the oath as a Mason, joining the Lodge of St Mary's Chapel in Edinburgh.

The trimming King Charles also gave Alexander what he desired, so that he and Sinclair divided control of the weapons trade in Scotland. The split Privy Council approved of neither right, while King Charles himself stood against any hereditary Sinclair right, for it was not under royal control. Both had powerful friends, for Bishop Spottiswood was now Lord Chancellor, while Alexander's father was the royal secretary in London. But with the sudden death of Alexander in 1637, King Charles again asked the Privy Council to approve another request from 'the masters deacons and freemen of the maisones and hammermen and uppoun there information that the overseeing and judging of there traide did from many adges belong to the Lairds of Rosline to signe a grant to that purpose to the now laird Sir William Sinkler'.

By this time, Scotland was riven by religious conflict, and the King's ratification of the Sinclair hereditary claims fell into abeyance. The time of troubles had begun, and the warriors and the armourers would be hired to serve on either side. The efforts by King Charles and Archbishop Laud to introduce the English Liturgy with its Catholic overtones and ritual was a spark in a powderkeg. So extreme was the royal insistence that, when the new Liturgy appeared in April, 1637, a proclamation was published, requiring all the King's subjects on pain of rebellion to conform themselves to the fresh form of worship. And riot and revolution would be the consequences of that act.

The Edinburgh mob of women 'of the bangster Amazon kind'

went berserk in St Giles during the reading of the 'Popish' book. Stools were thrown at the heads of bishops, while ministers were almost beaten to death. In another riot, Bishop Sydserf of Galloway, 'who was suspected of having a crucifix in his cabinet and another under his dress', was pursued by 300 viragos to the Council House, where some noble Earls hurled him through the doorway and put up a barricade. Such outbreaks led to many of the members of the Privy Council petitioning King Charles to withdraw his Liturgy, otherwise he would need 40,000 soldiers to enforce its use.

There was no royal withdrawal. Given the 'long boggling and irresolution of the King', a Covenant based on the old anti-papal Negative Confession was drawn up. As the historian William Law Mathieson noted:

> Nobles and lairds carried the Covenant with them for signature wherever they went; whole congregations swore to maintain it with uplifted hands; and all alike, men, women, and mere children, were admitted to the oath. Many subscribed with tears, cursing themselves to all eternity if they should prove unfaithful to their vow; and some even insisted on signing with their blood. The churches of Covenanting ministers were crowded to overflowing; and some female enthusiasts, in order to attest their Protestantism by sitting at communion, are said to have kept their seats from Friday to Sunday.

Such was the frenzy of the time that some feared that a religious civil war was approaching, as had happened in Holland and France with the Huguenots. As Robert Baillie wrote: 'No man may speak anything in publick for the King's part, except he would have himself marked for a sacrifice to be killed one day. I think our people possessed with a bloody devil, far above anything that ever I could have imagined.'

The royal plan of action was a naval blockade to prevent trained soldiers and arms being sent over from Holland, followed by seaborne assaults from Ireland in the west and a landing in the Firth of Forth in the east. The old idea of Hadrian's Wall and the shorter-lived Antonine Wall was revived by Sir William Monson – a fortification stretching from Glasgow to Stirling, excluding the Highlands 'where it is not fit for civil men to live'. With few resources, however, and with many of his own Members of Parliament supporting the Covenanters, King Charles could hardly muster an army or a fleet.

The Convenanters were far more efficient, ordering the lairds of each parish in the shires to make a list of all good men, along with their mounts and arms and ammunition. Committees of war were established by every presbytery, and these were in touch with the lodges of the armourers, who were threatened with 'Excommunication Without Cooperation'. Officers were appointed from the local gentry, but only as colonels and captains and ensigns. The specialist ranks of lieutenant-colonels and sergeant-majors, lieutenants and sergeants, were reserved for those with combat experience, returning from long service in the Thirty Years' War overseas.

These mercenary veterans were often wayward about their employers. The famous Alexander Leslie, a field-marshal in the Swedish army, considered fighting for King Charles, who meant to send forces to aid his nephew, the Elector Palatine, in Germany. But when this mission fell through, Leslie agreed to join the Covenanters. Another turncoat had set out for England, but found his ship landing in Scotland, and so signed on for Scottish pay, quoting the dangerous military maxim: 'So we serve our master honnestlie, it is no matter what master we serve.' And when a ship carrying twenty recruits for the Covenanters was captured by the royal navy in 1639, all became volunteers in the King's army.

The first Bishops' War began with skirmishes in the North-east, where the most powerful royal supporter, the Marquis of Huntley, had his castles and estates. The Covenanters chose as their commander, James Graham, Earl of Montrose, who would himself pass over to become the best guerrilla general that the King's side ever had in the Civil War. Raiding parties seized Huntley's arms and ammunition en route to Inverness castle, and Montrose with Alexander Leslie occupied Aberdeen. Most of the ill-equipped royal castles fell with hardly a fight, including Edinburgh and Dumbarton and Tantallon by the Firth of Forth. The King now seemed to have little support north of the Borders.

For his commander, King Charles had appointed the loyal James, Marquis of Hamilton, who had served under the King of Sweden, but was more of a diplomat and a courtier than a conqueror. Of the 5,000 men which Hamilton was meant to ferry from Yarmouth to join Huntley, only 200 had ever held muskets before. These raw troops needed a month's training and proper weapons. After this sea-sick rabble had arrived off Leith, Hamilton was further embarrassed when his mother, a firm Covenanter, threatened to 'rydis on the heides of hir troupes boith day and nycht with hir pistollis and carbine', ready to shoot her son on landing ashore. To stall, while the King gathered his army at York, Hamilton negotiated terms with the Covenanters, before sailing away in futility.

The King managed to gather some 21,000 men and camped at Birks near the border stronghold of Berwick. Meanwhile, the forces of the Covenanters advanced to Duns Law, a few miles off. Their ranks were depleted by royalist Highlanders attacking in the north; Aberdeen changed hands four times over. Complaints were sent back to Edinburgh that the Scots opposing the king had 'no horsemen at all, ther is no provision of victuals and money'. Yet God would surely grant the Covenanters the victory, and so their morale remained high and enabled them to call the King's bluff by threatening to advance to the Tweed river and 'lay down our leagues within shott of cannon to the King's trenches'.

A subsequent truce and treaty returned to the King and his party all of the property and castles seized in Scotland. For his part, Charles agreed to summon a General Assembly and Parliament in Edinburgh; all ecclesiastical matters would be subject to Kirk assemblies, while civil matters would be the terrain of Parliament. He declared that he had only intended to maintain his position, not to invade Scotland or to inflict innovations in religion and laws upon its people. Yet nothing specific was written, which would guarantee the ending of the rule of the bishops and the remission of their estates.

The result was the second inconclusive Bishops' War. Both the Scottish Reformers and the King found it difficult to raise an army. Sent to the north in 1640, the Duke of Northumberland wrote back to his royal master: 'Our wants and disorders are so great that I cannot device how we should go on with our designs for this year.' The Short Parliament at Westminster would vote no funds for a Scottish campaign, for many of the members there agreed with the King's adversaries. The Covenanters had done a little better, finding enough money to pay their Low-Country trained commanders, who had returned home at a steep price. They managed to put together a force again at Duns, and, to their surprise, Newcastle surrendered, followed by the garrison of Edinburgh castle. Charles I capitulated, and the friendly English Parliament voted £300,000 to pay off Covenanting army expenses.

Yet now another religious war saved the Royalist cause. A Catholic rebellion broke out in Ireland, and the Scottish Presbyterians were moved to protect their brethren in Ulster, 'planted by their own nation', and under the threat of massacre. By 1642, 11,000 men had been sent across the Irish Sea; this manoeuvre prevented their return to participate in a Civil War over the Borders.

At the beginning of the conflict between the English Parliament and King Charles, the Royalists were in the ascendancy. So the Puritan leaders in the south negotiated a Solemn League and Covenant, which might bring a Scottish army of 21,000 men to oppose the Cavaliers – their own forces had the nicknames of their helmets and their armour, Roundheads and Ironsides. While the Scots wished to impose their Presbyterian zeal on the whole island, the Parliament at Westminster demurred. 'The English were for a civill League,' a Scot complained, 'we for a religious Covenant.' Reluctantly, the Puritans agreed that the Church of England should be reformed 'according to the word of God', whatever that might be.

Such a phrase would never satisfy the extreme ministers of the Kirk. Their excesses were summed up in the words of Samuel Rutherford: 'Better the King weep for the childish trifle of a prerogative than Popery be erected and three Kingdoms be destroyed.' The unrepentant Scottish lords such as the great Graham, the Marquis of Montrose, and the Setons, were imprisoned and their estates were confiscated. But as yet, the Sinclairs of Rosslyn kept out of the conflict. Only with his release did Montrose remember his allegiance to the Stewart Crown, and he was appointed the royal commander in the north of Scotland. For, as he declared, the subject 'is obliged to tolerate the vices of his prince as he does storms and tempests and other natural evils, which are compensated with better times succeeding.'

Expecting an easy victory, the Covenanting army crossed the Tweed in the January of 1644, only to discover disillusion. The troops failed to take Newcastle or York; as Robert Baillie complained, 'we are exceeding sadd, and ashamed that our armie, so much talked off, hes done as yet nothing at all.' And at the decisive battle of Marston Moor, the right wing of the Parliamentarian forces collapsed, with its commander Alexander Leslie, now the Earl of Leven, taking to flight. But the Scots pikemen held the centre, while Cromwell's Roundheads in their pudding-basin helmets and Leslie's Border horse routed the Cavaliers on the left flank, then wheeled and destroyed the royalist infantry in the centre. Yet the city of Newcastle still held out, and the Scottish forces were stymied there.

Behind their backs, Montrose was proving himself to be one of the greater guerrilla generals in history. Reaching Perth in disguise, he met 1,200 trained Catholic soldiers, sent over from Ireland; their ranks were swelled by the same number of Highlanders. A charge broke the 5,000 levies at Tippermuir, and half the enemy were left dead. Perth surrendered, and Montrose could arm and supply his ragged army. He advanced on Aberdeen, where the Covenanters were stupid enough to leave the walls and face another charge. 'Thair was littill slauchter in the fight, bot horribill was the slauchter in the flight.' The city was given over to plunder and rape and more murder. The Irish, according to the Royalist Patrick Gordon, killed men with as little worry as they killed a hen for their supper.

Doubling forward and back through the Highlands, Montrose won three more brilliant victories, while the cause of King Charles I was destroyed by Cromwell at the battle of Naseby. Robert Baillie asked 'why our forces there have received defeat upon defeat even these five times from a despicable and inconsiderable enemy, while the forces of this nation obtaine victory upon victory by weak meanes against considerable and strong armyes'. So ferocious were the remaining Irish that 6,000 Covenanters were said to have perished at Montrose's sixth victory of Kilsyth near Glasgow. But at his final defeat against superior forces at Philiphaugh, all the Irish infantry with their women and children were massacred 'with such savage and inhuman cruelty', Gordon wrote, 'as neither Turk nor Scythian was ever heard to have done the like'. Montrose himself would escape to Norway and France, but in terms of barbarity, the Presbyterian sword of the Lord and of Gideon was far bloodier than the occasional mercies which had been doled out by the Scottish nobleman.

After his own defeats, King Charles I began to negotiate with the Covenanters. His orders were to disband all the Royalist forces, while their commanders should go to France. He was assured by David Leslie, Lord Newark and Lord John Sinclair that the Scottish army would protect him. He surrendered himself to their guardianship, and as Lord Lothian wrote, that action 'filled us with amazement and made us like men that dreame'. Yet Charles would not agree to the establishment of a Presbyterian Kirk in England, and Cromwell threatened invasion if the King were not yielded into English custody. On a payment of £400,000 in two instalments, the Scots sold their monarch, and their army left the soil of their old enemy.

Negotiations continued with the King, who eventually agreed to a separate peace with the Scots, which would confirm the solemn League and Covenant in the English Parliament, although neither he nor his subjects would be forced to subscribe to its terms. In return, Scotland would send an army into England to restore the monarch's authority. Old Royalist lords supported this engagement. Lord Sinclair had been imprisoned for calling David Leslie a traitor and perjurer, who had offered the King safety within the army, and then had abandoned him. They fought a duel, but neither was hurt. Soon the fortress towns of Berwick and Carlisle were seized, and the army was to be swelled to 30,000 men in order to impose the Kirk's commands south of the Border. Half that force advanced towards Preston, where they were routed at nearby Langdale by Cromwell's cavalry, which took some 10,000 prisoners. Since Solway Moss, there had been no greater Scottish disaster.

Cromwell's advance to Edinburgh led to the collapse of the moderate Reformers, who were trying to restore the King in England in order to impose a version of Presbyterianism there. On his return to London, however, Cromwell decided, as Queen Elizabeth had dealt with Mary, Queen of Scots, to have King Charles I executed. His intrigues in Scotland had made him too great a danger for England. But certain Lords, including the Marquis of Montrose and Lord John Sinclair, had gone to Holland to counsel the heir to the throne, who would become Charles II; he should go to Ireland and mount an invasion of Scotland. The Covenanters also approached the presumptive King, who was promised support if he would accept their religious dictates. He would not, preferring Montrose's advice, that he would 'signify nothing . . . Trust the justice of your cause to God and better fortunes; and use all active and vigorous ways.'

Faced with another English or a new Royalist invasion, the Kirk was silly enough to purge the army of its best professional soldiers, who were called Malignants. They were replaced by amateur zealots, 'minister's sons, clerks, and such other sanctified creatures, who hardly ever saw or heard of any sword but that of the spirit'. Meanwhile, Montrose was sent to Orkney, where he assembled an army of some 1,200 men. Without waiting for reinforcements, he landed in Caithness and advanced to Carbisdale in Ross, where he was surprised by light cavalry and his forces were butchered. He was soon captured with two of the local Sinclairs; all were hanged and quartered. As Archibald Campbell, the Marquis of Argyll, noted, 'the tragic end' of the stoical Montrose showed that he knew 'how to goe out of this world, but nothing at all how to enter in ane other', for he would not pray on the scaffold.

With the defeat of Montrose, Charles II appeared to accept the demands of the Covenanters and set sail for Scotland, where he was welcomed with bonfires and dancing and joy. Before he could be crowned, Cromwell crossed the Tweed with some 16,000 men – David Leslie had the same number of troops to oppose him near Musselburgh on the coast not far from Edinburgh. Soon Leslie doubled his forces, while Cromwell's men were suffering from disease and shortage of supplies. In a dawn attack in a howling storm from their camp at Dunbar, the Roundheads rode down the Scots, still asleep with wet matchlock muskets and unable to find their weapons and horses. One brigade fought to the bitter end, until they were trampled down. The Scottish horse and foot were 'made by the Lord of Hosts as stubble to the swords' of the Ironsides. And as Cromwell rightly predicted, 'Surely it is probable the Kirk have done their do. I believe their King will set upon his own score now.'

The descent of the Sinclairs of Rosslyn was now on a slippery slope. As Father Hay noted, 'John Saintcler, commonly called the Prince, kept out the House of Roslin against General Monke, after the battle of Dunbar, and after the surrenderie of the castle was sent prisoner by Cromwell to Tinemouth, where he remained during the troubles.' In a later petition to King James II of England, the widower Lady Rosslyn was more explicit about the ruin of her once wealthy family:

> The elder brother of your petitioner's husband held out the Castle of Roslin by a commission from King Charles the Second, of ever blessed memorie, when the archtraytor, Oliver Cromwell, with the rebells under his command, came into Scotland, and defended the said Castle until Generall Monke battered down one intire side thereof, and took it by force; and after plundering and takeing away all that was in the castle, sent the said elder brother of your petitioner's husband to Tinemouth Castle, where he continued prisoner a long time, dureing which he contracted more debt, with the former encumbrances, than the estate was worth: That your petitioner's husband, soon after his late Majestie's happy restoration, comeing home from beyond sea, redeemed and made purchase of the Barony of Rosline from the creditors, and was att considerable charges, by making raparations in the Castle; but a great part of it, as well as the Chapell, continues still very mutch out of repair.*

Yet, there was worse to come. At the end of the day, loyalty may deserve a sort of penury, and lead to loss of faith. And the irony was that the Kirk, dedicated to the quest of the free spirit towards the divine, the original doctrine of Sanctus Clarus, had become a tyranny, seeking to impose its narrow codes of worship on all and sundry.

* See Illustrations.

15

Woe to the Jacobites

Weapons again decided the final Royalist efforts against the Round-heads. Trying to supply a new Scottish force at Stirling, David Leslie found his levies without arms or even rations. Cromwell sent his 4,000 troops from Edinburgh into Fife under the command of General Lambert; they destroyed an equal force at Inverkeithing, with 500 Highlanders fighting to the last man. Cromwell now moved north to capture Perth, leaving open the south-western way for a counter-attack over the Borders. There was little alternative for the remnants of the Scottish army. As one of its commanders, William, Duke of Hamilton, wrote, 'We must either starve, disband, or go with a handful of Men into England. This last seems to be the least ill, yet it appears very desperate to me.'

When King Charles II invaded Cumbria, he had only 13,000 men with a few cannon and not enough cavalry. As Hamilton commented, 'We have quit Scotland, being scarce able to maintain it; and yet we grasp at all, and nothing but all will satisfy us, or to lose all.' The one good argument was despair: 'For we must now either stoutly fight it, or die.' When Cromwell doubled back to confront the Scottish marauders at Worcester, he outnumbered them three times over. The battle was hard fought for all that; in Cromwell's words, 'as stiff a contest for four or five hours as I have ever seen'. King Charles showed courage, charging at the head of his guards before his escape; but Hamilton was mortally wounded and his regiment of horse shattered by artillery fire.

Such was what Cromwell called 'a crowning mercy'. This was the end of the attempt by the Kirk to impose its Presbyterian revolution on Britain. The ministers would no longer try to rule the King and the Lords and the Assemblies in the name of their particular godliness. And when in 1660, General Monck reversed direction and crossed the Tweed to march south on London and expel the Rump of the Long Parliament and restore King Charles II to the throne, the bishops would return to Scotland with royal authority behind them. Little had been achieved by this last religious war on the mainland, although it would still continue across the Irish Sea.

The Scottish aristocracy, which had been split over the Covenant, relapsed into a conservative reaction in favour of the King, who no longer allowed the episcopacy to interfere with the nobility over privileges and estates seized from the Old Catholic Church. The alliance between lairds and bishops was demonstrated in 1662, when the new Archbishop Sharp entered St Andrews to take up his ecclesiastical throne, riding with the Earls of Leven and Newark, most of the Fife gentry and 600 horsemen.

In the south-western Borders, there was still support for the religious rebels, many of whom had fled to Ulster. This culminated in the Pentland Rising of 1666, when some 3,000 Covenanters, starving and half-drowned after many days of torrential rain, advanced within 3 miles of Edinburgh and Rosslyn. The survivors of an assault by the Lothian militia were tortured or hanged or transported to Barbados to serve as slaves. Such was the bitter end of this revolt in search of the free spirit, inquiring after the divine, which concluded in failed tyranny and ignominy.

The three sea wars of England and Holland after the Restoration were unpopular, as they destroyed the essential Baltic trade of the Firth of Forth. James, Lord Ogilvie, was ordered with a strong military force into Fife; all discontent was suppressed. As for the Sinclairs of Dysart and Roslin with their coal interests, their fortunes remained in decline. The last expedition of the Sinclairs to the Baltic had hardly been a success. In the Kalmar War of 1612, Denmark and Norway had fought Sweden, which had recruited troops in Scotland. A detachment of 400 men landed at Romsdalfjord in Norway near the ancient lands of the Møre ancestors of the Sinclairs and marched east towards Sweden.

The mercenaries lived off the land by looting, but in a mountain pass at Kringen they were ambushed by the local farmers. Warned by a horn blown by a village girl, Prillarguri, the Norwegians began a rockslide and charged and massacred the Scottish contingent, including one of its captains, George Sinclair. A ballad of the disaster is still sung in the schools of Norway, a monument to Jorgen Sinkler marks the bloody spot and the place is called Sinclair's Pass, or rather, impasse.

Although King Charles II had cleverly kept a sort of peace in Scotland, his brother James VII and II of England was heavy-handed and a devout Catholic, married to Mary of Modena, whom the remaining Covenanters thought to be a bastard daughter of the Pope. He was prepared to do little or nothing for the old supporters of the Stewart line. Of the other sons of Sir William Sinclair, who died in 1650, one expired in exile in France; another was killed in a siege; three more died young, while one was 'possessed by a spirit'. Of the two daughters, one married Hume, the laird of Foord, while the two 'bastard childering' ended one as the wife of the Tutor of Annandale, the other as a shopkeeper in Edinburgh.

The widow Lady Rosslyn had finally to travel to London at great expense to beg the mercy of the Catholic King and Queen. Although they turned down her petition for a pension or the privilege of coining farthings in America in order to educate her many children, her son James did become a Page of Honour at Court and a Cornet in the Queen's Guards. He would die at the Battle of the Boyne, fighting for King James. His father, James Sinclair, was 'a very civill and discreat man', according to Father Hay. Educated largely in France, he certainly had kept out of trouble during the Reformation. 'He was mutch taken up with building, and addicted to the Priests; those two inclinations spoiled his fortune. He died in a good adge, and with the reputation of ane honest man; yet . . . he was too easie.'

The ingratitude of the Stewart Kings to their most loyal subjects was again proven. As King Richard III in Shakespeare's play, they were often not in the giving mood today. Lady Rosslyn's complaint about 300 years of unrewarded faithful service fell on ears of stone:

That the Family of Roslin continued in a very splendid and opulent condition, as the petitioner doubts not but your Majesty well knows, for many adges, untill after the death of King James the Fifth, that the then Laird of Roslin takeing part, according to his duty, with Marie Queen Dowager of Scotland, against the Lords and others who engadged themselves in a rebellion for carrieing on a reformation, as they called it, he, with other loyall persons, were brought to a very low condition.

Although the ancestral lands had been forfeited for fighting for Mary, Queen of Scots, they had been restored by King James VI and I of England. Yet so great were the laird's debts that he had been forced to sell all his property except the Barony of Roslin, 'free of all debts, which was but a small part of the great estate formerly enjoyed by that family'. Once again beggared after the Battle of Dunbar and the imprisonment of the new laird, the Barony tottered on the edge of bankruptcy. And yet, King James VII and II would not lift a royal seal to help a fellow Catholic Scottish family, which would continue to shed blood for the Jacobite cause.

Indeed, the so-called Glorious Revolution of 1688 led to the final pillage of Rosslyn castle and chapel by the mob from Edinburgh. Father Hay chiefly mourned the sack of the famous library with its collection of medieval Catholic missals, many of them collected in the 16th century after they 'had been taken by the rabble out of our monasterys in the time of the reformation'. Hay himself lost 'several books of note, and amongst others, the original manuscript of Adam Abel', who was a Grey Friar from Jedburgh Monastery, the composer of the *Rota Temporum*, a history of Scotland from early to Tudor times. After this final attack, the chapel was left to nature with only its solid stone roof and sealed vaults protecting the mysteries within. 'But as nothing is done to keep it together,' Dorothy Wordsworth was to note on a visit, 'it must, in the end, fall.'

Although Prince William of Orange took over England in a bloodless invasion because of the flight of James II, fearing to be beheaded as his father had been, this Protestant coup led to civil wars in Scotland and Ireland. As King Charles II had said of his brother, 'I am much afraid that when he comes to wear the crown, he will be obliged to travel again.' If only James had not been such a stubborn Catholic, as were the Sinclairs of Rosslyn, then the Dutch interloper would not have lasted. 'If King James would but give the country some satisfaction about religion,' wrote Thomas Danby, later Earl of Leeds, 'which he might easily do, it would be very hard to make head against him.'

As it was, a loyal and romantic streak seemed to stir some Scottish lairds towards another Stewart restoration. John Graham of Claverhouse, Viscount Dundee, was reputed to have become the Grand Prior of the revived Knights Templars, wearing its insignia under his black armour. He declared to the Duke of Gordon, who was holding Edinburgh castle in the name of King James, that he was going 'wherever the spirit of Montrose shall lead me'. With a small detachment of the old Scottish Border horse and some faithful Highlanders, he surprised Orange's army in the narrow pass of Killiecrankie outside Blair Castle. Charging down the slope, Dundee routed the enemy, but was shot and killed by a stray bullet. The victorious Jacobites, however, were slaughtered in their turn outside the cathedral of Dunkeld by a regiment of Presbyterian Cameronians, whose commander also fell. And that resistance was that, for the time being, in Scotland.

In Ireland, the decisive battle at the Boyne was more international and more of a religious war, which has persisted to this day. For the first time, the Masonic lodges were influential among the corps of officers on either side: their conflict would continue for 300 years. William of Orange's army was a European stew of Scots from Ulster, English and Dutchmen, French Huguenots and Danes, Swedes and Prussians. They confronted a Catholic army of Irish and Frenchmen. An assault across the river led to another Protestant ascendancy over the unhappy green island, so close to the Old Faith.

In proof of Masonic influence, the wall chart of the Boyne Society still survives in the Ulster Museum in Belfast. This fledgling Lodge derived from the Ancient Scottish Rite, and it showed off Gnostic and Templar and medieval guild symbols.* These signs would serve as the teaching aids for members of the Orange and Arch Purple and Black

* See Illusrations.

Orders, which would dominate politics in Ulster in the 19th and 20th centuries. The Boyne Society became the 1st Loyal Orange Boyne Society, Armagh, dedicated to the Union with Great Britain and the British monarchy.

In a sense, the Jacobite movement was nostalgic and patriarchal, with the Highland clans and chiefs holding out against the material values of the Protestant industrial revolution in the Lowlands. Isolated Catholic families, such as the Setons and the Sinclairs in Fife and Lothian, were rejected to the margins. They longed for past glories, even in pursuit of lost causes. To be a Jacobite near Glasgow or Edinburgh was a probable path to ruin.

When the economic disaster of the Darien Scheme was followed by the Union with England in 1707, an abortive invasion from France the following year was put under the guidance of the young Stewart heir, who came to be known as the Old Pretender. Storms and the English fleet soon chased him back from Aberdeen to Dunkirk. But with the death of Queen Anne of England and the accession of the Hanoverian King George I, all links between the Crown and Scotland appeared to be severed, in spite of their common Parliament. And so the Jacobite rebellion of 1715 was hatched.

A key figure and a scathing chronicler was John, Master of Sinclair, the eldest son and heir of Henry, Lord Sinclair of Herdmanston, the only peer to protest publicly against the accession of William of Orange to the throne. John the Master had served under the Duke of Marlborough in the Low Countries, where he had shot and killed two members of the Schaw family, once the patrons and supporters of the Lords of Rosslyn. He escaped trial and served in Prussia, before returning to the family seat of Dysart in Fife. He was never to inherit the Baroncy, because of his actions in the Jacobite rebellion.

A first strike was the botched attempt to seize Edinburgh castle and its armaments. The Master of Sinclair put down the failure to the delay of the plotters in drinking and 'powdering their hair'. He knew that his commander, John, the Earl of Mar, and his Highlanders lacked the weapons, which the Sinclair family had long supplied to the Stewart cause throughout their mastery of the crafts and guilds and lodges of hammermen and smiths. 'While every one was building castles in the air,' Sinclair declared, 'and making themselves great men, most of our arms were good for nothing; there was no method fallen on, nor was the least care taken to repair those old rusty broken pieces, which, it seems, were to be carried about more for ornament than use, though gunsmiths were not wanting.'

In his traditional role, the Master of Sinclair decided to seize with 80 horsemen a merchant ship carrying a cargo of arms, which was anchored off Burntisland. His forces only captured some 350 firearms and 4 barrels of gunpowder, but these supplies did galvanize Mar and his troops into taking over most of Scotland above Glasgow and Edinburgh. As Sinclair noted, munitions remained a problem, although Mar could have sent to Holland for more gunpowder, while powderhorns and flints to strike a spark were available. The Romanies were still travelling behind the troops: 'Ram's horns were there in plenty and gipsies to make them into powder flasks,' while flints could be shaped from those picked from the seashore.

Although a battalion of Highlanders crossed the Firth of Forth, briefly taking the port of Leith and meeting supporters on the Borders, Sinclair derided these reinforcements of Cavaliers as 'an army of fox-hunters armed with light dress-swords'. They passed through Penrith and Kendal and Lancaster, only opposed by the Westmoreland militia, carrying pitchforks. They reached Preston, where they were besieged by professional royal dragoons. They surrendered with their arms, 200 nobles and gentlemen with 1,400 footsoldiers, mainly from the Highlands. This penultimate Border campaign ended in humiliation. As the Scot Robert Campbell noted, 'None but fools would have stayed to be attacked in that position, and none but knaves would have acted when there as they did.'

On the day of the capitulation, a pitched battle was fought at Sheriffmuir near Stirling and Perth. The Earl of Mar's motley forces had swelled to 12,000 men, four times the size of those of the Duke of Argyll. As Campbell noted of their array:

> There were country gentlemen from Angus and Aberdeenshire, riding on stout horses, with sword and pistol, each dressed in his best laced attire, and each attended by serving-men, also armed, and also on horseback. Then there were Highland gentlemen in the more

picturesque garb of their country, with obeisant retinues of clansmen on foot. The mass of the army was composed of Lowland peasants, with arms slung over their plain gray clothes, and of mountaineers, nearly naked, or at least wearing little more than one shirt-like garment. Two squadrons of cavalry, which Huntly had brought with him, excited, under the name of light-horse, the derision of friends and foes; being composed of stout bulky Highlandmen, mounted on little horses, each with his petit blue bonnet on his head, a long rusty musket slung athwart his back, and not one possessed of boots or pistols, those articles so requisite to the idea of a trooper.

Across the bleak moor of low hills, the troops confronted each other. Argyll had drawn up his dragoons and infantry in a compact order, where they had slept all night. The forces of the Earl of Mar were, as the Master of Sinclair wrote, 'never so constant in any thing as our being disorderly'. Had they been attacked, they would have been scattered, for not 'since the invention of powder were so many troops packed in one small place. It cannot properly be said we had a front or rear any more than has a barrel of herrings.' No assault came until the Sunday morning, when the Highlanders on Mar's left flank fired their guns and charged the enemy, who answered with artillery. 'No sooner that begun, the Highlandmen threw themselves flat on their bellies; and when it slackened, they started to their feet. Most throw away their fuzils, and drawing their swords, pierced them every where with an incredible vigour and rapidity.'

Taken in the flank by Argyll's dragoons, the ferocious High-landers were driven back into the river Allan, where some were drowned. But the Earl of Mar's right wing outflanked Argyll's left, and another Highland charge overwhelmed the opposing cavalry and infantry, which took to flight in the direction of Perth. Neither commander took advantage of their lopsided triumph. They re-formed their forces, stared at one another for a while; then they retired. The Master of Sinclair's own squadron of horse was never ordered to fight or pursue. As the Jacobite lament put the matter, some said that we won, and some said that they won, and some said that none won:

There's but ae thing, I'm sure,
That, at Shirramuir,
A battle there was, that I saw, man.
And we ran, and they ran,
And they ran, and we ran,
And we ran, and they ran awa, man.

That was the end of Jacobite hopes in this rebellion. For the High-landers returned to their mountains, and the young Old Pretender had not yet sailed to Scotland. He eventually reached Dundee and Perth and took up residence in the old palace at Scone, where he announced his forthcoming coronation. Before that event, the advance of Argyll's army forced him to retreat to France again after a stay of less than two months in his homeland. 'I took the party to repass the seas,' he advised his supporters, 'that by that I might leave such as cannot make their mistake . . . in full liberty to take the properest measures for avoiding at least utter ruin.'

He was followed by the Master of Sinclair, who fled to his clan stronghold in Orkney, and then to the Jacobite haven of France. George Seton, the Earl of Wintoun, was accused of being an armourer as well as a rebel, for he had once worked as a bellow-blower and a smith's helper. Although he was condemned to death at Tyburn, he managed to escape from the Tower of London and proceed to Rome and safety. Yet to become a refugee was no refuge from royal ingratitude. As the Master of Sinclair wrote in his *Memoirs* of the long Sinclair attachment to the Scottish Crown, the result was that the family was left:

> . . . Without anie other thanks, having brought upon us considerable losses, and among others that of our all in Cromwell's time; and left in that condition, without the least relief, except what we found in our own virtue. My father was the only man of the Scots nation who had courage enough to protest in parliament against King William's title to the throne, which was lost, God knows how; and this at a time when the losses in the cause of the royall familie, and their usual gratitude, had scarce left him bread to maintain a numerous familie of eleven children, who had soon after sprung up to him, in spite of all which he had honourably persisted in his principle. I say, these things considered,

and after being treated as I was, and in that unluckie state, when objects appear to men in their true light, as at the hour of death, could I be blamed for making some bitter reflections to myself, and laughing at the extravagance and unaccountable humour of men, and the singu-laretie of my own case (an exile for the case of the Stewart family), when I ought to have known that the greatest crime I or my familie could have committed, was persevering, to my own destruction, in serving the royal familie faithfully though obstinately, after so great a share of depression, and after they had been pleased to doom me and my familie to starve?

Although the Hanoverian governments passed Disarming Acts, the Highlanders did not surrender their sturdy swords or their greased long guns. While General Wade tried to pacify the mountain people with the building of military roads and Forts Augustus and William, they were waiting for another last adventure for the Stewart cause. This would nearly come about in 1744, with a planned invasion by the Young Pretender, Prince Charles Edward Stewart, along with a French fleet and the seasoned Marshal Maurice de Saxe and his regiments. Once again, as with the Spanish Armada and the troops of the Duke of Parma, a Channel tempest wrecked the troop transports in Dunkirk, and that attempt was lost in the deluge.

The following year, the Young Pretender was backed secretly by the French in a minor incursion, although it was provided with proper armaments. In a brilliant comparison, the historian of the Jacobite Risings, Bruce Lenman, wrote: 'If Montrose was baroque, Charles was rococo, a style which contrasts with the baroque from which it evolved by its lightness and surface quality. It is a style which in porcelain charms and surprises, and in all media it relies at its best on a subtle blend of the audacious, the skilful and the irresponsible.'

On a French privateer, *du Teillay*, and guarded by the 64-gun battleship, *L'Elisabeth*, both loaded with munitions from the Ministry of Marine, the Young Pretender set sail for the Outer Hebrides. He was to be supported by a Franco-Swedish regiment, but it would not arrive in time for the final battle. The Macdonald chiefs were contacted and the arms unloaded in western Scotland, where the

Jacobite standard was raised at Glenfinnan. There, Prince Charles Edward was joined by Cameron of Lochiel with 700 men. This Highland chief already had extensive contacts with New York and North America, where a later rebellion against the Hanoverians would erupt. In his own case, the exiled Lochiel would be given command of a French regiment that would see service in time across the Atlantic.

As with Mussolini's later march on Rome, Prince Charles Edward conquered Scotland north of the Borders by a simple ramble to Edinburgh. The few English troops in the way abandoned the northlands and shipped to Dunbar for a stand there. The two little armies of 2,500 men on each side confronted each other at Prestonpans, where the Highlanders charged along a tramway leading from the coal pits to the harbour, and then massacred their enemies, before the English artillery could be brought to bear. Yet most of the Scots lairds remained sitting on the fence. Few, except those who were broken by the Reformation, joined the Jacobite cause. As the Earl of Kilmarnock said, he did not care a farthing for the two Kings and their rights, 'but I was starving, and, by God, if Mahommed had set up his standard in the Highlands, I had been a good Musselman for bread.'

The south-western Borders remained staunchly Presbyterian, and Prince Charles Edward could only raise 5,500 men for the daring last Scottish dash over the Borders into England. Against all advice, the Prince had expected volunteers to flock to his colours. Yet only in Manchester did a Catholic ex-officer in the French army, Francis Townley, raise a few hundred recruits for a brigade. The Prince, however, decided to turn back at Derby and not advance on London, for three large armies were already converging on him. Although his troops fought a good rearguard skirmish near Penrith and later won an action at Selkirk, the Prince's cause was doomed and awaiting an apocalypse on Culloden moor.

After the Battle of the Boyne in 1689, the Irish resistance fighters called the Wild Geese had fled to fight for France, while tens of thousands more left for America. The massacres committed by the Protector Cromwell at Drogheda and William of Orange's forces at Limerick were never forgotten; but equally, the atrocious murders in Ulster of 12,000 immigrant Scots Protestants at the beginning of the Irish rebellion of 1641 were consigned to oblivion, although not by their descendants. Fighting for the French, the Irish Brigade at the Battle of Fontenoy in 1745 defeated the Duke of Cumberland and the English with a ferocious charge, shouting, 'Remember Limerick!'.

'Butcher' Cumberland was then recalled to Scotland to put an end to the pretensions of the Young Pretender. He intended revenge against the Scottish rebels. 'There is good reason to believe they will soon be dispersed or destroyed,' he wrote back to Lord Granville before the conflict in a letter still preserved in its green dispatch case in the Royal Archives at Windsor, 'and that a little case of *examples* will restore this Country to a perfect state of tranquillity.'

The Duke of Cumberland believed in terror tactics and the scorched-earth policy of old Border wars. A marauding detachment sent to Glenesk was ordered 'to destroy all them . . . in arms and to burn the habitations of all those who have left them and are with the rebels.' The English forces must 'pursue and hunt out these vermin amongst their lurking holes'. No quarter should be shown, and if anyone was captured, he should be subject to military execution. A final battle was to be the prelude for the ethnic cleansing of the Highland clans.

With an army well-supplied from a fleet at sea, Cumberland drew up his regiments with artillery positioned between the front lines, and his dragoons on the left and right wings. He told his men to meet the inevitable Highland charge with broadsword and target. 'Depend my lads on your bayonets.' The shivering and starving and badly-equipped twin lines of the Jacobites were soon decimated by barrages from the English cannon and muskets. Even so, they charged the enemy ranks time and again, before breaking and running with the royal cavalry hacking them down in flight. As one fusilier stated, 'I never saw a field thicker of dead.' And curiously enough, although none of the Sinclairs were held to be there, their battle standard was fallen and captured on that sad day. And the Young Pretender escaped to little purpose.

Retaliation is often given the name of pacification. 'Butcher' Cumberland resolved to quell the Highlands for ever. Lord Loudon was ordered to proceed from Skye to Fort Augustus, with instructions to 'drive the cattle, burn the ploughs and destroy what you can belonging to all such as are or have been in the rebellion, and burning the Houses of the Chiefs'. Many other commanders were told to sweep the country with fire and sword. The troops behaved worse than the old Border reivers, adding rape and arson to their plunder of cattle and sheep, horses and goats. Unless all weapons were surrendered, death or transportation were the consequences. Even the wearing of Highland dress, the tartan and the kilt, were prohibited, as they were the marks of a Jacobite uniform. An English Lord, Henry Pelham, referred to this enforcing Act of Parliament of 1747 as 'one for disarming and undressing those savages'.

Another proposal that met the serious consideration of the Duke of Cumberland was the shipping of whole clans to the American colonies, because 'I believe with great reason, that while they remain in this island their rebellion and thievish nature is not to be kept under without an army always within reach of them.' Cumberland even wrote about his fears to his fellow Duke of Newcastle: 'All the good we have done is a little blood-letting, which has only weakened the madness, not cured it . . . This vile spot may still be the ruin of this island and our family.'

His fears were made groundless by changes on the ground. The old clan system would be destroyed by forts and roads and sheep, and its chieftains bought by the chance to turn clan land into personal property. The American Revolution would transplant ancient wrongs and grudges into a battle for liberty, reflected in the struggle between the independent mountain men – mainly Scots and Irish in ancestry – and the tidewater plantation owners, mainly loyal to the British Crown.

Mass immigration to America and France was already under way from Scotland and Ireland. Through the exiled Freemasons and their Lodges, nurtured for so long by the Sinclairs of Rosslyn, two revolutionary movements would help to organize their respective nations, because of the military structure of these secret societies. This would serve as yet another paradox of history. The free spirit of the Celtic Scots and Irish was being sent abroad to conspire against Crown and church and establishment. And in the forking of the paths, that urge for freedom would aid in the creation of the world's greatest democracy, yet also the terror of the French revolution. So often has the search for liberty, as in the case of the Kirk, been the prelude to tyranny.

16

The Radical Lodges

History may repeat itself in tragedy, but also in influences and revolutions. The apparent destruction of the Knights Templars, outside their continuance through the Setons and the St Clairs of Rosslyn, had led to the passing of many of their practices into the ancient Scottish Rite of the emerging Masonic Lodges. The revival of the Military Order by the tutor of the Young Pretender could not help the Prince's rebellion in Scotland, as once the original Templars had aided Robert the Bruce at Bannockburn. Yet their enduring ideals and their brilliant organization would infuse American and European Freemasonry, particularly those Lodges which served in the armed forces or were set up as secret societies against the state. After the Stewart defeat in 1715 in Scotland, the flight to France of the Jacobites had resulted in a revival of the Templars. A mystic and tormented figure played the role of another St John the Baptist in this resurrection. Andrew Michael, the Chevalier de Ramsay, had been born in Ayr in 1686 and had studied at Edinburgh, Leyden and Oxford. Elected as a Fellow of the Royal Society, he nonetheless wrote: 'All my ambition is, that I should be forgotten.'

This fate was not to be. As a young man, he had campaigned in Flanders with the Duke of Marlborough's victorious armies against the French forces and their supporting Jacobite contingents. Attracted to the spiritual teachings of Archbishop François de Fénelon of Cambrai, Ramsay changed sides and became Fénelon's pupil until his master died. The seminary had become a hospital for the war-wounded and the starving. Charity and chivalry were foremost in Fénelon's teaching. There Ramsay had met the Old Pretender, who chose him as the tutor to his son, Prince Charles Edward Stewart, and his younger brother Henry, afterwards to be appointed by the Pope as the Cardinal of York. Ramsay revived the Military Order of the Scottish Knights Templars and became Grand Master of its Grand Lodge in Paris. In 1736, he made a speech to a sympathetic group of Catholic aristocrats:

> At the time of the crusades in Palestine many princes, lords and citizens associated themselves, and vowed to restore the Temple of the Christians in the Holy Land. They agreed upon several ancient signs and symbolic words drawn from the mysteries of the faith in order to recognize each other in bringing back the architecture of the Temple to its first institution.
>
> The fatal religious discords which embarrassed and tore Europe in the 16th century caused our order to degenerate from the nobility of its origin. Many of the rites and usage that were contrary to the prejudices of our times were changed, disguised, suppressed. Thus it was that many of our brothers forgot, like the ancient Jews, the spirit of our laws and only retained the letter and the shell. The beginnings of a remedy have already been made. It is only necessary to continue until at last, everything be brought back to the original institution.

Recollecting the ancient wisdom of the Military Orders brought from Scotland to France, perhaps through the Royal Order instituted by Robert the Bruce, Ramsay went on to allude enigmatically to a high degree or caste of knightly priests and princes in a revived Order of Melchizedek, the followers of the example of the sacred King of Israel:

> The word Freemason must therefore not be taken in a literal, gross or material sense, as if our founders had been simple workers in stone, or merely curious geniuses who wished to perform the arts. They were not only skilful architects, desirous of consecrating their talents and goods to the construction of material temples; but also religious and warrior princes who designed to enlighten, edify, and protect the living Temples of the Most High.

Pope Clement XII soon forbade Catholics from becoming Freemasons under threat of excommunication, out of the usual fear that, as the Knights Templars, they might form a state within the state. Two years before the rebellion of the Young Pretender, the Chevalier de Ramsay died – fortunately for him, since many of the Jacobites met their end in that failed adventure. His legacy, however, was left to Karl Gotthelf, Baron von Hundt, who revived in Germany the Ancient Order of the Temple, after the defeat at Culloden and the harrying of the Highlands had extinguished all Stewart hopes.

Von Hundt's diary stated that in 1742 he was initiated into the Templar Order in Paris in the presence of Lord Kilmarnock – soon to be executed by the English for treason – and that he later met the Young Pretender. Von Hundt was a Protestant as well as a Mason; nevertheless, he revived this old Order, signing on twelve German princes, led by the Duke of Brunswick, to join the resurrected body. This creation was opposed by a rival Swedish Order, which also held to the ancient Scottish Rite, as received by King Gustav III of Sweden.

Whatever the truth of the schism, the Jacobite connection was maintained in northern Europe. The early work of Nicolas de Bonneville during the French Revolution testified to the importance of the ancient Scottish Rite. For him, 'the secret of the Freemasons is explained by the history of the Knights Templars.' He told of strange ceremonies, including the exchange of blood by sword-point for the initiate, then being used in Lodges of the revived Swedish Rite. The novice Mason received a white apron and black gloves, the colours of the Cistercian monks and the Templars. The three pillars of Masonry were Jachin, Boaz and Mac-Benac, making up the initials JBM or Jacq. Burg. Molay, the name of the martyred last Grand Master of the Order. Mac-Benac was also the pseudonym of Aumont, the Templar leader of those knights, who had fled to Scotland.

De Bonneville also recognized that the Templars, as did the Muslims, worshipped a single God or Divine Creator and Intelligence. This led to their wrongful condemnation for denying the divinity of Jesus and spitting on the Cross. He even spoke of a secret tradition among the Templars, that the great Saladin, before his conquest of Jerusalem, had been received into the Order by the knight Hugo of Tiberias. The cry of 'Yah-Allah' was a recognition of an affinity with

Islam, while the worship of the head may have sprung from ancient Gnostic Orphite rites involving the dragon serpents, which guarded the Greek paradise, the Garden of Hesperides. Above all, the Masonic ceremony of venerating the image of a skeleton in a coffin was taken from the Templars, the skull being separate and representing the beheaded St John the Baptist.

For the Chevalier de Ramsay, the illumination of the mind towards universal truth was important for the revived Templars. 'All the Grand Masters in Germany, England, Italy, and elsewhere exhort all the learned men and all the artisans of the Fraternity to unite to furnish the materials for a Universal Dictionary of all the liberal arts and useful sciences, excepting only theology and politics.' His two exceptions were ignored by the authors of the *Encyclopédie*, an inspiration of the French Revolution. Freemasons always specified the organization of their lodges and the *Encyclopédie* as the opposition to the Bourbon dynasty. At a later Congress of the Grand Orient, the Freemason Bonnet declared:

> Liberty, Equality, Fraternity. The Revolutionary seed quickly germinated among this elite of illustrious Freemasons, D'Alembert, Diderot, Helvetius, d'Holbach, Voltaire, Condorcet completed the evolution of minds and prepared the new era. And when the Bastille fell, Freemasonry had the supreme honour of giving to humanity the charter (the Declaration of the Rights of Man), which it had elaborated with devotion.

Bonnet went on to claim that, at the beginning of the French Revolution, the Constituent Assembly had 300 Masonic members, and that the Declaration of the Rights of Man was the work of the hero of the American Revolution, the Marquis de Lafayette, who presented the key of the Bastille to the American President George Washington. Actually, the Rights of Man was mainly derived from the work of Tom Paine, but also from another major aristocratic contributor to the *Encyclopédie*, the Marquis de Condorcet. He was a utopian and a pioneer in moral science with views on history improving the lot of society through successive changes.

After the Revolution, Condorcet did not succeed. Unlike the Comte de Mirabeau and the Marquis de Lafayette, he joined the triumphant Jacobins too late. He worked with Paine, and yet his *Plan for a Constitution* was gutted, and when he protested, he was condemned. In hiding, he wrote a historical sketch on the progress of the human spirit. He affirmed the laws of nature and morality. He still believed in social betterment, during even what would be called the 'Terror'. 'How welcome to the philosopher is this picture of humanity, freed from all its chains, released from the domination of chance and from that of the enemies of its progress, advancing with a firm and sure step in the path of truth, virtue and happiness.'

The Comte de Mirabeau was a key player in the Constituent Assembly. In his papers, he admitted to being a Freemason, influenced by the mysterious Rosicrucians and the Bavarian Illuminati, whom he praised in his *History of the Prussian Monarchy*. He said that the Illuminati were modelled on the Jesuits in their secrecy and double logic, while opposing faith in God for faith in Reason. They wished to abolish royalty and serfdom and unjust taxation and superstition, while bringing in liberty of the press and universal toleration for all religions. Two later radical thinkers, Louis Blanc and George Sand, attested to the success of the European conspiracy of the mystic Illuminati from Germany, and particularly to its brilliant organization.

An inspired intriguer, Adam Weishaupt, was its founder. He drew an ancient diagram of the secret society organized in cells. A hierarchical system led upwards to a Grand Master, whose will was supreme. Yet no lieutenant or cell communicated with each other.* As a commentator on Weishaupt wrote:

> He knew how to take from every association, past and present, the portions he required and to weld them all into a working system of terrible efficiency – the disintegrating doctrines of the Gnostics and Manicheans, of the modern philosophers and Encyclopaedists, the methods of the Ismailis and the Assassins, the discipline of the Jesuits and Templars, the organization and secrecy of the Freemasons, the philosophy of Machiavelli, the mystery of the Rosicrucians – he knew, moreover, how to enlist the right elements in all existing associations as well as isolated individuals and turn them to his purpose.

* See Illustrations.

So strong was the influence of the Illuminati that the genii of German literature, Goethe and Lessing, became members of the society. Percy Bysshe Shelley even wrote a bad novel, *St Irvyne or the Rosicrucian*, about a Protestant brotherhood of the Rosy Cross opposing the Habsburg Emperors: Elizabeth Barrett Browning called it 'boarding-school idiocy'. Shelley also presumed that the Assassins and their vision of paradise had inspired the Illuminati, while Mary Shelley set the home of Count Victor Frankenstein in Ingoldstadt, the spiritual centre of the cult. The disruption caused by his man-made monster, meant to be beautiful, was a commentary on the Illuminati strategy of destroying the social and political and religious institutions, which shackled the individual in the chains that Rousseau in his *Social Contract* wanted to cast off.

By 1789, there were 2,000 Lodges in France affiliated to the Grand Orient with some 100,000 members. Most of the leading radicals in the Constituent Assembly were informed by Illuminati beliefs in a social revolution. These included the Duc d'Orléans, the Marquesses de Condorcet and de Lafayette, the Comte de Mirabeau, and also their later opponents, Danton and Desmoulins, Marat and Robespierre himself. They used the techniques of conspiracy, cells and Lodges and summary judgement, to overthrow the government and rule the people with a series of revolutionary groups. These plotters practised an internecine struggle against each other in order to acquire the levers of power for their hidden purposes. That this blood-letting by the Jacobins ended in a regime of fear was merely another demonstration of the maxim: *After the Revolution, who shall win the Revolution?*.

The American Revolution was also inspired by the ancient Scottish Rite. While the Grand Lodge of England, soon headed by Hanoverian dukes such as 'Butcher' Cumberland, only offered limited degrees, the Grand Lodge of Ireland gave out the higher chivalric degrees of Jacobite Freemasonry. Such rituals as the Royal Arch or Royal Ark Mariner degrees with their Templar connotations were particularly attractive to the uniformed officers and men of the colonial armies. In 1761, the Grand Lodge of France appointed Stephen Morin as the Grand Inspector of the New World, with the power of authenticating lodges according to the ancient Scottish Rite. The St Andrew's Lodge of Boston, Massachusetts, was instituted by the Grand Lodge of Scotland, and it was the first to institute in 1769 a new ranking – the Knights Templars degree, founded by the Jacobite Old Stirling Lodge during the 1745 rebellion. The Grand Master of the Boston brethren, Joseph Warren, was appointed by Scotland to be the Grand Master of all of North America; other members of the Lodge were Paul Revere and John Hancock, so famous in the history of the revolution to come.

One year later, British troops put down a riot in the 'Boston Massacre'. After another three years, local resistance against British taxes resulted in the 'Tea Party', when a mob disguised as Mowhawk Indians boarded a merchantman and threw hundreds of chests of tea into the cold kettle of the harbour. At least thirty present and future members of the St Andrew's Lodge were responsible for stirring the pot on that epic day of resistance.

When war broke out with England, John Hancock convened the Second Continental Congress, which authorized the raising of an army under the leadership of the prominent Freemason from the old colonial British Army, General George Washington. His officer corps was organized from the Catholic and Protestant and Continental Lodges. One of his major-generals, Arthur St Clair, who was descended from the Lords of Rosslyn, had fought with Wolfe at Quebec, but he now joined the Continental Army. Sent to command the far-flung forts in the wilderness at Ticonderoga against a counter-attack from Canada, St Clair, with his 2,000 men and corps of artillery, conducted a brilliant night escape from a trap, sprung by the overwhelming British forces under General Burgoyne. St Clair knew that such a retreat before a superior foe was 'perhaps the most delicate and dangerous undertaking in the whole circle of military operations, and that it never will be effected without prudence, fortitude and secrecy.' In spite of a final flurry, St Clair managed the difficult job. There would not be another Culloden here, with all that rout and slaughter.

Following the Americans, Burgoyne now tripped into his own snare; surrounded at Saratoga, he had to surrender with all his men. As the triumphant American commander Horatio Gates declared: 'If Old England is not by this lesson taught humility, then she is an obstinate old slut, bent upon her ruin.' General Washington, however, was losing to better British generals with their trained troops and superior naval forces. He was forced to retire from New York and Philadelphia to winter with his ill-supplied Continental Army at Valley Forge. The only thing which kept his troops from desertion and despair was the discipline and morale of the professional officers under his command, usually Freemasons in their brotherhood and beliefs. One of them was Arthur St Clair, who later became the President of the last Continental Congress and Governor of the North-western Territories for fourteen years, but was beggared, as usual, by faithfully serving the state.

In political terms, the leading Freemason and intellectual, Benjamin Franklin, had long been Congress's ambassador to France, where he had joined two Lodges, one of which had included Voltaire. He knew of the growing importance of the ideals of the Freemasons in French social life, and of their grouping in cells, copied from the Illuminati. He had met the Marquis de Lafayette, who would have such an influence on America, both in war and peace. And he helped to draft the Declaration of Independence with a fellow-Mason, while some twenty other brethren signed the document in Congress, all insisting on total severance from the British Crown, along with pushing for liberty and equality and the 'rights of man' – for most people, naturally, who were not black or female.

In the Highlands of Scotland and in Ireland, there was much support for the Declaration of American Independence. 'Here are none but rebels,' a clergyman of the Church of Ireland wrote back to the Under-Secretary for the Colonies in London. 'All our newspapers abound with intelligence favourable to the rebels. The King is reviled, the ministry cursed, religion trampled under foot.' Early in the struggle, the young Lieutenant Ridsdale informed the *Hibernian Magazine* that the troops which 'kept up the spirit and life of the rebellion were totally Scotch and Irish'. And as Ebenezer Wild noticed in Valley Forge, St Patrick's Day produced a noticeable change in camp, a celebration by the Irishmen born in America or refugees there, reinforced by deserters from the British lines.

Although Scottish regiments under British officers fought their fellow-countrymen in the colonial war, as did some of the Loyalist Volunteers of Ireland, there were six mutinies among Scottish troops raised for America, which resulted in the discharge of the levies.

Without doubt, the Declaration of American Independence provoked strong support from the Gaelic nations. 'Here we sympathize more or less with the Americans,' an Irish Member of Parliament wrote from Dublin. 'We are in water colour what they are in fresco.'

A certain understanding also existed between the military Lodges in the opposing armies. The Mowhawks were allies of the British, and their chief, Joseph Brant, had become a Freemason on a visit to London. When he discovered that his American prisoners were brethren by their secret hand signals, he tended to release them rather than take their scalps off their heads. And if the refugee Irish and Scottish Freemasons were still revenging themselves on the British army, they took after the mercenary Hessians as if they were Hanoverian Kings, while they were less brutal with their enemies from the Old Countries, who might themselves be members of Masonic Lodges and share their general beliefs.

When the War of Independence was effectively ended by the intervention of French troops and the French fleet, which forced in 1781 the surrender of Lord Cornwallis at his base at Yorktown, the principles of Freemasonry were bound to affect the structure and the wording of the Constitution of the new Republic. The crafts and the guilds and the Lodges in the countries on both sides of the Atlantic worked in a loose federal system under a Grand Master, just as the thousands of commanderies of the Knights Templars had also followed the Rule of their Grand Master. And so the thirteen United States of America would be federated under a President, checked by two Houses of Congress and a Supreme Court, intended to approach King Solomon in his wisdom – a prominent Freemason, John Marshall, was the first Chief Justice.

In the year of 1789, when George Washington was elected as the President of the United States, a National Assembly was formed in France and the Bastille was stormed, beginning another revolution. Washington himself and his influential Irish Secretary of War, McHenry, were leading brethren, and so Templar and Masonic symbols were stamped on the currency, which survive to this day. On the dollar bill, the eye enclosed in the triangle echoed the apocalyptic visions of the medieval seer Joachim de Fiore, the three Ages evolving to that of the Spirit. The pyramid, left unfinished, suggested that the pinnacle of human wisdom and achievement had not been reached. These Masonic symbols were also millennial, for the American Revolution was inspired by the hope and belief in building a heaven on earth as well as a better society.

The very design of the new capital of the United States was influenced by the sacred architecture of the Knights Templars. The French architect, Pierre l'Enfant, was ordered by the President to modify his grid pattern and reproduce around the White House and the Capitol the eight-pointed emblem of resurrection within the circle of the cosmos. And when George Washington himself laid the cornerstone of the Capitol, he blessed it with corn and wine and oil, as if he were consecrating an ancient temple. His Masonic apron, embroidered by the Marquise de Lafayette, is still preserved with its Templar black-and-white pavement design; also his gavel and his silver trowel, his square and his level, all used to found the American legislature.

The history of Freemasonry in England after the defeat of the Jacobites was an exercise in control, deletion and suppression. The Grand Lodge of that country was created on St John's Day, the sacred date of the Templars, in 1717, a year after the failure of the rebellion of the Old Pretender. More than fifty Lodges were engulfed within seven years by the new Grand Lodge under Protestant control. An effort to capture English Freemasonry for the Jacobite cause was easily scotched, and the *Constitutions* of 1723 by James Anderson, a Scottish minister, became the Rule of the Grand Lodge in London. His father had been Master of the Lodge in Aberdeen, and the son's work claimed to be compiled 'from the old Records'. His new Rule prohibited a Mason from being engaged 'in Plots and Conspiracies against the Peace and Welfare of the Nation'.

These *Constitutions* were followed by *New Constitutions* fifteen years later. They confirmed the influence of the ancient Scottish Rite over English Freemasonry, also the long royal connections through the ancient crafts and guilds with the Lords of Rosslyn. As Anderson stated:

> The Kings of Scotland very much encouraged the Royal Art; from the earliest Times down to the Union of the Crowns, as appears by the

Remains of glorious buildings in that ancient Kingdom, and by the Lodges there kept up without Interruption many hundred Years, the records and Traditions of which testify the great Respect of those Kings to this honourable Fraternity, who gave always pregnant Evidence of their Love and Loyalty, from whence sprung among the old Toast among Scots Masons, viz., God Bless the King and the Craft!

Nor was the royal Example neglected by the Nobility, Gentry and Clergy of Scotland, who join'd in every thing for the good of the Craft and Brotherhood, the Kings being often the Grand Masters, until, among other things, the Masons of Scotland were impower'd to have a certain fix'd Grand Master and Grand Warden, who had a Salary from the Crown, and also an acknowledgement from every New Brother in the Kingdom at Entrance, whose Business was not only to regulate what might happen amiss in the Brotherhood, but also to hear and finally determine all Controversies between Masons and Lord, to punish the mason, if he deserv'd it, and to oblige both to equitable Terms: At which Hearings, if the Grand Master was absent (who was always nobly born) the Grand Warden presided. This Privilege remain'd till the Civil Wars, but is not obsolete; nor can it well be receive'd until the King becomes a Mason, because it was not actually exerted at the Union of the Kingdoms.

The *Constitutions* further declared that 'James the Sixth of Scotland, succeeding to the Crown of England, being a Mason King, reviv'd the English Lodges; and as he was the First King of Great Britain, he was also the First Prince in the World that recover'd the Roman Architecture.' As for the listed Grand Masters and Grand Wardens of the crafts and guilds, one of those who were not Kings of Scotland was named as William St Clair, the Earl of Orkney and builder of Rosslyn Chapel, 'a Master Piece of the best Gothic'. A later *Pocket Companion* of Anderson's Masonic works in 1761 asserted that the St Clairs had been presiding over the crafts and guilds of Scotland since the 13th century, when the Kings gave them the office of Grand Masters of the original Kilwinning Lodge. By this time, the authors were already aware that the last of the Sinclairs of Rosslyn had resigned his claims on his hereditary position. 'A real Mason, and a gentleman of the greatest candour and benevolence, inheriting his predecessors' virtues without their fortune, [he] was loth that the office of Grand Master, now vested in his person, should become vacant at his death.'

Conscious of the growing power of the Lodges in the armed forces, the Hanoverian commanders had begun a purge of Free-masonry after the second Jacobite disaster of 1745. The royal dukes such as Cumberland became Grand Masters, while the possession of literature or evidence sympathetic to the Stewart or Catholic cause was a matter of treason. The records of the long St Clair control of the Catholic crafts and guilds of Scotland had already been destroyed by Protestant mobs. Now the books and minutes of the early Lodges of the Ancient Scottish Rite were expunged and replaced by a history of Freemasonry, based on English Lodges after the Refor-mation. This process of autocracy and deletion by the British Crown became more stringent with the knowledge of the significance of Freemasonry in America and France, resulting in the overthrow of royal authority.

At the formation of the Grand Lodge of Scotland in 1736, the old ways were recognized by a formal surrender to the new dominance. The first Grand Master was William St Clair or Sinclair, the last of the long line of male Sancto Claros, who had ruled at Roslin for seven centuries and had preserved the mysteries of the Templars and the Masons and the faith of the Middle Ages. A member of the Royal Company of Archers, the King's bodyguard for Scotland, he was admired by Sir Walter Scott, who wrote of him:

The last Roslin was a man considerably above six feet, with dark grey locks, a form upright, but gracefully so, thin-flanked and broad-shouldered, built, it would seem, for the business of war or chase, a noble eye of chastened pride and undoubted authority, and features handsome and striking in their general effect, though somewhat harsh and exaggerated when considered in detail. His complexion was dark and grizzled, and as we schoolboys, who crowded to see him perform feats of strength and skill in the old Scottish games of Golf and Archery, used to think and say amongst ourselves, the whole figure resembled the famous founder of the Douglas race . . . In all the manly sports which require strength and dexterity, Roslin was unrivalled; but his particular delight was in Archery.

Through his bowmanship, and as a member of the Royal Company of Archers, William St Clair had kept his faith in the Stewart cause. The *Annals of Scotland* of 1724 described the Company 'all through the reigns of Anne and the first George [as] a sodality composed almost exclusively of the Jacobite aristocracy, and, in fact, a sort of masked muster for the cause of the exiled' Old Pretender on its parades. Nine years later, the *Caledonian Mercury* named William St Clair as a brigadier of the Royal Company on a showy march through Edinburgh behind a standard bearing a Lion Rampant and the motto: PRO PATRICIA DULCE PERICULUM [For the Patricians, Peril is Sweet]. After an archery contest, the Scottish nobles watched the killing of a king and the usurpation of a throne in Shakespeare's tragedy of *Macbeth*.

When Walter Scott compared William St Clair to 'the famous founder of the Douglas race', he was referring to the giant who had died five centuries before, in Spain, with the heart of Bruce and another Sir William St Clair, whose Templar tombstone still lies in Rosslyn Chapel. But this 'last Roslin' surrendered his family's hereditary role as Grand Master of the crafts and guilds and Orders of Scotland in order to become the first elected Grand Master of the Grand Lodge of his country by a unanimous vote. The document yielding his inherited rights confirmed their existence:

> I, William St Clair of Rossline, Esquire, taking to my consideration that the Masons in Scotland did, by several deeds, constitute and appoint William and Sir William St Clairs of Rossline, my ancestors, and their heirs to be their patrons, protectors, judges, or masters; and that my holding or claiming any such jurisdiction, right, or privilege, might be prejudicial to the Craft and vocation of Massonrie, whereof I am a member, and I being desirous to advance and promote the good and utility of the said Craft of Massonrie to the outmost of my power, doe therefore hereby, for me and my heirs, renounce, quit, claim, overgive, and discharge all right, claim, or pretence that I, or my heirs had, have or any ways may have, pretend to, or claim, to be patron, protector, judge or master of the Massons in Scotland, in virtue of any deed or deeds made and granted by the said Massons, or any grant or charter made by any of the Kings of Scotland . . .

This renunciation by the 'last Roslin' of the great role he had inherited was the final proof that the St Clairs were the bridges between ancient aristocracy and future constitutional democracy. He also lost control of the family chapel and castle, for his fortunes were gone in the Stewart cause, and he had eight children, but only one daughter, Sarah, survived. As the Crown of Scotland had once passed with a lass, so did Rosslyn pass with a lass, who married an Erskine and a Wedderburn, later Lord Loughborough, then Lord Chancellor, then the first Earl of Rosslyn.

William St Clair only served as Grand Master of the Grand Lodge of Scotland for one ceremonial year. But on his death, a song was sung by four hundred Masonic mourners to the tune of *'Rosslyn Castle'*.

> St Clair to dust its claim resigns,
> And in sublimer regions shines,
> Let us, whom ties fraternal bind,
> Beyond the rest of humankind,
> Like St Clair live, like St Clair die,
> Then join the Eternal Lodge on high.

As for the Order of the Knights Templars and the Royal Order of Scotland, an expert on Masonic history and ritual, Alexander Deuchar, breathed life into the ancient practices. He took two of the older Scottish Templar groups and had them chartered from the revived Templars within the Irish Grand Lodge, which had also restored the Order in North America. By 1811, when the Hanoverian Duke of Kent had taken over the Masonic Templars in England, Deuchar obtained a charter nominating himself as the Grand Master for life of 'The Knights of the Holy Temple and Sepulchre, and of St John of Jerusalem'. And so the two historic progenitors of modern Freemasonry were born again in the rituals of our times.

17

Phantoms and Myths

With the penury and resignation of William St Clair, some repairs were made to Rosslyn chapel and castle. For they had been thoroughly pillaged in 1688 during the Glorious Revolution. As the memoir of a Pentland merchant, James Currie, testified:

> On this same night, some men went over to Rosslyn Castle, and burnt their images and many of their Popish books, I telling them where they would find their Priests' robes; but withall I desired some to go after them and hinder them from taking or hurting anything, except what belonged to their idolatry; for at this time the Prince of Orange was come to England.

When General Sir James St Clair Erskine acquired the estate of Roslin, he became the Grand Master Mason for Scotland between 1810 and 1811, and he had the shattered windows of the chapel reglazed. The roof was also repaired to some degree, while the old floor of ceramic tiles was relaid with flagstones, obliterating the maze patterns of the Middle Ages. Yet the ruined castle became more ruinous. In his book on *Old and New Edinburgh*, Grose wrote of the place as 'haggard and utterly dilapidated – the mere wreck of a great pile riding on a little sea of forest – a rueful apology for the once grand fabric whose name of "Rosslyn Castle" is so intimately associated with melody and song.'

Those melodies and songs, which created the myth of Rosslyn, were chiefly the works of Lord Byron, and the Lake poet, William Wordsworth, and Sir Walter Scott, the greatest romancer of his age. Byron lamented the ruin of the castle:

Oh Roslin! time, war, flood, and fire,
Have made your glories star by star expire.
Chaos of ruins! who shall trace the void,
O'er the dim fragments cast a lunar light,
And say, 'here was or is,' where all is doubly night.

Alas! thy lofty castle! And alas
Thy trebly hundred triumphs! and the day
When *Sinclair* made the dagger's edge surpass
The conqueror's sword, in bearing fame away.

For Wordsworth, the desolate chapel was a relic of a past age:

The wind is now thy organist – a clank
(We know not whence) ministers for a bell
To mark some change of service. As the swell
Of music reached its height, and even when sank
The notes in prelude, Rosslyn! To a blank
Of silence, how it thrilled thy sumptuous roof,
Pillars, and arches, – not in vain time-proof,
Though Christian rites be wanting!

The imagination of Sir Walter Scott, based on tradition, created the persistent myth of the chapel in his 'Dirge of Rosabelle', a ballad that appears to preface the poems of Edgar Allan Poe. The legend was that the chapel shone with the mysterious light of the divine spirit at the death of any member of the family:

O'er Rosslyn all that dreary night,
  A wondrous blaze was seen to gleam;
'Twas broader than the watch-fire's light,
  And redder than the bright moon-beam.

It glared on Rosslyn's castled rock,
  It ruddied all the copse-wood glen;
T'was seen from Dryden's groves of oak,
  And seen from caverned Hawthornden.

Seemed all on fire that Chapel proud,
  Where Rosslyn's chiefs uncoffined lie;

Each Baron, for a sable shroud,
   Sheathed in his iron panoply.

Seemed all on fire within, around,
   Deep sacristy and altar's pale;
Shone ever pillar foliage-bound,
   And glimmered all the dead men's mail.

Blazed battlement and pinnet high,
   Blazed every rose-carved buttress fair –
So still they blaze, when fate is nigh
   The lordly line of high St Clair.

The question of those who made the armour of the burning knights was also illuminated by Sir Walter Scott. In his novels, he gave leading roles to some of the Border travellers, so welcome at Rosslyn. He noted of the Lochmaben gypsies that they had been granted four small villages near the ancient castle there, since the days of Robert the Bruce. 'They themselves are termed king's rentallers, or kindly tenants; under which denomination each of them has a right, of an allodial nature, to a small piece of ground.' These were the descendants of the wandering smiths and hammer-men, who had fought at Bannockburn and were protected by the St Clairs, the masters of royal weapons. Arms maketh the King as well as the man.

The new Earls of Rosslyn did restore the chapel in the Victorian style, and they refurbished the castle, so that it was fit to live in, although not to defend. At the west end of the chapel, an apse and baptistery were constructed with an organ chamber above. This addition defaced the outer aspect of the ragged wall, which supported the two pillars of the Temple of Solomon, the legacy of its founder, Earl William. The stained glass windows within were a testament to the Gothic and Templar revival of the period. One was of St Longinus, the blind centurion of the Grail legends, who had pierced the side of Christ on the Cross and was made to see again by the Blood of the Saviour, trickling into his dead sight. Curiously, this was also the legend of the original Sanctus Clarus, whose holy water healed the inflammation of the eyes.

The other new windows featured two warrior saints, St Michael and St George, the patron saint of England, presumably a reference to the Union of the two kingdoms with the slaying of the dragon of discord. As for St Michael the Archangel, he was the patron saint of the Knights Templars, because he was held to be the divine messenger, bearing the Word between earth and heaven. As for the fourth blessed soldier in stained glass, St Maurice, he was beheaded with his Christian soldiers for refusing to worship the pagan gods of Rome, another reference to the Protestant martyrs who had refused the authority of the Papal See.

Two other stories emerged about Rosslyn. One was a letter from a later Dean of Worcester, written about 1670:

> The lairds of Rosling have been great architects and patrons of building for these many generations. They are obliged to receive the Mason's Word which is a secret signal Masons have thro'out the world to know one another by. They alledge 'tis as old as since Babel when they could not understand one another and they conversed by signs. Others would have it no older than Solomon.

And indeed, the Victorian Earls of Rosslyn were occasionally elected Grand Masters of both the Scottish Grand Lodges and of the revived Templar Orders.

The other legend was connected with the vaults under the chapel and the courtyard of the Castle. While we were investigating there, a whole buried circular staircase fell in, leading only to mud and rubble. Yet the antiquarian Slezer, in his *Theatrum Scotiae* of 1693, had claimed that 'a great treasure, we are told, amounting to some millions, lies buried in one of the vaults. It is under the guardianship of a lady of the ancient house of St Clair, who, not very faithful to her trust, has been long in a dormant state. Awakened, however, by the sound of a trumpet, which must be heard in one of the lower apartments, she is to make her appearance and to point out the spot where the treasure lies.'

A later legend of the valuables hidden in the vaults was ascribed to tradition. The Victorian *Tales of Roslin Castle* also resurrected the original significance of the name of Sanctus Clarus, the bearers of the Holy Light; its radiance might strike people blind before restoring their sight:

Historical tradition has likewise insinuated, that the treasure of the unfortunate Darnley was secreted in the castle, and lost among its ruins. And ever since its demolition, there has been a traditionary prediction through Scotland, that these immured treasures would ultimately be discovered, but by a blind person only, as, like most other ancient castles, they were supposed to be guarded by an angel lady, of such dazzling purity, that mortal eye could not long look upon her and live. In consequence of this prediction, many of the blind from every quarter of Scotland, in fond anticipation of the wealth they would acquire by such a happy discovery, have visited the castle, and with the acute sense of feeling with which the blind are ever possessed, every seam and chink, every arch and flaw in the walls, every bolt and rivet of iron within their reach, has been examined, and re-examined, with eager touch, and scratch of finger and nail, but without effect.

Of such stuff are phantoms and legends made. Obscure and rather neglected, Rosslyn chapel was pulled from a glass darkly by the authors of the cult success, *The Holy Blood and the Holy Grail*. Although containing some original research, the book associated the St Clairs and their chapel with the unlikely bloodline of Jesus and Mary Magdalene, also the bogus Priory of Sion, a mystic Rosicrucian and Catholic organization modelled on the Knights Templars. This clique was said to include a St Clair at the time of the crusades, as well as Leonardo da Vinci and Isaac Newton and Jean Cocteau. Anyone with a famous name could be recruited into this ridiculous conspiracy.

The author of this hoax, as ingenious as the spurious *Ossian*, was a certain Pierre Plantard, who assumed the name of de St Clair. He had no right to it. He was a collaborator with the Vichy régime in France, and was convicted for crimes of deception. He conspired with Philippe, the Marquis de Cherisey, in fabricating Secret Dossiers, which established the untruth of the Priory of Sion. These were placed in leading French institutions and libraries, to which the authors of *The Holy Blood and the Holy Grail* were directed. They associated these forgeries with an attempt to restore the ancestry of Jesus through the Merovingian and Bourbon Kings of France to the throne of that country.

The first book of this Rosslyn Trilogy, *The Sword and the Grail* of 1992, was a serious work, which would spawn a host of horrors. When I found the first Templar Grailstone, ignored and broken in a corner of Rosslyn chapel, I thought I would restore to recognition the magnificent and noble creation of Rosslyn chapel. Alas, I became another Count Frankenstein, who had intended his monster to be a splendid work of his art. He was soon disillusioned. As Mary Shelley made him say:

> His limbs were in proportion, and I had selected his features as beautiful. Beautiful! – Great God! His yellow skin scarcely covered the work of muscles and arteries beneath; his hair was of a lustrous black, and flowing, his teeth of a pearly whiteness; but these luxuriances only formed a more horrid contrast with his watery eyes, that seemed almost of the same colour as the dun white sockets in which they were set, his shrivelled complexion and straight black lips.

Fortunately, the extraordinary beauty of Rosslyn chapel will survive the plethora of idiocies heaped upon its superb stones. Some twenty books on the meaning of the fabulous place of Earl William St Clair have since appeared in print. Their authors are beyond name or shame. The head of Jesus and the Grail have been discerned within the 'Apprentice' Pillar, although that solid support of the stone roof has no hollow within, or the whole place would fall down. The agony of the last Grand Master of the Temple, Jacques de Molay, is seen in the carvings; the Essene Scrolls have reached there with the Knights Templars, also the worship of the earth mother goddess Ishtar. There is another worldwide conspiracy of a Rex Deus bloodline, connected to the St Clair family. And there are geomantic patterns, which link Rosslyn to Glastonbury, also to St Sulpice in Paris and on to Carcassonne and Barcelona. This is piffle piled on nonsense.

And now Rosslyn is afflicted with a thriller, *The Da Vinci Code*, much influenced by the previous pointer to the St Clair chapel, *The Holy Blood and the Holy Grail*. Its plot is preposterous, its message is pernicious, its history a bungle and a muddle. The claimed conspiracy of the Priory of Sion has been exploded, while the attack on the evil machinations of the Catholic Church is no more convincing than were the fictional Protocols of the Elders of Zion, once used against the Jews. The key image in this bad novel is that of the dead body of Jacques Saunière, arranged in a pentagram before he dies, said to be in the manner of Leonardo's most famous drawing, 'Vitruvian Man'. But Leonardo's masterpiece does not have four limbs and a head, but double arms and legs, composing the principle of sacred architecture, the octagon within the circle and the square. The head served as the cornerstone of a holy building. That blessed shape, as Leonardo intended to show, has been a subject of this book. Yet it was originally a symbol of baptism, new beginnings, perfection and spiritual rebirth: and not of a ritual murder.

Yet *The Da Vinci Code* is only a thriller, using a mishmash of esoteric texts, often wrongly, to create a tragic farce about the Grail. And it is no *Parzival*, although its curious clues take the readers to a true Chapel of the Grail at Rosslyn. And there, its final builder, Sir Oliver Sinclair, was a contemporary of Leonardo. And in the story of sacred architecture in Scotland, there is a more interesting and truthful tale to be told.

Leonardo da Vinci had been brought from Italy to complete his final building works in *châteaux* along the Loire. Because of Vitruvius, Leonardo had always believed in the octagon. Around 1490, he drew a sketch for an octagon supporting the dome of a church, surrounded by eight other eight-sided chapels. In his drawing of 1519 for a pavilion at the centre of the labyrinth of the Duke of Milan at Cloux near Amboise, he drew another octagon containing eight other octagons, enclosed in a circular canal – very similar to the remarkable Castel del Monte of the mystical Emperor Frederick II near Bari. And he also proposed a structure of eight inward mirrors, in which anyone inside might see themselves reflected infinitely.

Yet Leonardo's nearest approach to the secret of life was his creation of the Double Helix staircase at the *château* of Chambord, which was later reproduced at Holyrood House. Going up the winding stairs and going down, we interweave with passing passengers. Leonardo had discovered the structure of genetics. A friend of mine at Harvard, James Watson, and a colleague of mine as a Founding Fellow of Churchill College at Cambridge, Francis Crick, discovered the structure of DNA, a major scientific advance, which led to the award of the

Nobel Prize. The shape was the Double Helix, the title of Watson's book, although the inspiration was claimed by a third collaborator, Professor Maurice Wilkins. They did not acknowledge Leonardo, so often a prophet before his time.

More curious would be the influence of Leonardo, not only on the architecture of Rosslyn chapel, but on the biotechnological laboratory outside the village of Roslin, built by Earl William St Clair in the shape of a cross to house his masons. At the modern institute, Dolly the Sheep was first cloned. And if there was a *Da Vinci Code* leading to the Grail, there it was cracked. For the Grail is only the grace of God. The search for it seeks the enigma of Creation.

A medieval scroll in Orkney had suggested to me that the Ark of the Covenant might possibly be buried in Rosslyn Chapel. Yet the ground-plan was probably a symbol, not a reality. Historical research showed that the St Clairs of Rosslyn were the keepers of royal treasures in bad times. These would have included the Holy Rood, which disappeared at the time of Mary of Guise. With their close connection to the Knights Templars, the lairds of Rosslyn certainly grew wealthy after the excommunication and flight of members of that Military Order, perhaps with the jewelled containers from Constantinople of the Holy Shroud and Veil. And yet, the only proven treasure is that Chapel of the Grail itself, a mystery and a maze and a puzzle in stone. Each of us may try to penetrate to the heart of its light, but we will never reach its radiance. But as all living is only an inquiry towards the divine, we already know that Rosslyn is a beginning without

THE END

Notes

1. The Labyrinth and the Bull

Robert Graves, *Greek Myths* (London, 1955) is still incisive on the ancient Greek beliefs about creation. George St Clair, *Myths of Greece Explained and Dated* (2 vols., London, 1901) and C.H. Moore, *The Religious Thought of the Greeks* (Cambridge, Mass., 1916) have been helpful on the Orphic and Mithraic cults. Charles Bertram Lewis, *Classical Mythology and Arthurian Romance* (Oxford, 1932) stresses the Greek origins of the Arthurian cycle, while G.R. Levy, *The Sword from the Rock: An Investigation into the Origins of Epic Literature and the Development of the Hero* (London, 1953) is original and compelling. And Rudyard Kipling wrote his Hymn to Mithras in *Puck of Pook's Hill* (coll. ed., London, 1925).

In a remarkable piece of linguistic detection, Robert Craig Maclagan ferreted out *Scottish Myths: Notes on Scottish History and Tradition* (Edinburgh, 1882). Also important are W. Croft Dickinson, *Scotland from the Earliest Times to 1603* (rev. ed., Oxford, 1977); R. Forbes, *Calendars of the Scottish Saints* (Edinburgh, 1895); S Baring-Gould, *Myths of the Middle Ages* (2 vols., London, 1872); and F.W. Skene, *Celtic Scotland* (2 vols., Edinburgh, 1876–80).

For works on the Celtic churches, see M.V. Hay, *A Chain of Error in Scottish History* (London, 1927); H. Delehaye, *The Legends of the Saints* (London, 1907); Louis Duchesne, *L'Église au VIe siècle* (Paris, 1925); Louis Gougaud, *Les chrétientés celtiques* (Paris, 1911); E. Martin, *St Columban* (Paris, 1905); Thomas Dempster, *Historia ecclesiastica gentis Scotorum* (London, 1623); E. Ledwich, *Antiquities of Ireland* (Dublin, 1790); John Macpherson, *On the Caledonians, Picts, etc.* (Edinburgh, 1768); James Ussher, *A Discourse of the Religion anciently professed by the Irish and British* (London, 1631); George Chalmers, *Caledonia* (3 vols., London, 1807–24); John Jamieson, *An Historical Account of the Ancient Culdees of Iona* (Edinburgh, 1811); W.G. Todd, *History of the Ancient Church in Ireland* (London, 1845); D. MacCallum, *History of the Culdees* (Edinburgh, 1855);

J. Dowden, *The Celtic Church in Scotland* (London, 1894); J. Heron, *The Celtic Church in Ireland* (Dublin, 1898); and H. Zimmer, *The Celtic Church in Britain and Ireland* (London, 1902).

2. Sanctus Clarus

The three indispensable sources on the early history of the St Clair family are Father Hay, *Genealogie of the Sainteclaires of Rosslyn* (Edinburgh, 1835), Roland William Saint-Clair, *The Saintclairs of the Isles* (Auckland, 1898), and L.-A. de Saint Clair, *Histoire généalogique de la famille de Saint Clair et de ses alliances (France-Écosse)* (Paris, 1869). Essential reading is Louis-Paul Blanc, *Le Mont 'Saint-Clair'*, (Nimes, 1994): more than any other, he has researched the origins of the name St Clair in France. The recording of the St Clair chant against blindness is by B.L. Fontana in *Dictionnaire des Saints Bretons* (Paris, 1979).

The Gnostic Scriptures by Bentley Layton (London, 1987) is seminal, as are two books by Elaine Pagels, *The Gnostic Gospels* (New York, 1979) and *Adam, Eve, and the Serpent* (New York, 1988). Also valuable is the concise survey by Benjamin Walker, *Gnosticism: Its History and Influence* (London, 1983). I am also grateful to Malcolm Lee Peel for his edition of *The Epistle to Rheginos: A Valentinian Letter on the Resurrection* (London, 1969).

3. King Arthur and the Grail

I have leaned on a previous book of mine, *The Discovery of the Grail* (London, 1998). John Passmore's excellent work on *The Perfectability of Man* (London, 1970) suggested the connection between the Pelagian heresy and Arthurian literature and Protestantism. Saint Augustine's *Confessions* showed that he was a heretic and a Manichean before his conversion to Christianity and the doctrine of original sin. Essential in studies of the historical truth of Arthur are John Morris, *The Age of Arthur: A History of the British Isles from 350 to 650* (London, 1973), and Leslie Alcock, *Arthur's Britain: History and Archaeology, AD 367–634* (London, 1971), which is particularly significant on excavations at Iron Age hill forts and their use in the 6th century.

In his works, Roger Sherman Loomis is the authority on the Irish and Welsh origins of the Grail theme, particularly *The Grail: From Celtic Myth to Christian Symbol* (Cardiff, 1963). There is a fine Penguin Books edition of Geoffrey of Monmouth, *The History of the Kings of Britain* (tr. and intro. by Lewis Thorpe, London, 1966). I am again grateful to Loomis, 'The Oral Diffusion of the Arthurian Legend', in the book edited by him, *Arthurian Literature in the Middle*

Ages: A Collaborative History (Oxford, 1959). His magisterial treatment of this subject and of the Celtic roots of Arthurian literature leave all scholars in his debt. Richard Barber spoils *The Holy Grail: Imagination and Belief* (London, 2004) by a narrow interpretation of the Grail as a mere Christian chalice invented by Chrétien de Troyes, thus ignoring its classical and Celtic origins.

I am also indebted to the excellent translation of *Perceval* or *The Story of the Grail* by Ruth Harwood Clive with introduction and notes (Georgia, 1985). Jean Frappier's works on *Perceval* are most important, particularly his *Chrétien de Troyes et le Mythe du Graal* (Paris, 1972). A brilliant pamphlet by Leonardo Olschki, 'The Grail Castle and its Mysteries' (Manchester, 1966), alone stresses the power of the Grail as representing the Light of God, deriving from the Gospel of Saint John and Gnostic heresies in the 12th century. The remarkable *Visio Pacis: Holy City and Grail* (Pennsylvania, 1960) by Helen Adolf relates the Grail quest to the loss of Jerusalem and the search for a heavenly city.

4. The Knights of Black and White

All inquiries into the crusades still begin and end with Sir Stephen Runciman's *A History of the Crusades* (3 vols., Cambridge, 1951–4). Generally useful on the subject are Zoé Oldenburg, *The Crusades* (London, 1966); Richard Barber, *The Knight and Chivalry* (London, 1970); Amin Maalouf, *The Crusades Through Arab Eyes* (London, 1984), and Hans Eberhard Mayer, *The Crusades* (Oxford, 1990). Jonathan Riley-Smith is admirable on the motives of the crusades in *The Crusades: Idea and Reality 1095–1294* (London, 1982), and Norman Housley, *The Later Crusades, 1274–1580: From Lyons to Alcazar* (Oxford, 1992) is fine.

Particularly significant on St Bernard is *Vézelay et Saint Bernard* (Jacques d'Arès ed., Croissy-Beaubours, 1985), and *The Second Crusade and the Cistercians* (Michael Gervers ed., New York, 1992). For St Bernard's views on the crusades, see G. Constable, 'The Second Crusade as seen by Contemporaries', *Traditio*, 9 (1953) and J. Leclerq, 'L'encyclique de St Bernard en faveur de la croisade', *Revue bénédictine* 81 (1974). Essential reading in its field is Alan MacQuarrie, *Scotland and the Crusades, 1095–1560* (Edinburgh, 1995).

Most interesting of recent works on the Knights Templars are Gérard de Sède, *Les Templiers sont parmi nous* (Paris, 1962); Louis Charpentier, *Les Mystères Templiers* (Paris, 1967); Guy Tarade, *Les Derniers Gardiens du Graal* (Paris, 1993); Michel Lamy, *Les Templiers* (Bordeaux, 1997); Patrick Rivière, *Les Templiers et leurs mystères* (rev. ed., Paris, 1997); and Alain Desgris, *L'Ordre des Templiers* (Paris, 1994).

The brilliant book by the librarian at Montségur, Raimonde Reznikov, *Cathares et Templiers* (Toulouse, 1993), proves that the Knights Templars both attacked and supported the Cathars in the Langue d'Oc. Michel Roquebert, in

Les Cathares et le Graal (Toulouse, 1995), considers the Grail texts as orthodox and Catholic, and so he denies the title of his book, stating that the Cathars as heretics had nothing to do with the Holy Vessel. Zoé Oldenbourg, *Massacre at Montségur: A History of the Albigensian Crusade* (New York, 1961), remains magisterial on the subject.

The extraordinary Curator at the Royal Library, Copenhagen, Sigfús Blöndal, wrote *The Varangians of Byzantium* (Cambridge, 1978). An excellent translation of the *Orkneyinga Saga* is that of Herman Pálsson and Paul Edwards (London, 1978).

5. The Knights of the Stone Grail

In his seminal work, *War and Human Progress* (London, 1950), John U. Nef argued that weaponry changed cultures through industrial advances. Most useful on tactics and weapons are J.F.C. Fuller, *Decisive Battles: Their Influence upon History and Civilisation* (2 vols., London, 1939); E.S. Creasy, *The Fifteen Decisive Battles of the World* (London, 1852); A.H. Burne, *More Battlefields of England* (London, 1952); and Peter Young and John Adair, *Hastings to Culloden* (London, 1964).

For studies on Wolfram von Eschenbach's text, I recommend David Blamires, *Characterisation and Individuality in Wolfram's 'Parzival'* (Cambridge, 1966); Margaret F. Richey, *Studies of Wolfram von Eschenbach* (London, 1957) and Hugh Sacker, *An Introduction to Wolfram's 'Parzival'* (Cambridge, 1963). The translations from the original are largely mine, and I have also made use of a previous book by myself, *The Discovery of the Grail* (London, 1998).

6. The Matter of Bannockburn

On Border warfare, George Macdonald Fraser, *The Steel Bonnets* (London, 1971) is definitive, although he is brief on its origins in the 13th century. I am indebted to John E. Morris, *Bannockburn* (Cambridge, 1914), who quotes extensively from contemporary chroniclers. Also important are R. Borland, *Border Raids and Reivers* (Glasgow, 1910); J.C. Bruce, *Handbook to the Roman Wall* (Newcastle, 1947); J. Nicolson and R. Burn, *History and Antiquities of Westmoreland and Cumberland* (London, 1977); James L. Mack, *The Border Line* (Edinburgh, 1926); George Ridpath, *The Border History of England and Scotland* (Berwick, 1858); Sir Walter Scott, *The Border Antiquities of England and Scotland* (2 vols., London, 1869); and Daniel & Samuel Lysons, *Magna Britannica, Volume the Fourth Containing Cumberland* (London, 1816).

7. The Makers of Weapons

From the medieval scriptorium and library of Rosslyn, five manuscripts, all signed by the St Clair family, remain in the National Library of Scotland. Others survive in the Bodleian Library at Oxford. For my information on the Romanies, I am indebted to John Townsley for his personal examination of the gypsies in Scotland in the unpublished *The Mark of Gaginus*, 2002, and to Neil Sinclair and Peggy Rintoul for their work on 'The Sinclairs cum MacNokairds of Argyllshire', 2002, also to the Scottish Women's Rural Institute, 'Taynuilt: Our History', 1966. For wandering workmen and the early guilds, R.A. Leeson, *Travelling Brothers* (London, 1979) is essential.

   In addition to the invaluable *Scotland from the Earliest Times to 1603* (*op. cit.*), I have found useful E.M. Barron, *The Scottish War of Independence* (Inverness, 1934); G.W.S. Barrow, *Robert Bruce and the Community of the Realm of Scotland* (London, 1965) and *The Kingdom of the Scots* (London, 1973); Ronald Nicholson, *Edward III and the Scots* (Oxford, 1965); E.L.G. Stones (ed.), *Anglo-Scottish Relations, 1174–1328* (London, 1965); and R.L. Graeme Ritchie, *The Normans in Scotland* (Edinburgh, 1954). The quotation from the medieval chronicler Bartholomew in his *De proprietationibus rerum* is translated by H.R. Schubert, *A History of the British Iron and Steel Industry* (London, 1957), while the quotation about the London masons is from the excellent Heather Swanson, *Medieval Artisans: An Urban Class in Late Medieval England* (Oxford, 1989). There is an admirable edition by William Beattie of the *Border Ballads* (London, 1952), while Jean Gimpel, *The Medieval Machine: The Industrial Revolution of the Middle Ages* (London 1976) is essential reading.

8. The Northern Commonwealth

I have fully dealt with the career of Henry St Clair and the Zen voyage in the first book of my Rosslyn trilogy, *The Sword and the Grail* (London, 1992). I have added much new material on his role as a shipbuilder and the strategy of the Northern Commonwealth. For information on the first cannon, I am indebted to a pamphlet by H.W.L. Hime, 'Our Earliest Cannon, 1314–1346', 2002. The claims of Henry St Clair to the Earldom of Orkney are fully documented in the 'Deduction concerning the genealogies of the Ancient Courts of Orkney, from their First Creation to the Fifteenth Century. Drawn up from the most authentic Records by Thomas, Bishop of Orkney, with the assistance of his Clergy and others' (Kirkwall, 1446), translated in T. Sinclair, *Caithness Events* (Wick, 1899).

   Séan O'Faolain wrote his admirable *The Irish* (Dublin, 1955). The Hakluyt

Society published in London in 1873 a bilingual version of Nicolò Zeno's *Narrative and Map*, edited and introduced by Richard H. Major. The most important modern supporters of the accuracy of the *Zeno Map* are Captain A.H. Mallory, *Lost America* (Columbus, 1954) and Charles H. Hapgood, *Maps of the Ancient Sea Kings* (New York, 1966). See also Frederick J. Pohl, *Prince Henry Sinclair: His Expedition to the New World in 1398* (New York, 1974). I am also grateful for the unending researches of Niven Sinclair and his friends on the Zen Voyage and the Northern Commonwealth.

9. Renaissance and Defeat

Essential in the sources and interpretation of this chapter are *Scotland from the Earliest Times to 1603 (op. cit.)* and the excellent Jamie Cameron, *James V: The Personal Rule 1528–1542* (East Lothian, 1998). Also important in the Scottish Record Office for this period are the *Acts of the Lords of Council*, and the *Acts of the Lords of Council and Session*, and the *Acts and Decreets*, as they will be in the succeeding chapters of this book. To be consulted are William Drummond, *History of Scotland from the Year 1423 until the year 1542* (London, 1861); A.H. Dunbar, *Scottish Kings: A Revised Chronology of Scottish History 1005–1625* (Edinburgh, 1906); David Hume, *The History of the House and Race of Douglas and Angus* (Edinburgh, 1748); R.K. Hannay and D. Hay (eds.), *The Letters of James V* (Edinburgh, 1954); and W.C. Dickinson (ed.), *John Knox's History of the Reformation in Scotland* (Edinburgh, 1949).

Also to be considered are P.D. Anderson, *Robert Stewart, Earl of Orkney, Lord of Shetland: 1533–1593* (Edinburgh, 1982); W.A. Armstrong, *The Armstrong Borderland* (North Berwick, 1969); C. Bingham, *James V: King of Scots* (London, 1971); I.B. Cowan and D. Shaw (eds.), *The Renaissance and Reformation in Scotland* (Edinburgh, 1983); Pamela E. Ritchie, *Mary of Guise in Scotland, 1548–1560* (East Lothian, 2002); W. Ferguson, *Scotland's Relations with England: a Survey to 1707* (Edinburgh, 1977); N. Macdougall, *James III: A Political Study* (Edinburgh, 1982) and *James IV* (Edinburgh, 1989); C. McGladdery, *James II* (Edinburgh, 1990); S. Ross, *The Stewart Dynasty* (London, 1993); M.W. Stuart, *The Scot who was a Frenchman; being the life of John Stewart, Duke of Albany in Scotland, France and Italy* (London, 1940); and B.C. Crawford, 'William Sinclair, Earl of Orkney and his Family: a study in the politics of survival' in K.J. Stringer (ed.,), *Essays on the Nobility of Medieval Scotland* (Edinburgh, 1985).

10. The Sacred Shape of the Stones

For sacred architecture, I would recommend the reading of Helen Rosenau, *The Ideal City: Its Architectural Evolution* (New York, 1972); Kevin Lynch, *The Image of the City* (Cambridge, Mass., 1960); S. Giedion, *Space, Time and Architecture* (London, 1954): P. Soleri, *Arcology, The City in the Image of Man* (Cambridge, Mass., 1969); G. Munte, *Idealstädte* (Berlin, 1957); Marco M. Olivetti, *Il Tempio Simbolo Cosmico* (Rome, 1967); Joseph Rykwert, *The Idea of a Town* (London, 1976); John Michell, *The Dimensions of Paradise* (London, 1988); Hermann Kern, *Through the Labyrinth* (Munich, 2000); and Jean Paul Richter (ed.), *The Literary Works of Leonardo da Vinci* (London, 1883).

Essential reading on Rosslyn chapel are two books by Robert Brydon, *The Guilds, the Masons and the Rosy Cross* (Roslin, 1994) and *Rosslyn and the Western Mystery Tradition* (Edinburgh, 2003). I deal with the subject fully in my two previous books, *The Sword and the Grail* (London, 1992) and *The Secret Scroll* (London, 2001). Also recommended is Karen Ralls, *The Templars and the Grail: Knights of the Quest* (Wheaton, Illinois, 2003).

11. The Chapel of the Grail

J. Huizinga, *The Waning of the Middle Ages* (London, 1924) is a supreme example in prose of how to describe the essence of a period. Also important is Craig Wright, *The Maze and the Warrior* (Cambridge, Mass., 2001). I am grateful to the Scottish and English National Heritage guides to the Cistercian abbeys of Melrose, Newbattle and Rielvaux. Also valuable are Hubert Fenwick, *The Auld Alliance* (Kineton, 1971) and Maurice Vieux, *Les secrets de Bâtisseurs* (Paris, 1975); in this book are the illustrations taken from the album of Vilart de Honnecourt. The musical notes carved on the rib vaulting behind the altar at Rosslyn were discovered by Shawn Williamson, who believes them to signify the lost and sacred hymn of St John the Baptist. Lewis Spence wrote 'The Arthurian Tradition in Scotland' for the *Scots Magazine*, April, 1926.

I deal fully with the Kirkwall Scroll in the second volume of my Rosslyn Trilogy, *The Secret Scroll* (London, 2001.) The radio-carbon dating of this medieval hanging places it in the 15th century, thus making it unique in Scottish history. It should receive a large grant for its restoration and be put on permanent exhibition. Vital in researching early accounts of Rosslyn is John Thompson, *The 1893 Guide to Rosslyn Chapel, Castle and Hawthornden* (rev. ed., Bakewell, Derbyshire, 2004).

12. An Eden of Stone

Much of this chapter is derived from Andrew Sinclair, *Jardins de gloire, de délices et de Paradis* (Paris, 2000). Other works recommended are John Armstrong, *The Paradise Myth* (London, 1969); Germain Bazin, *Paradeisos: The Art of the Garden* (London, 1990); Jean Delumeau, *Mille ans de bonheur: Une histoire du paradis* (Paris, 1995); Northrop Frye, *The Return of Eden* (Toronto, 1965); Georges Riat, *L'Art des Jardins* (Paris, 1900); E. Sinclair Rohde, *Garden – Craft in the Bible* (London, 1927) and *The Story of the Garden* (London, 1932); C. Thacker, *The History of Gardens* (London, 1979); John Harvey, *Medieval Gardens* (London, 1981); Sylvia Landsberg, *The Medieval Garden* (London, 1995); W. Braunfels, *Monasteries of Western Europe* (London, 1972); Sir Frank Crisp, *Medieval Gardens* (2 vols., London, 1924); Donald Campbell, *Arabian Medicine and Its Influence on the Middle Ages* (2 vols., London, 1926); Jonas Lehrman, *Earthly Paradise: Garden and Courtyard in Islam* (London, 1980); and Celia Fisher, *Flowers in Medieval Manuscripts* (London, 2004).

13. A Loyal Downfall

I am wholly indebted to Robert L.D. Cooper for his edition of *Genealogie of the Sainteclaires of Rosslyn* by Father Richard Augustin Hay (Edinburgh, 2002). The Curator of the Grand Lodge of Scotland Museum and Library meticulously lists the St Clair Charters. The most important of these are the *Charta Whillielmi Comitis Orcadiae Baroniae de Roslin Facta Olivero de Sancto Claro*, MCCCCLXXVI; *Charter of William Earl of Orkney made for Oliver de Sinclair of Lands of Herbertshire, 1476; Queen Dowager's Bond to Sir William Saintcler, 1546*; the *Retour of Sir William Sinclair* and the *Premonition to Matthew Sinclair, 1558*; and the *Charter of Justiciar granted to Sir William Sinclair, 1559*. Also essential is William Forbes-Leith SJ, *Narratives of Scottish Catholics under Mary Stuart and James VI* (Edinburgh, 1885). He quotes on the character of the Bishop of Ross from Tylter's *Life of Sir Thomas*.

Invaluable is the admirable biography by Antonia Fraser, *Mary, Queen of Scots* (London, 1969). She quotes William Patten, *Diary of Somerset's Campaign*, 1547. Also important is Gordon Donaldson, *All the Queen's Men: Power and Politics in Mary Stewart's Scotland* (London, 1983) and *The Reformation in Scotland* (Cambridge, 1960); G. Seton, *A History of the Family of Seton* (2 vols., Edinburgh, 1896); J.K. Cameron, *The First Book of Discipline* (Edinburgh, 1972); Duncan Shaw (ed.), *Reformation and Revolution* (Edinburgh, 1967); D.H. Willson, *James VI and I* (London, 1956); and D.L.W. Tough, *The Last Years of a Frontier* (Oxford, 1928). Sir Walter Scott's *Provincial Antiquities* was first published in Edinburgh, while he quoted from the first volume of Chambers, *Domestic Annals of Scotland*.

14. Faith and Penury

I am again heavily indebted to George MacDonald Fraser, *The Steel Bonnets* (*op. cit.*) for his magisterial account of the pacification of the Borders: the quotations are his. The quotation on the 1618 troubles came from the essential work of William Law Mathieson, *Politics and Religion: A Study in Scottish History from the Reformation to the Revolution* (2 vols., Glasgow, 1902). He also quotes Lindsay, *True Narrative of the Perth Assembly* and provides his own comments. Also essential is David Stevenson, *The Origins of Freemasonry: Scotland's Century, 1590–1710* (Cambridge, 1988), although he is determined to prove the Protestant origins of Scottish masonry, despite the evidence in this book. See also Sir Richard Maitland and Alexander, Lord Kingston, *The history of the house of Seytoun* (Edinburgh, 1829), and Lord J. Somerville, *Memorie of the Somervills; being a history of the baronial house of Somerville* (Sir Walter Scott ed., 2 vols., Edinburgh, 1815). I have again quoted from Father Hay (*op. cit.*)

David Stevenson has also written two excellent books: *The Scottish Revolution 1637–1644: The Triumph of the Covenanters* (Newton Abbot, 1973), and *Revolution and Counter-Revolution in Scotland, 1644–1651* (London, 1977). The quotations from Robert Baillie are taken from *The Letters and Journals* (D. Laing ed., 3 vols., Edinburgh, 1841–1842); see also, F.N. McCoy, *Robert Baillie and the Second Scots Reformation* (London, 1974). The turncoat with the dangerous maxim was James Turner, who persecuted the Covenanters, whom he knew well, after the Restoration.

15. Woe to the Jacobites

See G. Burnet, *History of My Own Times* (O. Airy ed., 2 vols., Oxford, 1897–1900), also S.R. Gardiner (ed.), *The Hamilton Papers* (London, 1880), also P. Gordon of Ruthven, *A Short Abridgement of Britane's Distemper* (J. Dunn ed., Edinburgh, 1844). E. Hyde, the Earl of Clarendon, *The History of the Rebellion and Civil Wars in England Begun in the Year 1641* (W.D. Macray ed., 6 vols., Oxford, 1888) remains indispensable. See also G. Wishart, *The Memoirs of James, Marquis of Montrose, 1639–50* (Edinburgh, 1893), and J. Buchan, *Montrose* (London, 1931), as well as W.S. Douglas, *Cromwell's Scotch Campaigns, 1650–51* (London, 1898); J.K. Hewison, *The Covenanters* (2 vols., Glasgow, 1913); W.M. Lamont, *Godly Rule, Politics and Religion, 1603–1660* (London, 1969); C.S. Terry, *The Life and Campaigns of Alexander Leslie, First Earl of Leven,* (Edinburgh, 1899); and H. Cary (ed.), *Memorials of the Great Civil War* (2 vols., London, 1842).

For the Jacobite rebellions, I am grateful to Sir Charles Petrie, *The Jacobite Movement: The First Phase, 1688–1716* (London, 1948); Bruce Lenman, *The Jacobite Risings in Britain, 1689–1746* (London, 1980); Audrey Cunningham, *The*

Loyal Clans (Cambridge, 1932); J.P. Kenyon, *Revolution Principles* (Cambridge, 1977); A. and H. Taylor, *1715: The Story of the Rising* (London, 1936): C. Sinclair-Stevenson, *Inglorious Rebellion: The Jacobite Risings of 1708, 1715 and 1719* (London, 1971); R. Campbell, *The Life of the Most Illustrious Prince John, Duke of Argyll and Greenwich* (London, 1745); John, Master of Sinclair, *Memoirs of the Insurrection in Scotland in 1715* (Sir Walter Scott ed., Edinburgh, 1858); J. Baynes, *The Jacobite Rising of 1715* (London, 1970); G.P. Insh, *The Scottish Jacobite Movement* (Edinburgh, 1952); Eveline Cruickshanks, *Political Untouchables: The Tories and the '45* (Oxford, 1981); and the Duke of Cumberland's papers in the Royal Archive, Windsor Castle.

16. The Radical Lodges

For Irish conspiracies, essential are the essays in T. Desmond Williams (ed.), *Secret Societies in Ireland* (Dublin, 1973). See also Andrew Sinclair, *An Anatomy of Terror* (London, 2003); Nesta H. Webster, *Secret Societies and Subversive Movements* (London, 1924); George Rudé, *The French Revolution* (London, 1988); and J.M. Roberts, *The French Revolution* (Oxford, 1978).

For information on the influence of Freemasonry on the American Revolution, I am indebted to the brilliant work of Michael Baigent and Richard Leigh in *The Temple and the Lodge* (London, 1989), also L.C.W. Cook (ed.), *Colonial Freemasonry* (Missouri, 1973–4); A. Cerza, 'The American War of Independence and Freemasonry', *Ars quatuor coronatorum* (vol. lxxxix, 1976); J.H. Lepper and P. Crossle, *History of the Grand Lodge of Free and Accepted Masons of Ireland* (2 vols., Dublin, 1925); L. Einstein, *Divided Loyalties* (London, 1933); J.A. Anderson, *The Constitutions of the Freemasons* (London, 1723); William Alexander Laurie, *The History of Free Masonry and the Grand Lodge of Scotland* (Edinburgh, 1850); David Murray Lyon, *History of the Lodge of Edinburgh* (Edinburgh, 1873); Robert Freke Gould, *The History of Freemasonry* (2 vols., London, 1885); and Robert L.D. Cooper, 'The Knights Templars in Scotland – The Creation of a Myth', *Quatuor Coronati*, Vol. 115, November, 2003. He appears to be determined, as so many others are, to write the Templars and the Catholic crafts and guilds and Lodges out of history, even when the earlier and contemporary Scottish Masonic historians present a different case. I remain grateful to Robert Brydon for his work on William St Clair and the Royal Company of Archers, also on Alexander Deuchar and the revival of the Templar Orders.

17. Phantoms and Myths

Essential again is *The 1893 Guide to Rosslyn Chapel, Castle and Hawthornden* by the
Reverend John Thompson. In this work, the evidence of James Currie appears,
also Grose's comment on the ruin of Rosslyn castle, and Slezer's legend of the
dormant Lady St Clair. M. Baigent, R. Leigh, and H. Lincoln were the three
authors of *The Holy Blood and the Holy Grail* (London, 1982). The work made a
greater myth out of Rennes-le-Château than of Rosslyn. An admirable Time-
watch BBC programme, 'The History of a Mystery', produced by William Cram,
secured a confession from Pierre Plantard of his forgeries. See also Dan Brown,
The Da Vinci Code (New York, 2003).

For an understanding of Leonardo da Vinci read A. Richard Turner,
Inventing Leonardo: The Anatomy of a Legend (New York, 1993). James Watson,
The Double Helix, was published in New York in 1968, while Maurice Wilkins
published *The Third Man of the Double Helix* at Oxford in 2003. I remain
grateful to the unpublished work and research of Judith Fisken, Robert
Brydon, and Niven Sinclair and his many friends.

Index

Note: Names beginning with 'St' are indexed as spelt, but Christian saints are indexed under their name. At some time the St Clair family began to be known as Sinclair. Anything relating to the families in general is indexed under St Clair, but individuals usually referred to as Sinclair in the text are indexed under that name. The abbreviation '*fl.*' (flourished) with a date has in a few cases been used to distinguish people of the same name.